Work and the Well-Being of Poor Families with Children

Work and the Well-Being of Poor Families with Children

When Work Is Not Enough

Andrea L. Ziegert and Dennis H. Sullivan

LEXINGTON BOOKS

Lanham • Boulder • New York • London

Published by Lexington Books
An imprint of The Rowman & Littlefield Publishing Group, Inc.
4501 Forbes Boulevard, Suite 200, Lanham, Maryland 20706
www.rowman.com

6 Tinworth Street, London SE11 5AL, United Kingdom

British Library Cataloguing in Publication Information Available

Library of Congress Cataloging-in-Publication Data Available

ISBN 978-1-4985-5677-4 (cloth : alk. paper)
ISBN 978-1-4985-5679-8 (pbk. : alk. paper)
ISBN 978-1-4985-5678-1 (electronic)

∞™ The paper used in this publication meets the minimum requirements of American
National Standard for Information Sciences—Permanence of Paper for Printed Library
Materials, ANSI/NISO Z39.48-1992.

This book is dedicated to all poor families who struggle to do the best for their children and to our students past and present who challenge us to do this work.

Contents

Acknowledgments

The authors would like to thank Professor Christopher Wimer and the team at the Center on Poverty and Social Policy at Columbia University for preliminary access to historical SPM data series.

The authors would like to thank Jingwei Mao for expert technical assistance with tables, charts, and manuscript preparation.

Acronyms

ACA	Affordable Care Act (2010)
ACTC	Additional Child Tax Credit
AFDC	Aid to Families with Dependent Children
AMI	Area Median Income
ARRA	American Recovery and Reinvestment Act (2009)
ASEC	Annual Social and Economic Supplement of the Current Population Survey
CA	Child Allowance
CBO	Congressional Budget Office
CBPP	Center on Budget and Policy Priorities
CCDBG	Child Care and Development Block Grant
CDCTC	Child and Dependent Care Tax Credit
CEA	Council of Economic Advisors
CHIP	Children's Health Insurance Program
CTC	Child Tax Credit
EITC	Earned Income Tax Credit
GAO	Government Accountability Office
GDP	Gross Domestic Product
HUD	US Department of Housing and Urban Development
IPTW	Involuntary Part-Time Work
IPUMS-CPS	Integrated Public Use Microdata Series-Current Population Survey
LARC	Long-Acting Reversible Contraceptive
LIHEAP	Low-Income Home Energy Assistance Program
LIHTC	Low-Income Housing Tax Credit
MOOP	Medical Out-of-Pocket Expenses (and Medicare Part D)
NSLP	National School Lunch Program

OASDI   Old Age, Survivors, and Disability Insurance Program
OECD   Organization for Economic Co-operation and Development
OPM   Official Poverty Measure
PRWORA   Personal Responsibility and Work Opportunity Reconciliation
            Act (1996)
PTER   Part-Time for Economic Reasons
SBP   School Breakfast Program
SDDI   Social Security Disability Insurance
SNAP   Supplemental Nutrition Assistance Program
SPM   Supplemental Poverty Measure
SPMa   Supplemental Poverty Measure-anchored
SSI   Supplemental Security Income
TANF   Temporary Assistance for Needy Families
UI   Unemployment Insurance
USDA   United States Department of Agriculture
WIC   Special Supplemental Nutrition Program for Women, Infants
            and Children

Introduction

Children are a nation's future. Healthy, well-educated children are tomorrow's leaders, innovators, producers, and consumers. Unfortunately, in 2019 nearly one in seven children were poor in America; children were nearly a third of the 34 million poor. Children have the highest poverty rates in America (14.4 percent), more than one and a half times the poverty rates of individuals age 18 to 64 (9.4 percent) and those over 65 (8.9 percent) (Semega et al., 2020). And America's child poverty rate is the highest of highly developed OECD nations (OECD, 2020).

US child poverty is stubbornly persistent with long-term consequences. A lack of family resources during childhood compromises a child's ability to grow and achieve success in adulthood: poor children have lower educational attainment, more difficulty obtaining and keeping steady employment as adults, and higher likelihood of risky behaviors likely to lead to incarceration for men, or non-marital births for women (Garcia, Heckman & Ronda, 2021). Research by Chetty and co-authors (2014) shows that the family a child is born into, its race, family structure, neighborhood, and family resources strongly determine a child's life opportunities as an adult. Inequality of opportunity at birth compounds over a lifetime. When compared to other children, children born into families in the bottom quintile of the distribution of income are more than twice as likely to be poor as adults, and 70 percent will have adult incomes only in the bottom two quintiles (Smeeding, 2016; Urahn et al., 2012). In short, poor children in America are likely to become poor adults.

But demography need not be destiny. Public investment in families with children to insure against the risk of poverty improves social welfare now, and in the future, both for the family and the larger society. There are several good reasons to support poor families with children. First, there is a moral obligation: every child deserves a chance for a happy, productive life; children are not responsible for childhood circumstances which can affect their life chances. Second, investing in children is an investment in the future and is efficiency enhancing. Folbre (1994, p. 86) suggests children are public goods: "All citizens of the United States enjoy significant claims upon the earnings of future working-age adults through Social Security and public debt." We all have a stake in helping children grow up to be productive adults.

Furthermore, Black and Rothstein (2019) suggest that a private market economy underinvests in families with children, and public support is needed to remedy this market failure. For example, abundant research supports the conclusion that investment in children's health and education in the earliest years of life can have the greatest returns, yet key characteristics of these investments lead to underinvestment in children. Such investments are "lumpy" not evenly spread out over a child's life: most costs are borne by parents over a relatively short period of time, while the benefits are enjoyed by a child over their lifetime. Furthermore, investing in children in the earliest years may be particularly difficult for parents who are typically just beginning their working careers and have relatively lower incomes. Because parents are unable to borrow against their own or their child's future earnings to help finance these early investments, parents invest less in their children than is socially optimal.

In a comprehensive review of US safety net investments in children, Hoynes and Schanzenbach (2018) find that programs such as Medicaid, tax credits (Earned Income Tax Credit [EITC] and Child Tax Credit), and nutritional and cash welfare all have substantial benefits for children and society over the long run. Children who have had access to these programs have improved health, educational attainment, and economic productivity as adults. Hendren and Sprung-Keyser (2020) find that direct investment in the health and education of low-income children yields the highest returns, providing a fivefold return on average. Research by Goodman-Bacon (2021) suggests recipiency of Medicaid in childhood reduces mortality and disability and increases labor market outcomes in adulthood, while Chester and Alker (2015) find that children who receive Medicaid were less likely to drop out of high school and more likely to graduate from college. And while investments in younger children often have the highest returns, Garcia (2017) argues that there are high returns to investing in disadvantaged children of all ages. Furthermore, Hendren and Sprung-Keyser find that many of these investments in children pay for themselves: the long-run impacts were large enough to fully offset the initial program expenditures.

Because of the potential benefits, in 2015 Congress charged the National Academy of Sciences to convene a group of experts to produce a road map to reduce the child poverty rate by half. They found that child poverty is indeed expensive, costing between $800 billion and $1.1 trillion *every year* due to worsened health, lower earnings, and increased crime when poor children become adults (National Academy, 2019). This research, *Work and Well-Being of Poor Families with Children: When Work Is Not Enough*, complements the National Academy's findings by providing an in-depth study of poor families with children, their demographic characteristics, work and labor market experience, and government program participation and benefit receipt. In effect, we provide the details for how and why various policy approaches can address poverty among families with children. To do this, we make use of a new measure of poverty, an anchored supplemental poverty measure (SPM).

MEASURING POVERTY

In 1963 the US official poverty measure (OPM) was devised by Mollie Orshansky, an employee of the Social Security Administration. To construct her measure, Orshansky used estimates of the cost of US Department of Agriculture's 1961 Thrifty Food Plan for families of different size and composition. Based on information in the 1955 Household Food Consumption Survey, which suggested that the average family spent one-third of their budget on food, Orshansky multiplied the cost of a family's economy food plan by three to get an estimate of the minimum level of family expenditures required to avoid poverty. The result was a series of "poverty thresholds" based on the number and age of family members (for greater detail, see Fisher, 1997). A family was poor if their gross pre-tax income was less than their relevant poverty threshold. Despite widespread and persistent criticism, these thresholds (updated annually for changes in prices) and this definition of family resources describe how official poverty is calculated to this day.

In 1992, Congress charged the National Academy of Sciences to convene a panel of economists and policy makers to discuss alternative measures of poverty. The result was not one, but several SPMs (National Research Council, 1995). Finally, in 2010 the US Census Bureau and Bureau of Labor Statistics began publishing a SPM. Though not a replacement for the OPM, it is widely viewed as a significant step forward in poverty measurement.

The SPM thresholds improve upon the OPM thresholds in several ways. First, the thresholds are based on mean expenditures on food, clothing, shelter, and utilities for all two-child consumer units in the 30th to 36th percentile range based on data from the Consumer Expenditure Survey, then multiplied by 1.2 to account for additional miscellaneous expenditures. These thresholds are then adjusted for geographic differences in housing costs by tenure, and a three-parameter equivalence scale is used to adjust for family size and composition. These thresholds are updated annually using a five-year moving average of expenditures on food, clothing, shelter, and utilities. As such, these thresholds are a "quasi-relative" measure of poverty, since this adjustment process allows for changes in standard of living over time.

Second, the SPM measures use a revised measure of the "income" to be compared to the poverty threshold to determine poverty status. When Orshansky created her poverty measure in the 1960s, cash government payments were relatively more important than government in-kind assistance such as food stamps, housing subsidies, or medical assistance. Today non-cash, in-kind benefits are more numerous and important contributions to the well-being of a poor family, and the OPM's failure to consider these benefits misses increasingly important components of a poor family's resources. Furthermore, the OPM uses pre-tax cash income, which fails to account for the impact of both taxes paid and tax credits received on family resources.

The SPM directly addresses these criticisms by defining family resources as the sum of cash income from market and government sources plus government non-cash benefits received to meet a family's food, shelter, and utilities needs, minus taxes net of credits. In addition, work expenses, childcare expenses, out-of-pocket medical expenses, and child support payments to another household are subtracted from this family resource measure since these resources are not available to meet family needs (Blank, 2008).

Finally, the SPM measures use an updated concept of the family unit. Families today differ significantly from families in Orshanky's time. The OPM defines a family as a group of individuals related by blood, marriage, or adoption who share a residence. The SPM broadens the definition of "family" to include unmarried partners and their relatives, co-resident unrelated children, and foster children (Provencher, 2011). Table 0.1 summarizes the key differences between the OPM and SPMs.

Though not adopted as the official measure of poverty, the Census Bureau has published the SPM annually since 2010 (Short, 2011–2015; Renwick and Fox, 2016). A growing number of researchers are using the SPM to better understand poverty in the United States. Recently, a group of researchers (Fox et al., 2015a) have used data from the Consumer Expenditure Survey and the March Current Population Survey to create a historical data series of the SPM dating back to 1967. This series allows comparisons of OPM and SPM poverty over time. The historical SPM differs from the Census SPM in one important way: the historical SPM does not adjust thresholds for geographical differences in rental costs. This topic and some less consequential problems are thoroughly discussed in Fox et al. (2015a). Fox et al. (2015b) use this series to study trends in deep poverty (families with resources less than 50 percent of SPM poverty) from 1968 to 2011.

Table 0.1   A Comparison of the OPM and SPMa

	OPM	SPMa
Family Unit	Family head and relatives, including those related by marriage or adoption	OPM family unit plus unrelated children, foster children, unmarried partners, and their relatives
Poverty Threshold	Real* value of three times the cost of 1963 food budget	Real* expenditures on necessities** in 2012 at 30th–36th percentile of two-child consumer families, multiplied by 1.2 to allow for incidental expenses
Threshold Adjustments	Varies by number of adults, number of children, and age of head	Revised formula varies by number of adults and number of children
Resource Measure	Pre-tax cash income including cash transfer payments	OPM resource measure Add: Tax credits plus in-kind transfer payments that pay for necessities** Subtract: Taxes paid, work and childcare expenses, and out-of-pocket medical expenses

*The measures use slightly different versions of the Consumer Price Index.
**Necessities include Food, Clothing, Housing, and Utilities.
Source: Renwick & Fox (2016), p. 2.

Wimer et al. (2016) compare OPM and SPM poverty over time to investigate poverty trends. In order to make a more accurate comparison between OPM and SPM poverty, the authors use an "anchored" SPM measure of poverty (SPMa), which essentially keeps the market basket of goods and services used in the threshold calculations constant over time as the OPM does. Figure 0.1 compares SPM anchored poverty based on a fixed 2012 market basket to OPM. Our research uses the unique characteristics of the anchored SPM to analyze progress on reducing poverty for families with at least one child under age 18.

While both poverty measures are sensitive to business cycles and follow similar trends, SPM poverty exceeded OPM poverty prior to the Great Recession (2007–2009) but showed significantly less poverty than OPM during and after the recession. Chapter 3 will suggest why this was the case.

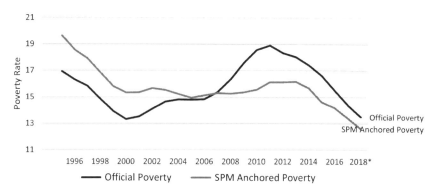

Figure 0.1   Official versus SPM Poverty Measures; All SPM Families with Children Under 18, 1995–2018. *Source*: Authors' calculations based on Current Population Survey: IPUMS-CPS, University of Minnesota and Historical SPM data, Columbia University.

DATA

To conduct our analysis, we use data from the 1995–2020 March Supplement to the Current Population Survey (ASEC) and historical SPM data provided by Columbia University's SPM Project Team. Like Wimer et al. (2016), we use a historical measure of SPM anchored at 2012, hereafter referred to as SPM poverty. Our unit of analysis is an SPM unit with at least one child under age 18. In defining variables used in our analysis, we have made decisions consistent with those made in constructing the historical SPM. For ease of exposition "SPM poverty" refers to an SPM poverty measure anchored in 2012.

We limit our analysis to three racial/ethnic groups based on the racial or ethnic identity of the SPM unit head: non-Hispanic white, non-Hispanic black, or Hispanic. "Hispanic" is an ethnicity rather than a race, though two-thirds of Hispanic individuals consider their ethnicity a racial classification (Gonzalez-Barrera and Lopez, 2015). The Office of Management and Budget defines Hispanic heads as persons of Cuban, Mexican, Puerto Rican, South or Central American, or other Spanish culture or origin, regardless of race. In our analysis, Hispanics are further divided into two groups: native-born or foreign-born. Native-born Hispanics are born in the United States or its territories and currently reside in the United States; they are citizens by birth. Foreign-born Hispanics were born outside of the United States but currently reside in United States; foreign-born Hispanics may or may not have US citizenship and if a non-citizen, their legal status is unknown. For ease of exposition, we will refer to non-Hispanic whites as "whites," non-Hispanic blacks as "blacks," and Hispanics as a separate "racial" group distinct from non-Hispanic blacks or whites.

"Families" refers to SPM units with at least one child under 18 years of age, and the phrase "All Families" refers to black, white, and Hispanic with both native- and foreign-born families combined. We consider children to be in married couple, single non-partnered parent (henceforth "single parent"), or cohabiting couple families based on the status of the SPM family head. As such, the families we study are not exhaustive of all poor families with children, ignoring, for example, Asian families and their children, for whom the samples are often too small to generate reliable statistics

In order to better analyze subsamples in our data, a "year" in our data is a three-year moving average centered on a particular calendar year. The advantages of the three-year moving average are discussed in greater detail in Gundersen and Ziliak (2004). For example, variable values for 1995 are based on data for calendar years 1994, 1995, and 1996 (survey years 1995, 1996, and 1997). The principal advantage is that the resulting datasets are large—always more than 39,300 white families in all, 4,900 of whom are poor; 6,800 black families, of whom 2,400 are poor; 4,800 native-born Hispanic families, of whom 1,500 are poor; and 5,600 foreign-born Hispanic families, of whom 2,800 are poor.

We take advantage of the unique construction of the SPM to investigate the relative role of private income, government cash and non-cash transfers, taxes and tax credits, and family work/medical expenses in impacting poverty for families with children. While the SPM offers several advantages over previous measures of poverty, reliance on the March Supplement to the Current Population Survey (ASEC) when compared to relevant administrative data has the well-documented problem of under-reporting of transfer programs benefits received by the low-income and poor families (Meyer and Mittag, 2019). This should be kept in mind when we analyze poverty spending in chapter 3. Additionally, poverty rates throughout this chapter measure the poverty of persons in SPM family units that have total resources (variously measured) below the SPMa threshold for that family. The poverty rates do not measure "child poverty" per se because the measure includes all of the adults in the family.

Our analysis proceeds as follows: Chapters 1 through 3 provide a comprehensive view of poverty among families with children. Chapter 1 reviews significant demographic changes over the last two decades including changing racial and ethnic composition of American society, significant changes in family formation, and increased educational attainment of adults in poor families. We also introduce the families who are the focus of our studies: non-Hispanic whites, non-Hispanic backs, and native- and foreign-born Hispanic families with children.

Figure 0.2 provides anchored SPM poverty rates for our four racial groups of interest. While all four groups exhibit declining SPM poverty over time,

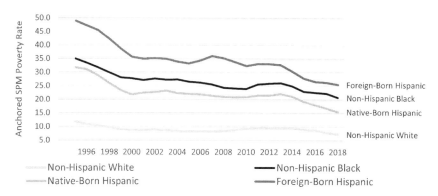

Figure 0.2 SPM Anchored Poverty by Race for Families with Children Under 18, 1995–2018. *Source*: Authors' calculations based on Current Population Survey: IPUMS-CPS, University of Minnesota and Historical SPM data, Columbia University.

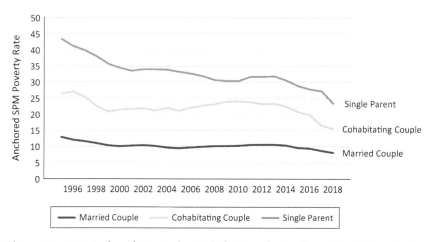

Figure 0.3 SPM Anchored Poverty by Marital Status, for Families with Children Under 18, 1995–2018. *Source*: Authors' calculations based on Current Population Survey: IPUMS-CPS, University of Minnesota and Historical SPM data, Columbia University.

there are significant differences in the level of poverty among our four demographic groups. The sensitivity of their poverty to changing demographics, labor market conditions, and benefit receipt will be discussed in the chapters that follow. Distinguishing between native- and foreign-born Hispanics is one of the advantages of our research design that makes it a contribution to the existing literature.

Similarly, figure 0.3 illustrates how SPM poverty varies by family type. As documented in chapter 1, how families are formed and shaped has changed over time; the SPM is particularly well suited to analyze the twenty-first century's diverse families. In particular, this research provides new information on how poverty among cohabiting couples differs from better understood poverty among married couple and single parents. As might be expected, coupled families with two potential adult workers will have lower poverty rates than single parent families. As discussed in chapter 1, cohabiting couples face unique issues which contribute to their poverty which is roughly twice that of married coupled families.

Chapter 1 concludes that many of the demographic changes shaping American families in the early twenty-first century have increased the likelihood of poverty in families with children. Increased immigration and the uncoupling of marriage and parenthood have increased the number of families who historically have the highest poverty rates, immigrant families, and families with unmarried heads. Chapter 1 also introduces the poor families who are the subject of our analysis throughout the book comparing them to their non-poor counterparts. Our families are representative of these larger demographic trends and provide important insights into poverty today.

Chapter 2 provides a review of the major economic trends that have shaped US labor markets over the past two decades with a special focus on the problems faced by poor and less skilled workers. In particular, we focus on work and wage gaps between poor and non-poor SPM families with children. Poor families are more likely to have higher levels of unemployment, more involuntary part-time work, and are more likely to have adults who do not or cannot work. Figure 0.4 illustrates SPM poverty rates based on work effort.

Work matters. Unsurprisingly, families without a worker have extraordinarily high poverty rates, though this rate has declined slightly over time. Part-time work effort decreases family poverty rates by 40 percentage points, though poverty rates still exceed 35 percent. Even if poor families have one or more full-time workers, their poverty rates remain stubbornly constant at just less than 10 percent. In part, these families suffer from low wages which

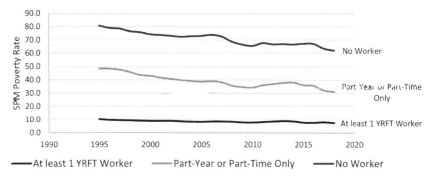

Figure 0.4 SPM Anchored Poverty Rates by Work Effort for SPM Families with Children Under 18, 1995–2018. *Source*: Authors' calculations based on Current Population Survey: IPUMS-CPS, University of Minnesota and Historical SPM data, Columbia University.

have stagnated or declined over time. Chapter 2 further explores these results on the basis of race and family structure to provide a better understanding of the work and wage gaps between poor and non-poor families with children.

Besides income from work, poor families have access to a variety of government benefits and tax credits. Chapter 3 begins with a brief review of the history of poverty spending in the United States. We then provide a step-by-step analysis of the anti-poverty effects of government programs by investigating the difference between private income poverty, a family's poverty based on labor and capital income and pensions, and SPM poverty, their poverty after all government benefits are added and work and out-of-pocket medical expenses are subtracted. This analysis is undertaken in six steps: first, we begin with private income poverty; in step two we study the poverty effects of taxes net of credits; in step three we consider the anti-poverty effects of non-means-tested government cash transfers such as social insurance; in step four we consider the anti-poverty impact of means-tested transfers, both cash and in-kind; in step five we analyze the impact of work expenses such as child care and out-of-pocket medical expenses on a family's poverty rate before ending at step six, their SPM poverty rate. This analysis is undertaken for each of our racial and marital status groups of interest. Figure 0.5 presents the beginning and ending points of our analysis for all SPM families with children.

As would be expected, private income poverty rates exceed SPM rates due to the impact of the social safety net. What is perhaps more interesting is the strong anti-poverty effects of government spending during the Great Recession: though the private income poverty rate increased by nearly 5 percentage points between 2007 and 2010, the SPM poverty rates barely budged. Chapter 3 explains why this is so by studying recipiency rates and mean real values of benefits received for each of our racial and marital status groups.

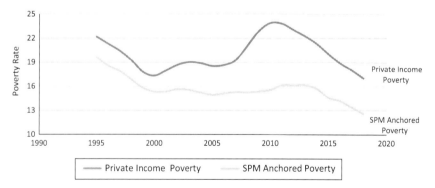

Figure 0.5   Private Income Poverty versus SPM Anchored Poverty, Families with Children Under 18, 1995–2018. *Source*: Authors' calculations based on Current Population Survey: IPUMS-CPS, University of Minnesota and Historical SPM data, Columbia University.

Chapter 3 finds that the difference between private income and SPM poverty is greatest for non-white families and single parent families. Chapter 3 details how different demographic groups differentially benefit from the various types of government spending by decomposing the difference between their private income and SPM poverty rates.

Chapters 1 through 3 provide the necessary background and context for the analysis we undertake in chapters 4 and 5. These chapters explore options for reducing poverty of families with children in 2018, the most recent year for which we can build a three-year (2017–2019) pre-Covid pandemic dataset. Specifically, they provide a series of simulations to determine which set of policies can reduce poverty rates by half for these families. We first investigate anti-poverty effects of reducing the work and wage gaps found in chapter 2. We find that unless guaranteed jobs are provided, reducing these gaps is not sufficient to reduce poverty rates by half for many of our demographic groups of interest. We then consider a variety of other policies, such as child allowance or increases in the EITC or increases in means-tested benefits which might be used singly or in combination to reach our stated goal. We also consider the anti-poverty impact of fully funding child care or eliminating out-of-pocket medical expenses. While many policies reduce poverty by a third or more among families with the highest poverty rates, we find that given the heterogeneous nature of the poverty population, there is no silver bullet that will reduce poverty by half for all families.

Chapter 5 continues the analysis begun in chapter 4 by investigating several specific policy proposals for poverty alleviation that have been advanced in recent years. We focus on proposals that directly affect poverty in families with children. In parallel with the chapter 4 simulations the specific proposals include policies that reduce the work gap (a job guarantee), reduce the wage gap (minimum wage increases), increase tax credits (enhance the EITC), alter means-tested benefits (increase the generosity of SNAP), introduce a child allowance, and consider a variety of combinations of these approaches, including the package of proposals advanced by the Biden administration. Many of these proposals combine an estimate of the extent to which poverty rates are reduced with an estimate of the effect of the policy on the federal budget, making it possible to approximate the cost per percentage points of poverty reduction, a measure of cost-effectiveness.

This book ends with a review of what we take to be the principal policy consequences of the analysis. While a few of the policy suggestions flow directly from the facts assembled in chapters 1 through 3, the main focus is on what was learned in chapters 4 and 5. In particular, we conclude that as a mechanism for dramatically reducing poverty in families with children, work-centered policies just don't work very well. That is not to say that the effects of reducing unemployment among poor adults are negligible, because they certainly are not, especially if the higher earnings are enhanced through higher wages or more generous tax credits that see to it that the unemployed poor are not simply converted into the working poor. It is to say, however, that if the true goal is to reduce poverty, the most cost-effective policy packages need to focus on providing poor families with income that is not directly tied to labor markets and on reducing expenditures for expenses on work, childcare and medical expenses that drive families into poverty despite their receipt of what appears to be adequate income.

Chapter 1

Twenty-First-Century Families with Children in the United States

Diverse demographic changes are central to the fabric of today's American life. Millions of individual choices—whether to marry or immigrate to America or have a child or get a degree—shape who we are as a society. The effects of these changes are easy to underestimate. They are not the product of public disputes in the way that policy changes often are, but simply the consequences of hundreds of millions of people living their ordinary lives, from birth (or immigration), to school attendance, to work and marriage and childbearing, and on into retirement. Many demographic changes are almost imperceptible from one year to the next, so they lack the drama of macroeconomic booms and recessions. But in the long run, demographic changes are very powerful indeed.

And these changes are important. From the standpoint of economic well-being, not all families are created equal: on average, married-couple families fare better than single parent families; Asian and non-Hispanic white families economically outperform black and Hispanic families; native-born families often have more income than do immigrant families; and better educated adults earn more than the less educated. An understanding of demographic characteristics and trends, such as education, immigration, and changes in racial and ethnic composition of the population and in family formation and size, is important to understand trends in the economic well-being of families.

This chapter documents some of these changes by reviewing the changing racial composition of American society and changing structure of families with children. First, we consider the ethnic and racial composition of the United States through a review of immigration and internal demographic changes which have shaped American society. Second, we investigate the changing education levels in the United States over the last several decades. Third, we review the changing trends in family formation and family structure. And finally, we introduce data on the SPM families analyzed throughout the book to more closely investigate how these demographic changes affect family poverty.

CHANGES IN THE RACIAL AND ETHNIC COMPOSITION OF THE UNITED STATES

The changing racial composition of the United States is the signature demographic change of the twenty-first century, as important to the nation as the Baby Boom Generation was to the twentieth century (Frey, 2018). Changes in past and present immigration trends have increased the racial and ethnic diversity of American from the outside while internal demographic changes—changes in number of women of childbearing age and relative fertility rates—have shaped the changing racial and ethnic composition of the population from the inside.

Immigration

Immigration has become a political lightning rod in recent years and for good reason: since 1990 the flow of immigrants has increased sharply. According to American Community Survey data the foreign-born population in 2016 was 44 million, representing 13.6 percent of the population. If current trends continue, by 2028 immigrants are projected to be 14.9 percent of the population, higher than any time since 1850.

Over the past decade, three basic principles have shaped legal immigration to the United States. First, two-thirds of permanent immigration involves family unification of immigrants with US citizens and lawful permanent residents. Second, employment-based visas based on the economic and labor-market needs of the economy represent another 20 percent of immigrants. Finally, refugees, asylum seekers, and winners of the diversity visa lottery account for the remainder (Hipsman and Meissner, 2013).

Over the past two decades, annual flows of lawful permanent residents into the United States have averaged just over one million per year (National Academy of Sciences, 2017). However, not all immigrants enter the United States legally. In the most recent available data, the Office of Homeland Security estimates that in 2014, nearly one in three foreign-born residents in the United States were unauthorized immigrants (Baker, Table 2, 2017). Over 70 percent of these immigrants are from Mexico and Central America; other 13 percent are from Asia, and 6 percent are from South America (Zong et al., 2018).

Immigrants' region of birth has varied over time. Europeans and Canadians dominated immigration flows in the mid-twentieth century, while immigration from Latin America and Asia characterize late twentieth- and early twenty-first-century migration. Though Mexican immigrants dominated immigration flows for decades, immigration from both India and China have surpassed Mexico since 2013. This represents both an increase in immigration from Asia over the last several years and a precipitous decline in immigration from Mexico since 2004. Nonetheless, 45 percent of immigrants in 2016 had Hispanic or Latino origins; of this group, Mexicans were by far the largest, Puerto Ricans were second largest, and other countries with more than a million immigrants each include El Salvador, Cuba, Dominican Republic, Guatemala, and Columbia (Flores, 2017). While these immigrant flows are substantial, in 2016, two-thirds of the 57.4 million Hispanics in the United States were native born (Zong et al., 2018).

Families with children are of particular interest to this research. The percentage of children under age 18 residing with at least one immigrant parent has doubled from 13 percent in 1990 to 26 percent in 2016, representing 18 million children. The vast majority of these children, 88 percent in 2016, were born in the United States and are citizens by birthright. And many of these children live in poor or low-income families: over half of children with an immigrant parent live in families with incomes less than twice the official poverty level (Zong et al., 2018). Poor families with citizen children but non-citizen parents complicate eligibility and recipiency of government programs designed to help the poor. Fear of arrest and deportation also contribute to the economic insecurity of these families.

Changing Internal Demographics

Though past and present immigration are important contributors to the changing racial and ethnic composition of the population, Frey (2018) suggests internal demographic changes are at least as important. In 2015, the median age of whites was 43.3 years compared to 33.8 for blacks, 28.7 for Hispanics, and 19.9 for mixed-race individuals. An aging white population with fewer women of childbearing age, combined with their lower fertility rates since the Great Recession, has led to a 10.8 percent decrease in white births between 1999 and 2016. As a result, 2016 was the first year the non-Hispanic white population actually declined, with the number of deaths exceeding the number of births in a majority of the 50 states (Saenz and Johnson, 2018).

At the same time, younger, minority families with more women of childbearing age and with higher fertility rates have resulted in a majority of minority children, suggesting that diversity comes "from the bottom up" (Frey, 2018, p. 6). The generation of children born since 2007 is the first minority, non-Hispanic white generation. Figure 1.1 provides US Census Bureau projections: by 2060 the share of children who are non-Hispanic white will fall

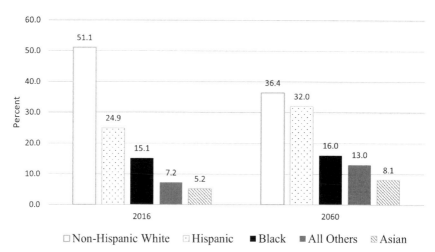

Figure 1.1   Racial and Ethnic Composition of Children Under 18, 2016 and 2060 Projected: The "All Others" group includes American Indian, Alaska Native, Native Hawaiian, and Other Pacific Islander; numbers do not add to 100 because Hispanics can be of any race. *Source*: Created by authors using data from Vespa et al., Current Population Reports, P25-1144, 2018.

from one-half to one-third, while Hispanics will make up nearly one-third of children, blacks 16 percent, and Asians 8.1 percent (Vespa et al., 2018, p. 8).

These internal demographic and immigration trends are changing the face of America. Population projections for select racial and ethnic groups over the next four decades suggests the fastest growing racial or ethnic group in the United States are individuals who are two or more races; their numbers are expected to grow 200 percent by 2060. The Asian population will double, and the number of Hispanics will nearly double over the next four decades (Frey, 2018; Parker et al., 2015). As a result, the non-Hispanic whites, 61.27 percent of the population in 2016, are projected to decline to 56 percent by 2030 and 44 percent by 2060.

The changing racial and ethnic composition of America has important implications for the poverty and low-income population, suggesting larger numbers of those groups who are disproportionately poor already: non-white families and immigrant families. As the next section will demonstrate, this higher likelihood of poverty is in part due to the educational attainment of these groups.

CHANGES IN EDUCATIONAL ATTAINMENT

Americans are better educated than ever before, as educational attainment has been steadily increasing in the United States since 1940. In 1980, a third of individuals age 25 and over had less than a high-school degree, and only 17 percent had a college degree or better. By 2018, only 10 percent of those 25 and older were high-school dropouts and 35 percent had a college degree or better.

These data, though encouraging, hide important differences in educational attainment among different demographic groups. Regardless of demographics, educational attainment has increased over time for all racial and ethnic groups. Graduation rates are similar for men and women of each demographic group. In 2018, nearly 95 percent of non-Hispanic whites have at least a high-school diploma closely followed by blacks, 88 percent. Though Hispanics have increased their high-school completion rates by more than other groups, they still lag behind at 72 percent. Many foreign-born Hispanics, especially those from Mexico, are less educated (Flores, 2017). In fact, 13 percent of foreign-born Hispanics lack a high-school diploma. The high proportion of US-born non-Hispanic whites without a high-school degree, 8 percent, in part reflects the age distribution of this population: many of these individuals are over age 50, having completed their education in an era when high-school graduation was less prevalent.

College completion rates have also increased over the last 25 years. Over the period, both men and women of all racial and ethnic groups were more likely to have graduated from college. In 1995, men were more likely to have a college degree than were women regardless of race or ethnicity; by 2018 non-Hispanic white men and women were equally likely to have graduated from college. Black and Hispanic women were more likely to be college graduates than their male counterparts: 26.9 percent of black women graduated from college compared to 23.2 percent of black men while 20.1 percent of Hispanic women were college graduates compared to 16.6 percent of Hispanic men. Compared to high school, racial differences in college graduation rates are more pronounced: non-Hispanic whites are nearly 50 percent more likely to graduate from college than are blacks and nearly twice as likely as Hispanics.

As we will discuss in chapter 2, educational attainment is more important than ever in today's labor markets: those with more education have a better chance of employment and wage growth over time and are less likely to be poor. The following section provides evidence that education is also important for family formation.

CHANGES IN FAMILY FORMATION AND THE LIVING ARRANGEMENTS OF CHILDREN

Just as the racial and ethnic composition of America has changed over time, the shape of families in America has changed dramatically over the last three decades. Some of these changes, such as smaller families and later childbearing, should reduce a family's chance of poverty. However, other changes such as the de-coupling of union formation from marriage and childbirth from marriage can increase a family's susceptibility to poverty.

The interaction between family structure and economic well-being is complicated. On the one hand, the number of adults and children in the family determines both potential economic support (number of workers) and economic needs of a family. On the other hand, economic well-being or lack thereof can shape family structure and stability. Increasingly, researchers report a "Diverging Destiny," for children based on socioeconomic characteristics of their mothers (McLanahan, 2004; McLanahan and Jacobsen, 2016). College-educated and more prosperous women are less likely to cohabit, more likely to marry later, form stable unions, and have children after marriage. Less educated women are more likely to exhibit a "retreat from marriage," and instead enter into cohabiting relationships early and often, often bearing children while cohabiting or unpartnered; when they do marry, the marriages are more likely to end in divorce than marriages of their better educated peers.

The section begins with a brief review of the theory of family formation, and why that theory is increasingly inadequate to explain today's diverse families. We then review the literature on non-marital births, cohabitation, and marriage.

Theories of Family Formation

The best-known economic theory of family formation is essentially a theory of marriage, with marriage portrayed as an economic decision generating production complementarities based on gendered roles, particularly for rearing children (Becker, 1991). Traditionally, a husband would specialize in market work outside the home, while his wife would specialize in household work and the rearing of children. Individuals would choose to marry if the benefits from marriage exceeded the benefits of remaining single, generating a marriage surplus. A "perfect storm" of social and economic changes over the last several decades has reduced the potential size of the marriage surplus:

- Changes in household technologies have increased household productivity and reduced the time needed for home production (Greenwood, Seshadri, and Yorukoglu, 2005).
- Introduction of birth control gave women greater control over their fertility while at the same time reduced the responsibility of men for an unplanned pregnancy of an unmarried partner (Hoffman, 2017; Akerlof, Yellen, and Katz, 1996).

- Changes in educational attainment and employment opportunities for women which have increased their economic independence (Blau and Kahn, 2000).
- Changes in the legal structure of marriage (divorce laws; changes in child support for children born out of wedlock) have reduced both the social and economic cost of non-marital births.
- Changes in social norms reduce the stigma for cohabitation and non-marital births so that increasingly marriage is less about joint economic production and more about personal fulfillment via shared consumption complementarities (Stevenson and Wolfers, 2007) or investment in children (Lundberg, Pollack, and Stearns, 2016).
- Demographic changes: increased longevity and declining birth rates suggest most of an adult's life is spent without children in the household; and
- Changes in government policy, whether workplace policies are family friendly, and determinants of the social safety net can all shape fertility behavior (McLanahan and Jacobsen, 2015).

Becker's model (1991) can also explain the retreat from marriage: advances in home technology reduced gains from household specialization and exchange while changes in the economy in the 1980s and 1990s, particularly the diminished economic prospects of less educated men and increased economic opportunities for women, reduced the potential marriage surplus for some couples. Lundberg et al. (2016) provide evidence that the gender wage gap for full-time male and female workers is smaller for workers without a college degree than for the college educated. The larger gains in mean earnings for less educated women, compared to the stagnation of less educated men's wages, is a possible explanation for the retreat from marriage for the less educated. Raley et al. (2015) argue that the economic uncertainty and declining labor-market conditions for less skilled men resulted in a "higher marriage bar," the level of economic resources considered necessary for marriage. Gould and Paserman (2003) suggest that changing wage differentials can explain about 25 percent of the decline in marriage over the last three decades.

Some researchers have gone further to suggest that the declining marriage surplus due to smaller gender wage gaps has resulted in a lack of "marriageable men" (Wilson and Neckerman, 1987; Craige et al., 2018). Lundberg, Pollack and Stearns (2016) note that the "marriageable men" hypothesis can only explain declining marriage rates if couples believe that the husband should be the primary breadwinner in the family. A recent survey by Pew Research Center (Parker and Stepler, 2017) found widespread support for this belief: seven in ten adults say, "it is very important for a man to be able to support a family financially to be a good husband or partner." By comparison, only 32 percent say it's very important for a woman to do the same "to be a good wife or partner"; in general, less educated and minority adults placed a higher value on the more traditional man's role as the primary financial provider than did better educated, non-minority adults.

While Becker's model can explain a retreat from marriage, it cannot explain the rise of non-marital fertility among couples, or why the association between marriage and fertility is much weaker for poor and near-poor individuals than for the more prosperous. An alternative theory proposed by Gibson-Davis (2009), the "Financial Expectations and Family Formation Theory," suggests that "cultural attitudes toward the perceived economic prerequisites for marriage, in combination with low economic resources, act as a barrier to marriage, but not childbearing" (p. 147). In effect, the decision to marry and the decision to have a child are different decisions governed by different principles. Indeed, many researchers have noted that poor and near-poor households value marriage and hold it in high regard (Cherlin, 2005), but believe they must attain middle-class economic standards in order to marry despite the lower likelihood of their attaining it (Edin et al., 2004; Waller and McLanahan, 2005; Gibson-Davis et al., 2005). As Cherlin (2005, p. 42) notes:

> marriage remains the preferred option for most people. Now, however, it is not a step taken lightly or early in young adulthood. Being "ready" to marry may mean that a couple has lived together to test their compatibility, saved for a down payment on a house, or possibly had children to judge how well they parent together. Once the foundation of adult family life, marriage is now often the capstone.

On the other hand, childbearing is a source of personal identity and meaning, and is often an expected and accepted part of young adulthood in many poor and low-income communities (Edin and Kefalas, 2011).

Diverse Families

"First comes love, then comes marriage, then comes baby in a baby carriage." This lyric from an American children's song describes a simpler time when family formation was typically a straightforward progression from dating, to marriage, and finally, to parenthood. Today, people travel a variety of different paths to form families. This section begins with a discussion of sexual activity and socioeconomic characteristics, and reviews data on age at first union, cohabitation, and marriage for demographic groups of interest.

Though family arrangements increasingly vary by socioeconomic characteristics, Reeves and Venator (2015) have found that sexual activity of single women aged 15–44 does not significantly vary based on income:

nearly two-thirds of women in this age group are sexually active, regardless of their income level. This suggests that differences in unintended pregnancy or childbearing are not explained by differences in sexual activity. Instead, affluent women whose incomes are greater than 400 percent of the official poverty level are twice as likely to use contraception, and in the event of an unintended pregnancy, are more than four times as likely to have an abortion than women whose income is less than 200 percent of the official poverty level. Furthermore, these gaps in contraception use and abortion cannot be explained by differences in preferences for births, as nearly two-thirds of women in each income group said they would be "very upset" or "a little upset" by a pregnancy. This supports Sawhill's (2014) contention that most non-marital births are unplanned, and that today's young women are a "generation unbound" and drifting into sex and parenthood.

How and at what age dating couples choose to form more permanent unions has implications for the stability of families and the care provided to children who live in these families. For example, McLanahan (2015, 2004) suggests age of mother serves as a proxy for maturity and potential quality of mothering. Age at first union, first cohabitation, and first marriage has changed over the last 40 years and can differ by race, ethnicity, and education.

The age at which a couple has formed their first "serious" relationship, known as first union, generally the early twenties, has remained stable over time and is similar for white, black, and Hispanic couples. The same cannot be said for differences in education. The least educated, those with a high-school diploma or less, form first unions earlier than do couples who are college educated: on average, men with a bachelor's degree are approximately five years older than male high-school dropouts, while college-educated women are nearly six years older than their less educated peers. A similar pattern exists for age at first cohabitation, largely due to the fact that over time, increasing numbers of couples choose to cohabit at first union. The exception is college-educated women whose probability of cohabiting at first union has remained remarkably stable over time while most recently, less educated women, and men of all education levels are more likely to do so. Historically, blacks are more likely than other groups to cohabit at first union.

Over time, age at first marriage has increased for all men and women, regardless of race or ethnicity. Historically, blacks have married later than other groups, though this difference has diminished with time. Similarly, while the college-educated have married at a later age than high-school educated couples, the difference has converged over time so that by the latest period, age at first marriage is similar for all education groups. In 2018, US Census data suggests the median age at first marriage was almost 28 for women and nearly 30 for men.

The importance of age and education in understanding how and when families form cannot be overestimated. The less educated form unions and are more likely to cohabit at younger ages than do the better educated, yet form legally binding unions (marriages) at ages similar to the better educated. As we shall see in the review of the literature to follow, younger, cohabiting couples may not be the most economically stable families for children.

Marriage

Though marriage rates have declined over the past 30 years, marriage remains the most common family structure; most adults will spend some part of their lives in a marital union. Furthermore, a 2019 snapshot of living arrangements of children under 18 suggests that 70 percent of children live with both parents, most of whom are married (Census, 2019). However, there are important differences in the stability of marriage based on age, race and ethnicity, and education.

Raley, Sweeney and Wondra (2015) describe the growing racial and ethnic divergence in marriage in the United States. While all groups are delaying marriage, there are significant racial and ethnic differences. Black women delay marriage by nearly four years longer than other groups, or are more likely to forego marriage altogether. When they do marry, they have higher rates of marital instability than do whites or Hispanics; divorce rates among blacks increased earlier and more rapidly for blacks than whites. Consequently, after accounting for women who have never married by their early forties, roughly half of all white and Hispanic women are in stable marriages compared to less than one-third of black women. Similarly, foreign-born Hispanics have higher marriage rates and lower divorce rates than do native-born Hispanics.

Marriage rates and stability also depend upon education: college-educated women are more likely to marry and their marriages are more stable than those of less educated women. Historically this is due to earlier marriages and higher divorce rates of the less educated, but more recently is associated with delays in marriage and a higher percentage of less educated women who forgo marriage altogether.

Although racial and ethnic differences in marriage persist across education levels, the gaps are greatest among the less educated. Raley, Sweeney and Wondra (2015) argue that marriage has increasingly become linked to employment, earnings, and economic opportunities. As a result, the legacy of discrimination often experienced by blacks and Hispanics has contributed to racial differences within educational groups. Increased economic inequality and stagnation of wages among the less educated of all racial/ethnic groups have resulted in increasing convergence of age at first marriage between the less and better educated.

Cohabitation

Cohabitation is an increasingly common family structure. Cohabitation provides the benefits of co-residence with less commitment and lower exit costs than marriage. Seventy percent of first marriages among women under age 36 began in premarital cohabitation (Kuperberg, 2019), and by age 12, 40 percent of today's children have spent some part of their childhood with parents who cohabit (Kennedy and Fitch, 2012).

A recent survey of US adults aged 18–44 conducted by Pew Research Center suggests that the share of adults who have ever cohabited, 59 percent, is greater than those who have ever been married, 50 percent (Pew, 2019). And they find important differences between the two groups. Married partners have higher levels of relationship satisfaction and trust than do cohabiting couples, and while love and companionship are top reasons for both marriage and cohabitation, nearly 40 percent of cohabiting couples cite finances (38 percent) and convenience (37 percent) as factors in their decision to live together. By comparison only 10 percent of married couples suggest convenience, and 17 percent suggest finances as reasons to marry. Furthermore, over half of cohabiting couples suggest finances are why they are not engaged or married to their current partner (Pew, 2019).

Pew researchers also find that a majority of adults age 18–44 who are either married or cohabiting have children under 18 in their homes. Seventy percent of married couples live with biological children they share, compared with only 35 percent of cohabiting couples. Among married couples there are few racial or ethnic differences in percentages of married couples who live with shared biological children; this is not true for cohabiting couples. Over half of Hispanic cohabiters live with shared biological children, while 44 percent of black couples and only 25 percent of white cohabiters do. Presence of children also varies by education: nearly three-quarters of cohabiters with a high-school education or less are raising children, while only 26 percent of cohabiters with a bachelor's degree or more have children at home.

Reeves and Krause (2017) find at least one important difference between cohabiting and married couples: the rate of unintended childbirth for cohabiting couples, 51 percent, is more than twice that of married couples, 23 percent. Furthermore, mothers in married couples are more likely to say that an unintended birth was mistimed rather than unwanted. Guzzo and Hayford (2014) find that for cohabiting couples, unplanned births are often associated with a higher risk of union dissolution, while couples who plan the birth of their child are more likely to transition to marriage.

A large literature suggests cohabiting relationships are less stable than married-couple relationships. In the late 1980s, most cohabiting relationships transitioned to marriage. Today, cohabiting relationships last on average only 22 to 24 months (Copen, Daniels and Mosher, 2013) and are more likely to end through separation. Higher levels of family formation and dissolution often lead to serial cohabitation and increased levels of multiple-partner fertility (Brown, Stykes, and Manning, 2016). In 2014, over 40 percent of cohabiting couples with children under 18 exhibited multiple partner fertility (Monte, 2019).

Consequently, children born into cohabiting families experience three times as many family transitions (creating or dissolving a family union) than do children born to married parents (Raley and Wildsmith, 2004; Brown, Stykes, and Manning, 2016). Nearly half of children born to cohabiting parents will experience a parental breakup before their third birthday compared to only 11 percent of married parents (Brown, Stykes, and Manning, 2016). By age 12, only one-third of children will have grown up in an intact cohabiting family, compared to three-quarters of children in married-couple families (Kennedy and Bompas, 2008).

Cohabitation transitions play a significant role in family instability, and this varies by race and ethnicity. More than half of black children, two-fifths of Hispanic children, and over a third of white children will live with a parent in a cohabitating relationship. Consequently, there is an increasing gap in family instability among children of different racial and ethnic groups (Brown Stykes and Manning, 2015).

Not only do children born into cohabiting families experience more instability, their living arrangements are often more complex. In 2016, of the children who lived in a heterosexual, cohabiting union, 53 percent lived with both biological parents while the remainder lived with a stepparent (Census, 2017). Nearly 40 percent children in cohabitating families lived with step and/or half siblings (Manning, 2015).

Children in cohabiting families experience less consistency in living arrangements, parental presence, and family income. That increased family instability is linked to negative impacts on child development and well-being is well established in the literature (Cavanagh and Huston, 2008; Cherlin et al., 1991; Fomby and Cherlin, 2007; Osborne and McLanahan, 2007; Wu, 1996; Wu and Martinson, 1993). Additionally, recent research suggests family structure can be an important determinant of intergenerational poverty and lack of socioeconomic mobility (Smeeding, 2016; McLanahan and Percheski, 2008).

Non-marital Births

Non-marital births include births to formerly married, divorced, or widowed women, plus births to never-married women. Non-marital births may be first, second, or higher-order births. The non-marital birth rate depends on both the proportion of women who are married and the relative fertility rates of married and non-married women. While marital fertility has declined in recent years, the most important factor has been the decline in marriage: women marry later or forego marriage altogether, yet do not necessarily forego union formation or parenthood. Consequently, nearly 40 percent of all births occur outside of marriage (Child Trends, 2018) and over half of these births are to cohabiting couples (Brown, Manning, and Stykes, 2015).

In 1960 non-marital births represented just 5.3 percent of all births; but between 1970 and 1990, non-marital fertility increased sharply from 10.7 to 28 percent of all births. Since then, the growth of non-marital births has slowed before peaking in 2009 at 41 percent of all births (Solomon-Fears, 2014; Curtin, Ventura, and Martinez, 2014). Non-marital births have declined to 39.8 percent of all births in 2016. Schneider and Gemmill (2016) attribute the decline in non-marital fertility to increased access to long-acting reversible contraceptive (LARC) methods and the effects of the Great Recession on fertility.

Just as union formation and the probability of cohabitation vary by race and ethnicity, so does the percentage of non-marital births. In 2019, black and Hispanic women had significantly higher percentages of non-marital births (70 and 52 percent respectively) than did non-Hispanic white women (20 percent). And not all Hispanic families are alike: Mexican and Central American families have higher birth rates and are more likely to marry, while Puerto Rican families have a strong tradition of consensual unions and are more likely to cohabit and have non-marital births (Cherlin, 2005).

The distribution of non-marital births by age of mother has also changed over time. In the past, non-marital births were disproportional to teens: in 1970 half of non-marital births were to young women under age 20 (Ventura, 2009). Non-marital birth rates for teens declined significantly between 1995 and 2012 so that the distribution of non-marital births by age of mother looks very different today than in the past. In 2016, teen births account for just over 10 percent of non-martial births, while nearly two-thirds are to women in their twenties.

The facts summarized in this section suggest that families today are more diverse, and perhaps more economically unstable, than in the past, with delays in marriage, increased levels of cohabitation, and more non-marital births providing children, particularly those with less educated parents, more precarious access to economic resources. These more varied paths to family formation pose particular challenges to our ability to measure poverty in these families.

OUR SPM FAMILIES

The dataset used in our analysis demonstrates many of the trends discussed in this chapter. Our choice of the SPM unit as our measure of a family is particularly well suited to many of the demographic changes described above. For example, use of the SPM unit permits an analysis of cohabiting couples and "other adults" who reside in families, something not easily accomplished with the official measure of poverty.

Changing demographic characteristics such as race/ethnicity, nativity, and family formation affect the composition of the poor. Table 1.1 illustrates how the demographic changes discussed in this chapter impact the incidence and composition of poverty of our SPM families over time.

The first three columns of table 1.1 describe demographic characteristics of all SPM families, the middle three columns of poor SPM families, and the last three columns detail poverty rates for individuals in SPM families. The data in the first three columns suggest that our SPM units reflect the demographic changes found in the general population of the last 20 years: they are less likely to be white and more likely to be Hispanic; they are less likely to be married and more likely to cohabit; and they are better educated with fewer SPM heads with a high-school education or less and more with some college or a college degree.

These changes in turn affect the poverty population. Demographic subgroups can make up large segments of the poor population because they have high population shares, high poverty rates, or both. For example, whites or married-couple families make up substantial portions of our poor SPM families (middle three columns), not because these groups have high poverty rates—the last columns suggest that these groups consistently have the lowest poverty rates—but because they make up the largest share of the population (first three columns). On the other hand, as a share of SPM families, blacks (15 percent) and single, non-cohabiting families (25 percent) have remained relatively constant over the last 20 years but make up an important portion of poor SPM families (last three columns) because of their relatively higher, though declining, poverty rates. Hispanics, both native and foreign-born, make up increasing percentages of poor SPM families, because of their higher relative poverty rates and increasing population shares. The following tables expand on this analysis by investigating these demographic trends through a more detailed comparison of poor and non-poor families with children under age 18.

Differences in poverty status may reflect differences in age; in general, we expect families headed by younger adults to have higher poverty rates because they are likely to have less work experience and may be less educated. Over time heads and spouses in both poor and non-poor families have

Table 1.1 Changing Population Trends and SPM Poverty in SPM Families with Children by Race, Marital Status, and Education of Head, Select Years 1995–2018

	Percentage of All SPM Families			Poverty Rate of Persons in SPM Families			Percentage of Poor SPM Families		
	1995	2006	2018	1995	2006	2018	1995	2006	2018
Race									
Non-Hispanic White	71.8	66.2	61.9	11.9	8.2	7.3	45.3	37.9	36.8
Non-Hispanic Black	15.2	15.0	14.7	35.0	26.2	20.7	27.2	26.2	24.5
Native-Born Hispanic	5.8	7.7	10.6	31.8	21.9	15.5	9.7	11.1	13.1
Foreign-Born Hispanic	7.2	11.1	12.8	49.0	34.4	25.5	17.8	24.8	25.6
Marital Status									
Married Couple	71.1	68.8	66.7	12.9	9.7	8.1	42.6	40.3	39.6
Cohabiting Couple	4.0	6.4	8.2	26.3	22.1	17.8	5.2	8.9	10.8
Single Parent	24.9	24.8	25.2	43.4	32.6	25.8	52.2	50.8	49.6
Education of Head									
Less than High School	16.4	14.0	10.3	46.0	38.5	31.6	38.7	35.8	26.3
High-School Graduate	32.8	29.2	24.6	20.0	17.7	18.0	34.7	35.2	35.7
Some College	28.0	29.2	28.9	13.6	11.0	10.6	20.2	22.1	25.5
College Graduate	22.7	27.6	36.2	5.6	3.8	4.3	6.4	6.9	12.5

Source: Authors' calculations based on Current Population Survey: IPUMS-CPS, University of Minnesota and Historical SPM data, Columbia University.

become slightly older on average. In 2018 on average, non-poor heads and spouses are older (42 years of age) than their poor counterparts (40 years of age), while adult children and parents of heads are of similar ages in both poor and non-poor families. The remaining adults in poor families are younger than their non-poor counterparts.

Table 1.2 describes our SPM families by race/ethnicity, marital, and poverty status. The changing racial and ethnic composition of the general population described at the beginning of this chapter affects our poor and non-poor SPM families alike: over time both groups have become less white and more Hispanic, while the proportions of the poor and non-poor that are black have remained relatively constant. The non-poor SPM families are more likely to be white than non-white, while poor SPM families are more equally divided between white families and non-white families.

Decreases in the probability of marriage and increases in the probability of cohabitation are also general trends affecting both poor and non-poor SPM families. The non-poor are much more likely to be married, slightly less likely to cohabit, and much less likely to be single parents than are poor SPM families.

As the literature at the beginning of the chapter suggests, there are significant differences in family formation among racial and ethnic groups, and our data reflect this. Regardless of poverty status, whites and foreign-born Hispanics have the highest likelihood of marriage, while blacks have the lowest probability of marriage and the highest probability of single parenthood. Furthermore, both poor and non-poor native-born Hispanics are more likely to cohabit than other groups.

Family size and composition are potential contributors to the poverty of SPM families. The number of adults determines the potential number of workers, while the number of children in the family determines the resource needs of the family. In 2018, the average poor SPM family had fewer adults (1.9) than non-poor SPM families (2.2); and until very recently had more children (2.1) than do non-poor SPM families (1.8). This is true for all racial and ethnic groups. Regardless of poverty status, married couples have slightly more children than do cohabitating couples, who in turn have slightly more children than single parent families. Hispanic families, whether native or foreign-born, have larger families than other racial/ethnic groups, with both more adults and more children. Poor white families have fewer children on average than do other groups. Finally, the averages above suggest that SPM families include adults who are neither the family head, spouse or cohabitating head or partner. The identity of these adults is important from a poverty perspective: if working age, they may be a potential source of resources for the family; if not, they may represent additional need for support. Table 1.3 provides information on these other adults.

Table 1.2   Overall Racial Composition and Marital Status by Race and Poverty Status

SPM Families with Children, Select Years 1995–2018 (percent)					
	Poor SPM Families			Non-Poor SPM Families		
	1995	*2006*	*2018*	*1995*	*2006*	*2018*
Racial Composition						
Non-Hispanic White	45.3	37.9	36.8	78.3	71.3	65.6
Non-Hispanic Black	27.2	26.2	24.5	12.2	13.0	13.2
Native-Born Hispanic	9.7	11.1	13.1	4.9	7.1	10.3
Foreign-Born Hispanic	17.8	24.8	25.6	4.6	8.6	10.9
Married Couple						
All	42.6	40.3	39.6	78.2	73.9	70.7
Non-Hispanic White	50.1	41.1	43.7	82.2	78.5	76.5
Non-Hispanic Black	17.9	18.0	18.2	53.3	49.2	46.8
Native-Born Hispanic	33.2	34.5	35.0	73.2	66.9	60.7
Foreign-Born Hispanic	66.5	65.2	56.5	80.8	79.0	73.9
Cohabiting Couple						
All	5.2	8.9	10.8	3.7	6.0	7.8
Non-Hispanic White	5.7	11.5	11.3	3.3	5.6	7.4
Non-Hispanic Black	4.9	6.6	8.0	5.7	7.4	8.3
Native-Born Hispanic	6.1	9.2	11.3	4.7	8.1	10.1
Foreign-Born Hispanic	3.9	7.1	12.7	3.1	5.3	7.0
Single, Non-Cohabiting						
All	52.2	50.8	49.6	18.2	20.1	21.5
Non-Hispanic White	44.2	47.4	45.0	14.5	15.9	16.1
Non-Hispanic Black	77.2	75.3	73.9	41.0	43.4	44.9
Native-Born Hispanic	60.7	56.3	53.8	22.1	25.0	29.2
Foreign-Born Hispanic	29.5	27.7	30.8	16.1	15.7	19.1

Source: Authors' calculations based on Current Population Survey: IPUMS-CPS, University of Minnesota and Historical SPM data, Columbia University.

Over the past 20 years, the likelihood of another adult living in SPM families has increased for poor and non-poor families alike: nearly 40 percent of families have an adult child, a parent, or some other relative living in their families. Poor and non-poor families are equally likely to have an adult child living at home, while the poor are slightly more likely to have a parent or other adult. Nearly half of foreign-born Hispanics have additional adults in the family, most often an adult child, but also other relatives. Whites are least likely to have other adult members of their families, while native-born Hispanics are more likely to have three generations living under one roof. Regardless of poverty status, cohabiting families are least likely to have other adults in their families, while single parents are most likely. While adult children are the most common other adult in single parent families, these families are twice as likely as coupled families to have a parent living with them. Additional adults may be a source of additional work effort for a poor family. While adult children could contribute to the work effort of poor families,

Table 1.3　Identity of Other Adults* by Race, Marital, and Poverty Status

SPM Families with Children, Select Years 1995–2018 (percent)

	Poor SPM Families			Non-Poor SPM Families		
	1995	2006	2018	1995	2006	2018
All						
Adult Child	22.2	25.1	19.6	24.5	26.1	19.1
Parent of head	3.7	6.4	6.1	2.9	4.9	4.2
Other	14.0	15.9	9.3	9.7	11.8	6.9
Percent with any of the above	33.8	39.0	26.0	31.8	35.8	25.7
Non-Hispanic White						
Adult Child	17.7	21.9	15.7	23.0	25.0	16.8
Parent of head	2.3	4.3	3.8	2.3	3.9	2.4
Other	10.2	12.7	6.9	8.1	9.8	4.9
Percent with any of the above	26.2	32.9	22.6	29.2	32.9	21.0
Non-Hispanic Black						
Adult Child	26.5	26.8	18.9	30.5	29.2	21.8
Parent of head	4.4	6.2	6.2	4.6	6.2	5.4
Other	13.3	14.0	8.1	12.2	13.5	8.0
Percent with any of the above	37.8	38.8	28.2	40.3	41.0	30.0
Native-Born Hispanic						
Adult Child	23.2	25.0	17.0	26.6	26.5	18.6
Parent of head	4.1	10.4	13.3	4.1	9.1	10.9
Other	12.9	18.0	12.1	12.2	16.3	11.2
Percent with any of the above	34.3	42.3	34.9	36.3	40.9	32.9
Foreign-Born Hispanic						
Adult Child	26.6	28.0	27.3	31.8	30.2	30.8
Parent of head	5.7	7.9	5.7	6.9	7.5	7.4
Other	24.8	21.8	12.3	24.9	22.3	13.6
Percent with any of the above	46.9	47.0	38.5	49.2	47.6	42.4
Married Couple						
Adult Child	23.0	27.3	22.8	23.9	25.7	18.9
Parent of head	2.8	4.9	3.7	2.1	3.5	2.1
Other	12.8	15.5	7.0	7.8	9.8	4.7
Percent with any of the above	32.5	39.5	29.6	29.6	33.5	22.9
Cohabiting Couple						
Adult Child	18.1	18.3	8.3	13.6	17.7	10.1
Parent of head	1.8	5.9	1.4	2.7	4.3	3.0
Other	11.9	14.2	9.3	10.3	11.5	8.1
Percent with any of the above	27.5	32.0	14.8	22.9	28.1	15.7
Single Parent						
Adult Child	22.0	24.5	19.5	29.3	29.8	23.2
Parent of head	4.6	7.7	9.1	6.3	9.9	11.7
Other	15.0	16.4	11.1	17.1	19.2	13.9
Percent with any of the above	35.5	39.8	32.9	43.2	46.4	38.8

*Person over 18 years of age who is neither a head, spouse, cohabitating head, or partner
Source: Authors' calculations based on Current Population Survey: IPUMS-CPS, University of Minnesota and Historical SPM data, Columbia University.

their contribution may be limited as they are likely among the youngest and least skilled workers. Additionally, some of these adult children may be students. Similarly, elderly parents of a head or spouse in married or cohabitating families may not contribute to work effort of the family, though they may contribute to other sources of income such as social security payments or provide child care which can support the work effort of other family members.

Overall, both poor and non-poor heads and spouses reflect the general population trend of increased educational attainment: there are fewer high-school dropouts, and more adults with some college (poor) or college degrees (both groups). Though both groups exhibit these trends generally, the educational attainment of the poor lags significantly behind that of the non-poor. Compared with the non-poor, adults in poor families are more likely to be high-school dropouts and less likely to have earned a college degree. This is typically true for all racial groups, though the magnitude of the difference between the poor and non-poor differs among racial groups.

Comparing educational attainment across racial groups suggest that by 2016, white non-Hispanic heads and spouses have appreciably more education than all other groups. Over half of these adults have been to college and 20 percent have earned college degrees, a college graduation rate twice that of non-Hispanic blacks and nearly three times that of native-born Hispanics. Foreign-born Hispanic heads and spouses are notable for their lack of educational attainment. Though they have become better educated over time, by 2016, nearly 60 percent did not have a high-school diploma and only 5 percent had graduated from college.

Table 1.4 also considers educational attainment by marital and poverty status. Unsurprisingly, the non-poor are substantially better educated than the poor, for each marital status group. However, both groups have increased their educational attainment over time, with fewer high-school dropouts and more college graduates. Furthermore, regardless of poverty status, heads and their spouses or partners are similarly educated, suggesting that our SPM families exhibit evidence of increased assortative mating, or like marrying/ cohabiting with like. For both poor and non-poor, married couples have the most education, while cohabiting couples are among the least educated; single parent heads are somewhere in between.

Finally, citizenship status for adults in poor SPM families with children is important. Given the immigration trends described at the beginning of the chapter it is not surprising that the number of families with non-citizen adults has increased over time for nearly every racial and marital status group; by 2018 nearly a third of poor families had a non-citizen adult member. Nearly all foreign-born Hispanics are non-citizens, though this number is declining over time. As noted earlier, studies suggest that though these adults are not citizens, the majority of their children were born in the states. Lack of adult

Table 1.4　Percent Educational Attainment of Heads and Spouses* by Race, Marital Status, and Poverty Status, Select Years 1995–2018

	Poor SPM Families with Children			Non-Poor SPM Families with Children		
	1995	*2006*	*2018*	*1995*	*2006*	*2018*
All						
Less than High School	42.5	39.9	31.0	11.2	10.9	9.1
High-School Graduate	33.1	34.1	34.8	33.8	28.6	23.9
Some College	17.7	18.8	21.7	28.8	28.8	27.2
College Graduate	6.7	7.2	12.6	26.2	31.7	39.8
Non-Hispanic White						
Less than High School	25.3	22.3	16.3	7.2	5.2	3.6
High-School Graduate	40.0	38.7	35.5	33.9	27.4	20.7
Some College	23.4	26.3	27.2	29.4	29.8	27.5
College Graduate	11.2	12.7	21.0	29.5	37.6	48.3
Non-Hispanic Black						
Less than High School	39.1	29.1	19.4	15.3	10.0	6.5
High-School Graduate	38.7	42.7	41.1	37.2	33.8	27.9
Some College	19.0	23.2	29.4	31.6	33.8	32.2
College Graduate	3.1	5.0	10.1	16.0	22.4	33.4
Native-Born Hispanic						
Less than High School	51.3	43.2	27.3	22.0	16.9	10.3
High-School Graduate	31.3	32.8	39.5	37.3	34.1	31.3
Some College	14.7	20.4	25.6	28.3	32.4	35.9
College Graduate	2.7	3.6	7.6	12.4	16.6	22.5
Foreign-Born Hispanic						
Less than High School	75.1	65.3	55.8	52.2	48.3	39.4
High-School Graduate	15.6	24.0	28.4	22.8	27.6	31.3
Some College	6.5	7.2	9.4	16.1	14.3	14.8
College Graduate	2.8	3.5	6.4	9.0	9.8	14.6
Married Heads & Spouses						
Less than High School	43.0	40.7	32.8	10.5	9.9	8.6
High-School Graduate	31.0	31.9	32.0	32.7	26.7	21.9
Some College	16.7	17.2	18.7	28.2	27.5	25.5
College Graduate	9.3	10.2	16.5	28.6	35.8	44.0
Cohabiting Heads & Partners						
Less than High School	45.9	40.7	36.8	19.0	17.4	12.7
High-School Graduate	38.0	40.0	39.6	46.8	41.1	37.5
Some College	15.1	16.3	18.6	26.9	30.2	32.7
College Graduate	1.0	3.0	5.0	7.3	11.3	17.1
Single Parent Heads						
Less than High School	40.2	34.9	24.6	17.9	14.8	11.5
High-School Graduate	35.8	36.8	37.4	34.6	31.3	28.4
Some College	20.7	23.1	29.4	32.7	35.6	36.1
College Graduate	3.4	5.2	8.5	14.8	18.2	24.0

*Spouses include the partners of cohabiting heads
Source: Authors' calculations based on Current Population Survey: IPUMS-CPS, University of Minnesota and Historical SPM data, Columbia University.

citizenship contributes to economic instability of these families and complicates their receipt of government support.

CONCLUSION

This chapter has reviewed a variety of demographic changes that are shaping families in America's twenty-first century. Increased immigration and differences in relative fertility rates suggest that America is becoming a more racially and ethnically diverse nation with fewer non-Hispanic white families and more black and Hispanic families. Adults are better educated: fewer will drop out of high school and more will have some college or a college degree. Educational attainment is increasingly important for family formation and stability. More education is associated with fewer children on average, and less education is associated with greater family instability. Adults without a college degree are more likely to cohabit or have children outside of marriage, and their relationships are less stable over time. As a consequence, children are likely to experience more instability in their living arrangements. All of these changes have important implications for poverty among families with children.

This chapter has also introduced the SPM families studied in this research. Our families are representative of these larger demographic trends: they are racially and ethnically more diverse, they are better educated, and they increasingly form diverse families, including families with other adult relatives. A third of SPM poor families have a non-citizen adult member. All of these factors impact the poverty levels of our SPM families. As we shall see in the next chapter, these demographic factors are also important in our understanding of families and labor markets.

Chapter 2

Work and Wages

Understanding the US Economy and the Poor

This chapter begins with a discussion of US labor markets over the past 30 years. Two major, recent US economic trends affect the ability of poor families to support themselves: changes in US labor markets that have led many workers to work less than they would like, or to drop out of the labor force entirely, and declining or slow-growing wages which have diminished the returns to work for many workers. This chapter begins by reviewing these major economic trends. We then investigate how these trends affect poor and low-skill workers in particular, focusing on unemployment, involuntary part-time work (IPTW), and poverty-level wages. We show the differential impact of these major trends and economic challenges by gender, race, and ethnicity. Finally, we illustrate how these issues affect our SPM families with children.

DECLINING LABOR-MARKET PARTICIPATION

The civilian labor force participation rate is an important indicator of the long-term health of the labor market. It measures the share of the civilian non-institutionalized population either employed or looking for work. As such it determines the relative amount of labor available to produce goods and services and thus is an important determinant of economic growth. Historically, labor force participation for youth (ages 16 to 19) and young adults (ages 20 to 24) is lower than for prime-age workers (ages 25 to 54), and labor force participation declines sharply after age 55 as increasing numbers of workers retire from the labor force. Generally, men participate in labor markets at higher rates than do women, and there are important differences by race and ethnicity as well.

Over the last several decades, a number of important changes have occurred in US labor markets that have impacted workers' labor force participation (Abraham and Kearney, 2020). For example, changes in worker tastes and preferences can affect the balance between work and leisure; demographic changes such as the aging of the baby boom cohort or increased immigration can alter the number of available workers; economic expansions or recessions cause cyclical changes in the demand and supply of labor; and structural changes in the economy, such as increased school attendance or changes in technology, outsourcing, and globalization of production, can affect the number of workers needed and available. Together, these changes have contributed to a general decline in labor force participation in the twenty-first century. Economists on the Council of Economic Advisors (CEA) (2014) estimate that since 2007, one-half of the decline in labor force participation is due to demographic change, one-third is due to structural factors, and the remaining one-sixth is due to cyclical factors.

After steadily rising for several decades, the overall labor force participation rate peaked at 67.3 percent in 2000 and has declined since, though this aggregate statistic obscures a variety of underlying changes. Men's participation in US labor markets has been declining for the last half-century. In 1950, 86.4 percent of men participated in the labor force, in 2000, 74.8 percent did, and by May 2019 only 71.6 percent of men age 20 and over were in the labor force. Women, on the other hand, increased their labor force participation over the last half of the twentieth century, from 33.9 percent in 1950, to a peak of 59.9 percent in 2000 before their labor force participation rate stagnated and declined slightly in the twenty-first century to 58.5 percent in May 2019 (US Bureau of Labor Statistics, Employment Projections). This pattern was true for women of varying race and ethnicities, educational backgrounds, ages, marital status, and for women with and without children alike. As a result, the gap between men and women's labor force participation has narrowed over time.

The aging of the "Baby Boom" cohort, those born between 1946 and 1964, also partially explains declining participation, as a large segment of the population has moved from an age group with higher participation rates to an older age group with lower participation. However, aging boomers are not the only group with declining participation. Since 2000, youth and young workers have experienced some of the most precipitous declines in labor force participation. Bauer et al. (2019) suggest that increased school enrollment, seasonal employment, decreased returns to work, reduced demand for low-wage work, minimum wage hikes, and competition from older workers or immigrants all play a role in explaining these declines. Both men and women with no more than a high-school diploma have experienced the largest declines. Furthermore, since 2000, young women with children under 18 are more likely to drop out of the labor force, with the largest declines for mothers with less than a college education.

Important differences in labor force participation also depend upon race and ethnicity. One of the most important changes in US labor markets in recent decades is the influx of Hispanic workers: in 1988, 7.4 percent of the labor force was of Hispanic origin, by 2016 they were 16.8 percent, and by 2026 they are projected to be one-fifth of the US labor force (BLS.gov). Hispanics are younger on average than other racial groups and many are immigrants who come to the US seeking better jobs and higher wages. Consequently, Hispanic men have higher participation rates than white men, while black men have the lowest rates of labor force participation. For women, the opposite is true: black women had higher participation rates and Hispanic women lower participation rates than white women. Different age profiles, fertility rates, and increased immigration help explain the changing racial and ethnic profile of the labor force; in 1996 one in four workers were non-white, by 2026 over 40 percent will be.

While recessions are associated with higher rates of unemployment and may lead to workers to drop out of the labor force temporarily, the persistence of lower rates of labor force participation suggests that more than just cyclical factors are at work. Most recently, increased globalization of production and trade has placed American workers in the tradable goods sector in competition with their counterparts in lower-wage countries. Autor, Dorn and Hanson (2021, 2019, 2013) suggest that increased trade has indirect negative effects on employment and marriage rates in communities exposed to import competition from trade. This has contributed to a decline in manufacturing employment, a sector particularly important for low-skill (high-school graduate or less) and middle-skill (some college) men. Muro and Kulkarni (2016) suggest that 7 million manufacturing jobs have been lost to globalization, offshoring, and automation since 1980. Baily and Bosworth (2014) suggest that of these jobs, 5.7 million were lost between 2000 and 2010. Charles, Hurst, and Schwartz (2018) find that manufacturing decline in the 2000s had large and persistent negative effects on employment rates, hours worked, and wages; they also show that declining local manufacturing employment is related to rising opioid use and deaths. In a study of manufacturing employment decline of black and white workers, Gould (2021) finds that between 1960 and 2010 the black community was particularly hard hit. The fifty-year decline in manufacturing employment led to a 14.7 percent decline in black men's wages, a 5.9 percentage point decline in employment, and 4.7 percentage point decline in marriage rates. As a consequence, black children are predicted to have an increased poverty rate of 11.4 percentage points.

Historically, manufacturing jobs have been important for low-skill workers because these jobs paid a wage premium significantly higher than other low-skill occupations. However, Mishel (2018) finds that while manufacturing jobs still pay a premium today, this premium has declined by 25 percent since the 1980s.

In *Men without Work,* Eberstadt (2016) argues that low and middle-skilled men displaced by loss of manufacturing jobs may drop out of the labor force because they have high reservation wages and are unwilling to accept lower paid service work. In support of this analysis, Koenig et al. (2016) suggest that reservation wages are linked to an individual's previous earnings, and Hogan (2004) finds that previous earnings have a larger impact on men's reservation wages than women's reservation wages, which tend to be more influenced by market wages. Furthermore, higher reservation wages of native-born men may also explain why low-skill immigrants with more limited expectations participate in labor markets at significantly higher rates than the native-born.

Technical change has led to a hollowing out of the labor force on the basis of skill. In recent years, computer and information technologies have increased the demand for highly skilled, college-educated workers, while replacing middle- and low-skilled male and female workers who perform routine, repetitive tasks such as assembly line workers or clerical staff, but with little impact on lower skill, labor-intensive service jobs (Autor, Goldin, and Katz, 2020; Autor, Katz, and Kearney, 2008; Autor and Dorn, 2013). Holzer (2015) describes this job market polarization as a "tale of two middles." While traditional middle-wage jobs such as production and clerical jobs have declined rapidly, technical change has led to an increase in other middle-skill jobs in health care, mechanical maintenance and repair, and some services. The job categories that are growing often require more post-secondary education or training than those that are declining, but worker skills have not kept pace. And these trends are likely to continue: Frey and Osborn (2017) suggest that at least 47 percent of US jobs are subject to potential automation in the future. Workers who lose their jobs and do not upgrade their skills often take part-time jobs in the lower paid service sector or drop out of the labor force altogether. Tuzemen (2018) argues that this polarization of the labor force due to skill-based technical change is a key factor in non-participation of lower and increasingly middle-skilled (some college) men, accounting for nearly 80 percent of the decline in prime-age male work effort between 1996 and 2016.

Institutional changes can affect labor force participation as well. While crime rates are roughly what they were in the past, Western (2006) notes that over the last three decades, the US prison population has increased more than sevenfold to more than two million people. Those who are incarcerated are disproportionately less educated non-Hispanic black and Hispanic men. For example, nearly 60 percent of black high-school dropouts in their thirties have spent some time in prison. Because the labor force participation rate is defined as the percent of the *non-institutionalized* population either employed or looking for work, the prison population is *not* included in this statistic, increasing the reported labor force participation rates for these groups. For example, Western and Petit (2010) report that while 40 percent of black high-school dropouts were listed as employed in 2008, including inmates in these population and employment estimates would reduce the employment rate to just 25 percent. Furthermore, incarceration is associated with lower labor force participation rates, lower wages, and greater economic disadvantage post release.

The loss of manufacturing jobs and the labor-market problems associated with incarceration are both trends that primarily affect men. Unlike men's labor force participation, which has been declining for the last 50 years, declining women's labor force participation is a more recent phenomenon. When asked why they are not working, women overwhelmingly cite family responsibilities as a reason for their non-participation. Staying home to care for family members is different than not working due to poor labor-market opportunities. Furthermore, Sandra Black and her colleagues (2017) note that the recent decline in women's labor force participation in the US is contrary to recently observed trends in other OECD countries; since 2000, out of all OECD countries, the US ranks second to last in percentage point growth in women's labor force participation (p. 7). While these countries face the same forces of technical change and globalization that affect all workers, the US is the only developed country without universal paid family leave, and also lags behind other nations in family-friendly policies such as paid sick days and access to high-quality, affordable childcare. Lack of these family-friendly options has disproportionally affected the labor-market choices of women.

There is evidence that a lack of affordable child care could make a difference. According to a recent government report (US Treasury, 2021), in a typical week in spring 2016, four in 10 children under the age of six were solely cared for by their parents, the remaining 60 percent, nearly 13 million children, received an average of 30 hours of care weekly from a non-parent. Middle- and low-income families are less likely to use licensed child care than are wealthier families; for these families cost and location constraints are important determinants of the type of care. For children under age five who are in some type of care, 80 percent spend some time with a relative, 47 percent spend some time in licensed care, and 24 percent spend some time in unlicensed, nonrelative care; most children are in multiple childcare arrangements (Malik, 2019).

Regardless of type of care, more than 60 percent of families are paying more than they can afford (US Treasury, 2021). Childcare costs have nearly doubled since the mid-1980s from an average of $87 to $148 weekly (in 2013$); care for preschoolers was more expensive averaging $179 weekly

(Herbst, 2018). Families with income below the official poverty level spent 30 percent of family income on paid childcare, roughly four times the percentage of non-poor families (Laughlin, 2013).

State and federal government subsidies for childcare are intended to reduce barriers to employment for parents and increase economic self-sufficiency of poor and low-income families with children. In 1996 as part of welfare reform, Congress consolidated several childcare programs into a single block grant, the Child Care and Development Block Grant (CCDBG). Re-authorized in 2014, CCDBG emphasized the dual role of economic self-sufficiency and healthy child development and school success. By 2018, state and federal governments provided $10.3 billion to subsidize care for poor and low-income families; roughly two-thirds comes from CCDBG and one-third from Temporary Assistance for Needy Families (TANF) and the Social Services Block Grant (Chien, 2021).

States define eligibility for CCDBG funds under broad guidelines from the federal government, typically requiring parents to be employed, looking for work or engaged in education or training activities (Matthews et al., 2015). In 2018, on average across the states, a three-person family was eligible for childcare subsidies if their income was less than $38,882 (57 percent of average state median incomes). Federal eligibility was slightly more lenient: that same family would be eligible for support if their income was less than 85 percent of average state median income ($58,004) (Chien, 2021).

Eligibility for aid however is not enough. In 2018 of the 12.8 million children eligible under federal guidelines, or 8.4 million children eligible under state guidelines, only 15 percent, 1.9 million children, received subsidies. Take-up rates vary significantly by state and by race and ethnicity. While some parents may not know about their eligibility for support, a recent US Government Accountability office (GAO) report (2016) found that states often did not have sufficient funds to meet the needs of eligible families; waitlists are long or may not even exist. Between 2002 and 2017, CCDBG funding has not kept up with inflation, declining 9 percent over the period. Only in FY2018 and FY2019 were additional funds authorized to implement the 2014 re-authorization (Ullrich, Schmit, and Cosse, 2019). In FY 2017, of the 1.9 million children who received childcare subsidies from all funding sources, recipients were most likely to be preschoolers in poor families (Chien, 2020). Of those who received CCDBG funding, nearly 40 percent were black, 26 percent white, and 23 percent Hispanic (Ullrich, Schmit, and Cosse, 2019).

In a review of the literature on child care and parental labor force participation, Morrissey (2017) finds that reduced-out-pocket costs for child care increase mother's labor force participation and hours worked, though there is substantial heterogeneity in the findings across studies. Davis and her co-authors (2018) find that childcare subsidy receipt leads to increased employment, in particular increased full-time employment among parents who otherwise would be less likely to be employed.

Studies of labor-market non-participants (Krueger, 2016; Krause and Sawhill, 2017; Tuzemen, 2018) often find that "illness or disability" are frequently cited for men's lack of labor force participation. Tuzemen suggests that the decline in men's labor force participation may be a result of a vicious cycle. First, technology has rendered the skills of many less educated workers obsolete, then the lack of job opportunities may lead to depression and illness among displaced workers, creating health conditions that further limit future employment (p. 27). Krueger (2016) finds support for this hypothesis; he reports that 20 percent of prime-age men not in the labor force have difficulty walking or climbing stairs, 16 percent have difficulty concentrating, remembering, or making decisions, while 50 percent take some type of pain medication daily. Similarly, Case and Deaton (2017) find that "deaths of despair" due to addiction, depression, and suicide are rising for prime-age white males and argue that this may be the consequence of deterioration of job opportunities for men with less education. Finally, Krause and Sawhill (2017) note that counties with the lowest rates of labor force participation among prime-age men, also have the highest rates of deaths of despair among this group, though causality is indeterminant.

While labor force non-participation may have negative health consequences for men, there is little evidence that their lost earnings have been replaced with disability benefits. Krause and Sawhill (May 2017) note that between 2004 and 2014 the number of men ages 25 to 54 who receive Social Security Disability Insurance increased by 117,000, while the number of non-labor force participants in the same age group increased by nearly 1.4 million over the same time period. Similarly, the CEA (2016) report that, at most, disability receipt explains 0.5 percentage points of an 8 percentage-point decline in men's labor force participation for this age group since 1976.

Another factor in the growth of non-participation is that non-participants often live in households with others who report income from a variety of sources. In a study of prime-age labor force non-participants Schanzenbach and co-authors (August 2017) find that 83 percent of non-participants live with another adult family member. Women are more likely to live with a spouse or partner and claim family responsibilities as a reason for not working, while men are more likely to be unmarried and live with their parents. Furthermore in 2016, 77 percent of female non-participants and 62 percent of male non-participants lived in households with earnings in the past year (p. 5). Only 11 percent of non-participants report income from safety-net programs, while nearly one million non-participant men and one million non-participant women live in households with retirement income.

The basic conclusion is that declines in labor force participation lead to lower incomes and higher poverty rates, with adverse implications for economic growth and individual well-being. The decline in work, particularly among less-skilled native-born men, may be associated with falling marriage rates (Sawhill and Venator, 2015), another factor that leads to lower family incomes. However, declining labor force participation is not the only problem; declining or stagnant wages adversely affect poor and low-skill workers as well.

WAGES IN SLOW MOTION: THE SLOW AND UNEVEN GROWTH OF WAGES

"It was the best of times; it was the worst of times . . ." So, begins one of the most famous lines in Western literature. But it could also be an apt description of wages in America since World War II. The first 30 years, 1949–1979 could be described as the "best of times:" a variety of data sources suggest that inflation-adjusted wages grew at approximate 2 percent per year over the period and that wage growth was spread evenly across the distribution of wages (Schmitt, Gould and Bivens, 2018). In fact, the lowest paid workers enjoyed wage growth slightly higher than that of the best paid workers, and economists often refer to this period as the "Great Compression" of American incomes (Goldin and Margo, 1992). During this period, a high-school educated worker could easily earn what would be considered a "middle class income" by the standards of the time. On the other hand, the last 40 years, since 1980 could comparatively be described as "the worst of times" as wages declined, stagnated or grew more slowly for low- and middle-wage workers, while better educated or higher-wage workers enjoyed significant gains—a period of a "Great Divergence" in wages.

This slow and uneven wage growth over the last 40 years is particularly troubling since American workers of the period were older, thus presumably more experienced, and better educated, than workers of the previous era. This section documents changes in wages in the American economy over the last 40 years with special attention paid to how these changes vary by sex, race, and ethnicity. The general trend is that the higher a worker's wage in the distribution of wages, the greater their wage growth over the period. For the first 15 years last four decades, low-wage workers were actually worse off than similarly situated workers in 1980; their wages began to grow slowly in the last several years so that by 2020, their wages were 19.5 percent higher than in 1980. Middle-wage workers saw little change in their wages until the economic expansion of the 1990s when wages grew; but for most of the twenty-first century, wages stagnated before finally recovering after

2010. But though their wages were 23.8 percent higher than a middle-wage worker in 1980, their annualized wage growth rate was only 0.58 percent, a fraction of the 2 percent annual wage growth enjoyed by workers during the Great Compression. In comparison, high-wage workers saw consistent wage growth over the last 40 years, with generally higher growth rates than either low- or middle-wage workers. Taken together, these trends have generated widening wage gaps between workers at the top, middle, and bottom of the distribution of wages.

Figures 2.1 and 2.2 consider wage growth for men and women separately and suggest that these trends differ significantly. Low-wage workers of both genders and middle-wage men saw little wage growth over the entire period. Indeed, for most of the period these workers were no better off, and usually

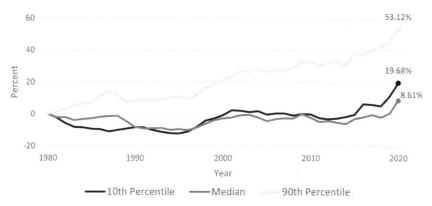

Figure 2.1   Cumulative Percent Change in Real Hourly Wages for Men at 10th, Median, and 90th Percentiles, 1980–2020. *Source*: Author's calculations from Economic Policy Institute, State of Working America Data Library, 2021.

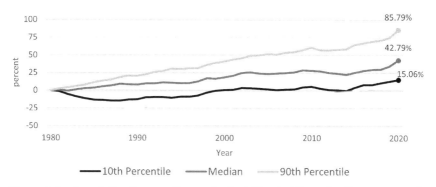

Figure 2.2   Cumulative Percent Change in Real Hourly Wages for Women at 10th, Median, 90th Percentiles, 1980–2020. *Source*: Author calculations from Economic Policy Institute, State of Working America Data Library, 2021.

worse off than similar workers in 1979. In an analysis of state-level wage data economists on the CEA suggest that when returns to work for men at the bottom of the wage distribution are particularly low, more men choose to drop out of the labor force (Council of Economic Advisors, 2016).

A review of figures 2.1 and 2.2 suggests that real growth rates for middle- and high-wage employees were higher for women than for men. Consequently, we would expect the gender wage gap to decline, as indeed it has. In 1980 middle-wage women wages were 63.7 percent of middle-wage men's wages; by 2020 they earned 83.7 percent of men's wages. The stagnation and decline of low- and middle-wage men's wages has also played a significant role in reducing the gender gap as well: Gould, Schieder and Geier (2016) estimate that 30 percent of the reduction in the gender gap is due to declines in men's real wages.

Wage growth also varies by education. In fact, only workers with a bachelor's degree or better have seen consistent wage growth over time, while wages of less educated workers are similar to or lower than wages in an earlier era. The increasing premium for college-educated workers may reflect differences in both the supply and demand for skill. While today's workers are generally better educated than were workers four decades ago, the supply of college graduates has not kept up with the growing demand for their skills (Autor, Goldin, and Katz, 2020; Goldin and Katz, 2009), resulting in mismatch of workers and needed skills. Autor (2014) provides evidence that the decline in the growth rate of the supply of college graduates between 1980 and 2000 explains the rise of the college wage premium during this period, while the surge in college attendance and graduation after 2004 explains the stagnation of this premium in recent years. Alternatively, Bressen (2014) suggests high-school educated workers have general skills but lack training in job-specific skills, while Cappelli (2014) finds that evidence of a skills gap can largely be explained by the decline in employer-provided on-the-job training.

The college wage premium varies by gender, race, and ethnicity, as table 2.1 shows. High-school-educated men have seen a slight decline in their real wages over time, and wage stagnation for black men has been particularly severe. Real wages for high-school educated women have increased, but more for white women than either Hispanic or black women. The college-educated have seen their real wages grow over the period, regardless of gender, race, or ethnicity, but white men and women have seen higher college wage premiums than blacks or Hispanics of either gender. College-educated women of each racial group have had greater wage growth than their male counterparts. These differential returns to education are important because they can affect an individual's decision to invest in further education.

Another approach to understanding wages over time is to consider the differences in wages between groups. For example, the difference between men

Table 2.1 Real Cumulative Change in Average Hourly Wages by Race, Gender, and Education, 1980–2020 (2020 dollars) (percent)

Education	All	Non-Hispanic White	Non-Hispanic Black	Hispanic
High School	8.7	12.8	6.0	10.5
Bachelor Degree	38.7	41.8	28.2	31.5
	Men	White Men	Black Men	Hispanic Men
High School	−0.3	3.5	0.0	4.7
Bachelor Degree	36.9	40.8	25.3	30.9
	Women	White Women	Black Women	Hispanic Women
High School	16.9	20.7	11.5	14.4
Bachelor Degree	54.3	58.4	30.8	39.6

Wages by education are the average hourly wages of workers disaggregated by the highest level of education attained. Wages are adjusted into 2020 dollars by CPI_U_RS. Sample is wage and salary, workers ages 16 and older.

Source: Data *Source* is CPS ORG. Economic Policy Institute, *State of Working America Data Library*, "Wages by Education," updated 2021.

and women's wages is the so-called "gender wage gap." The gender wage gap is a summary statistic that reflects gender differences in work, including differences in labor-market characteristics of men and women such as education and labor force experience, or differences in how men and women are treated in labor markets.

The data in table 2.2 suggest that average men and women's real wages improved over the last two decades for all levels of education. However, wages for workers with less than a high-school degree, or those with a college degree experienced more growth than workers with a high-school diploma, while those with some college saw little growth over the period. The gender wage disparity for workers with less than a college degree decreased before the Great Recession, as women's wages as a share of men's wages grew; the gender wage gap for the college educated saw little change. The gender gap for workers, regardless of education level, was larger after the Great Recession than it was before, suggesting that men's wages recovered more quickly than women's after the recession. More recently, Goldin and co-authors (2017) find an expanding gender earnings gap may be due to men's greater ability or preference to move to higher-paying firms or to their stronger capacity to advance within firms. These factors are more important the greater a woman's family responsibilities.

Claudia Goldin (2014) suggests that one of the defining characteristics of labor markets in the last 40 years is a "grand convergence" in gender roles of men and women that has narrowed the gaps between men and women in labor force participation, paid hours of work, hours of work at home, life-time labor force participation, occupations, college majors, and education where women have recently overtaken men (p. 1091). As men and women have become

Table 2.2   Real Average Hourly Wages by Gender and Education, 2000–2018 (2018 dollars)

		Less than High School	High School	Some College	College
ALL					
	2000	$12.59	$17.85	$20.32	$31.27
	2007	$13.03	$18.06	$20.46	$31.95
	2018	$13.68	$18.45	$20.34	$33.36
MEN					
	2000	$13.84	$20.15	$22.98	$35.54
	2007	$14.24	$20.08	$22.88	$36.52
	2018	$15.19	$20.35	$22.84	$38.60
WOMEN					
	2000	$10.75	$15.34	$17.82	$26.77
	2007	$11.12	$15.67	$18.24	$27.43
	2018	$11.47	$15.86	$17.94	$28.35
Wage Disparities—Women's Wages as a Share of Men's					
	2000	77.7%	76.1%	77.5%	75.3%
	2007	78.1%	78.0%	79.7%	75.1%
	2018	75.5%	77.9%	78.6%	73.4%

Source: EPI Wages 2018, Table 2.

more similar in these labor-market characteristics, the gender wage gap has decreased. In an extensive literature review, Blau and Kahn (2017) find that between 1980 and 2010, the total share of the gender wage gap explained by observable differences has increased from 51.5 percent to 62 percent. They find that by 2010 conventional differences in human capital variables such as education and experience no longer play a major role in explaining the gender wage gap. Instead, they find that gender differences in occupation and industry continue to be important in explaining the gap that remains. Furthermore, they find that differences in psychological attributes such as risk aversion or willingness to compete, or non-cognitive skills such as negotiation skills, can explain smaller though important fractions of the gender gap.

But what about the gender wage gap that remains after all these explanatory variables are considered, the so-called "residual" portion? Differences in wages can also signal differences in how men and women are treated in labor markets. Glynn (2018) suggests that the 38 percent of the gender pay gap that is unexplained reflects discrimination or gender stereotyping which encourages women to pursue jobs that are seen as more "suitable" for women than for men. In their review of the experimental literature on the gender wage gap (Goldin and Rouse, 2000; Neuman et al., 1996; Moss-Racusin et al., 2012; Reuben, Sapienza, and Zingales, 2014; and Williams and Ceci, 2015), Blau and Kahn (2017) suggest that labor-market discrimination cannot be overlooked.

Goldin (2014) on the other hand suggests that as men and women's labor-market characteristics become more similar, what remains is how firms reward individuals who differ in their desire for workplace flexibility. She argues that the gender wage gap will be further reduced only with labor-market changes in how jobs are structured and remunerated to enhance temporal flexibility. Workplace flexibility is particularly important to parents who combine home and market work. Research has found that poor and low-income women often take low-paying, part-time jobs because they enable them to work while their children are in school. Golden (2020) notes that part-time workers suffer a wage penalty, earning 29.3 percent less per hour than workers with similar demographic characteristics and education levels. And while the wage penalty for women, 15.9 percent is smaller than that for men, 25.8 percent, women bear the brunt of the wage penalty because they are twice as likely to work part-time as men (22.8 percent vs. 11.8 percent in 2019).

Gender differences in family responsibilities are linked to the gender pay gap: at least a portion of the gender wage gap is attributable to marital and parenthood status. In a study of 2012 median weekly earnings, Budig (2014) found the smallest gender pay gap for unmarried, childless women and men (96 percent), a slightly larger gap (93 percent) for childless women and men whether married or not, and a 76 percent pay gap for married parents and 83 percent for single parents.

A robust literature has developed over the last several decades that has generally found a fatherhood bonus—fathers make more than childless men—and a motherhood penalty—mothers make less than childless women. Budig and Hodges (2010, 2014) find that fatherhood increases men's wages by 6 percent after controlling for labor-market characteristics and differential selection into fatherhood. Budig and England (2001) find a wage penalty for motherhood of 4 percent per child that cannot be explained by differences in human capital, family structure, family-friendly job characteristics, or differences among women that are stable over time. However, not all men receive the same bonus nor do all women suffer the same penalty (Budig, 2014). The fatherhood bonus is highest for the most advantaged men: white men with college education, in professional occupations or occupations with high cognitive demands, while none of these traits alter the fatherhood bonus among black men, who have the lowest fatherhood bonus; Hispanic men fall somewhere in between. Among women, the motherhood penalty is largest for women at the bottom of the wage distribution, while evidence of a wage penalty for women with wages near the top of the wage distribution is mixed. Budig (2014) finds women with wages at the 90th percentile suffered no penalty at all, while Goldin and Katz (2008) find that for college-educated women 15 years after graduation, an 18-month break in work was associated with a decrease in earnings of 41 percent for those with an MBA, 29 percent for those with a JD or PhD, and 15 percent for those with an MD. In a study of the trend in family gaps from 1967 to 2013, Pal and Waldfogel (2016) find: that unmarried mothers face a larger motherhood wage penalty than their married counterparts; that while married women's motherhood wage penalties have decreased over time, unmarried mothers' have increased; and that cohabiting mothers face wage penalties in between those of married and unmarried mothers. While the motherhood penalty has been declining for women of all education levels, college-educated women had the smallest penalties while less educated women had the highest. They also find that black mothers had smaller motherhood wage penalties than white mothers until the beginning of the 1990s, but by 2013 had penalties that were two times those of white women. Over time, Hispanic women had no wage penalty or faced smaller penalties than either white or black women. Finally, consistent with research by Srivastava and Rodgers (2013), they find little evidence of a motherhood wage penalty for foreign-born mothers.

Just as differences in marital and family status can affect the gender wage gap, differences in educational attainment will affect racial and ethnic wage gaps. Table 2.3 provides evidence on real average hourly wages for white, black, and Hispanic workers, based on their education. In 2000 the racial/ethnic wage gap for workers with less than a high-school diploma was very small: black wages were 94.5 percent and Hispanic wages were 97.5 percent of whites' wages suggesting that these poorly educated workers were all paid similarly. However, as the level of education increases, the wage gap increases, as non-white workers earn a smaller fraction of white worker's wages. Before the Great Recession, whites and Hispanics experienced wage growth at every education level, while blacks saw stagnating or falling wages. Consequently, on the eve of the Great Recession, Hispanics gained ground relative to whites, while blacks actually lost ground. These trends continued after the Great Recession so that black workers were worse off relative to whites in 2018 than they had been in 2000, while Hispanics with a high-school diploma or less continued to gain ground. On the other hand, more educated black and Hispanic workers saw their wage gap stagnate or worsen slightly.

These trends are consistent with the existing literature. Bayer and Charles (2018) find that the gap in median earnings between black and white men narrowed between 1940 and 1970 but has since widened and today is as large as it was in 1950. Similarly, in a study of black and white workers, Daly, Hobijn and Pedtke (2017) find that black men and women earn persistently lower average hourly earnings than their white counterparts and that these differences have grown between 1979 and 2016. Differences in industry and occupation are the most important explanatory factors, explaining about 9 percent of the wage gap for men and 5 percent of the wage gap for women; however, controlling for these differences has become less important over time, especially for women. Differences in educational attainment is the

Work and Wages 49

Table 2.3 Real Average Hourly Wages by Race/Ethnicity and Education, 2000–2018 (2018 dollars)

		Less than High School	High School	Some College	College
Non-Hispanic White					
	2000	$12.81	$18.60	$20.98	$32.15
	2007	$13.18	$18.96	$21.19	$32.89
	2018	$13.77	$19.75	$21.58	$34.75
Non-Hispanic Black					
	2000	$12.10	$15.75	$18.02	$26.60
	2007	$12.22	$15.67	$18.16	$26.56
	2018	$11.42	$15.57	$17.15	$27.46
Hispanic					
	2000	$12.48	$15.88	$18.52	$26.62
	2007	$13.13	$16.48	$18.82	$28.36
	2018	$14.11	$17.28	$18.66	$28.49
Wage Disparities—Non-Hispanic Black Wages as a Share of Non-Hispanic White					
	2000	94.5%	84.7%	85.9%	82.8%
	2007	92.7%	82.6%	85.7%	80.8%
	2018	82.9%	78.8%	79.5%	79.0%
Wage Disparities—Hispanic Wages as a Share of Non-Hispanic White					
	2000	97.5%	85.4%	88.3%	82.8%
	2007	99.6%	86.9%	88.8%	86.2%
	2018	102.4%	87.5%	86.4%	82.0%

Source: EPI Wages 2018, Table 3.

second largest factor, consistently explaining about 5 percent of black-white wage gap for men over the period, but an increasingly important factor for women, explaining 2 percentage points of the black-white gap in 1979, but more than 5 percentage points in 2016. The remaining measurable variables: age, part-time status, and state of residence explain only a modest fraction of black-white wage differences. The authors find that a significant portion of the wage gap is unexplained, and this portion has grown over time. By 2016 the unexplained portion is 13 percentage points, nearly half of the total earnings gap for men; for women the unexplained portion of the wage gap had tripled to 18 percentage points. The authors suggest factors that are more difficult to measure, such as discrimination or differences in school quality or career opportunities play an increasing role in black-white wage gaps.

A NOTE ON THE GREAT RECESSION

Many of the changes described above refer to structural changes in the economy that have developed over the last three decades and have important consequences for low-skill workers. But cyclical economic change is important too, especially for non-white workers and those with fewer skills whose employment is more sensitive to cyclical change (De et al., 2021; Cajner et al., 2017). The Great Recession, December 2007 to June 2009, was, at the time, the longest recession since the Great Depression and was notably severe in several respects: real gross domestic product (GDP) fell 4.3 percent, the largest decline in post–World War II era, and the unemployment rate doubled from 5 percent in December 2007 to 10 percent in October 2009, resulting in job losses for more than 30 million people (Song and von Wachter, 2014). In addition, unlike most recessions that preceded it, the labor market was slow to recover, resulting in a "jobless recovery." Though the recession officially ended in June 2009, the unemployment rate for workers age 16 and over only returned to its pre-recession level by December 2015. During the Great Recession the number of persons unemployed for more than 27 weeks, the long-term unemployed, more than quadrupled and represented an unprecedented 45.5 percent of total unemployment in April 2010. While the long-term unemployment rate has declined since then, it had not reached its pre-recession value until April 2020.

Aggregate unemployment rates hide important differences for various demographic groups. The Great Recession sharply reduced employment for men, particularly younger workers and those with less than a college degree. And while unemployment rates doubled for all racial and ethnic groups, black and Hispanic workers were particularly hard hit. By 2017, unemployment rates for workers based on gender, race, ethnicity, and level of education had returned to their pre-recession levels.

Just because unemployment rates had returned to their pre-recession levels doesn't mean that the labor-market effects of the Great Recession have ended. In particular, rates of IPTW increased substantially during the Great Recession, and only returned to their pre-recession levels in February 2019. Blacks and particularly Hispanics, were unable to find full-time employment.

Furthermore, major labor-market disruptions such as the Great Recession introduce financial hardship and uncertainty which may affect family structures and household formation such as timing of marriage, divorce, cohabitation, and childbearing. For example, Cherlin and colleagues (2013) finds a 9 to 11 percent drop in fertility rates from 2007 to 2011, particularly among the poor and near-poor. Marriage and divorce rates declined, and cohabitation rates increased during the period, and while the Great Recession exacerbated these trends, these changes were a continuation of longer-term trends. Finally, Morgan, Cumberworth, and Wimer, (2011) find the Great Recession increased the likelihood of both unmarried and married young adults living with their parents.

Significant macroeconomic changes such as skill-based technical change and globalization of trade and production have created difficult labor-market conditions for less-skilled workers, particularly non-white workers. Declining or stagnant real wages over the last four decades have made it more difficult for many families to work their way out of poverty and may also have contributed to declining labor force participation. The next section of this chapter focuses more closely on the problems faced by the working poor.

THE LABOR MARKET AND THE POOR

The labor market directly affects poverty in two different ways: the work effort of potential workers, and how much they are paid when they do work. The adults in poor families may be less consistently employed than those in non-poor families. This difference in employment may arise from any one of the factors discussed above, including illness or disability, lack of job opportunities that match the worker's skills, or conflicts between work and family obligations. In addition, however, even those who work may find that their earnings are insufficient to escape poverty, the persons who are often known as "the working poor." We will discuss both aspects, beginning with a discussion of work status.

Of the nearly 33.9 million individuals who were considered poor by the official measure of poverty in 2019, about a third (11.3 million) were at least 16 years old and did not work at all (Census, 2020). Understanding the significance of this number requires both a comparison between poor and non-poor as well as a certain amount of historical context. Poverty among persons over age 15 who worked at full-time year-round jobs has been low (less than 3 percent) and has fallen since the recovery from the Great Recession. On the other hand, the poverty rate among persons over age 15 who did not work at all has been consistently over 20 percent.

Among the non-poor, over half of the persons over age 15 (57.0 percent in 2019) held a full-time year-round job, a number that fell by a few percentage points during the Great Recession, but then recovered. Among poor persons over age 15, only 12.1 percent held a full-time year-round job in 2019, a number that has improved some since the Great Recession. One might say that in 2019 there was a "full-time, year-round work gap" of: 57.0 − 12.1 = 44.9 percentage points. Another way to say it is that the percentage of poor persons over age 15 with no job has been falling and was by 2019 down to 60.8 percent. The corresponding share of the non-poor has also been falling, to 21.7 percent in 2019. The "no-work gap" by this measure is: 60.8 − 21.7 = 39.1 percentage points.

As discussed earlier, some of the changes in the number of non-workers among poor and non-poor alike have a demographic origin, as the Baby Boom generation moves into retirement or disability. Published Census data suggest that narrowing the population of "potential workers" to persons age 18–64 would cause both the work gap and the non-work gap to increase by 4–5 percentage points. Regardless of the exact measure chosen, it is clear that differences in work, particularly full-time year-round work, are closely associated with poverty. What is less clear is how many of the poor working-age adults who are not working would be capable of expanding their work effort. The Hamilton Project study by Shambaugh, Bauer and Breitwieser (2017) showed that about 65 percent of the non-working adults of working age were disabled, early retirees, or students, and another 25 percent were caregivers.

The most recent study of the work gap can be found in a 2018 report from the President's CEA. The report was focused on measuring the potential effects of stricter work requirements for three large government programs: the Supplemental Nutrition Program (SNAP, often called by its previous name, Food Stamps), Medicaid, and certain housing assistance programs. The CEA found that among non-disabled working-age adults who do not receive any of those benefits, 77 percent work and 67 percent work at least 30 hours per week. The most relevant group for comparison is SNAP recipients, since SNAP is available to a large percentage of poor families, but only a very small percentage of non-poor families. The CEA report shows that among non-disabled working-age SNAP recipients, only 46 percent work and only 30 percent work at least 30 hours per week, much less work than the non-recipients. However, a subsequent Hamilton Study report by Bauer, Schanzenbach, and Shambaugh (2018) shows that the CEA report fails to consider the extent to which the measured work efforts of the poor are affected by the instability of their actual work. As an example, they show that among SNAP recipients ages 18 to 49 with school-age children, 25 percent did not work at all during a one-year period, and only 15 percent did not work at all during a two-year period, numbers far smaller than those reported by the CEA report, which only looked at work during a single month.

THE WORKING POOR

Each year the Bureau of Labor Statistics provides a *Profile of the Working Poor*. The working poor are defined as persons who spend at least 27 weeks per year in the labor force (either working or looking for work) but whose earnings fell below the official poverty level. The working poor poverty rate (for a particular group) is defined as the ratio of:

$$\frac{\text{The number of Working Poor in a Group}}{\text{All persons in group who worked at least 27 weeks}}$$

In 2019, 6.3 million persons were working poor; nearly all, 5.1 million, worked full time.

The cyclical nature of the working poor rate is obvious, increasing during recessions and declining during economic expansions. This impact varied significantly among individuals. In a 2019 report on the working poor, researchers at the Bureau of Labor Statistics note that 4.0 percent of the labor force were classified as working poor. Women had higher working poverty rates than men regardless of race or ethnicity, and white working poverty rates for both men and women were approximately half those of black and Hispanic workers. Black men had higher working poverty rates than Hispanic men, while Hispanic women's working poor rate exceeded that of black women.

Similarly, working poverty rates vary by education, occupation, and family status. The less educated a worker is, the higher their working poverty rates. In 2019, high-school dropouts had the highest working poverty rates (12.8 percent), more than double that of high-school graduates (5.5 percent), and nearly four times that of individuals with some college or an associate degree (4.0 percent). Individuals with a college degree or more had the lowest rate at 1.4 percent. In 2019, nearly a third of the working poor were employed in low-skill service occupations, while workers in farming and construction occupations accounted for an additional 10 percent of the working poor.

In 2019, just over 3 million families with children under 18 were poor despite having at least one working family member. These working poverty rates vary significantly by family structure. While overall families with children had a working poor poverty rate of 7.8 percent, families maintained by a single woman had a working poor poverty rate of 20.3 percent, while married couple families with children had a 4.0 percent working poverty rate. Families with more than one potential worker are better able to balance work and home responsibilities in a way that reduces the probability of poverty.

Workers who are poor suffer from three major labor-market problems: periods of unemployment, IPTW, and low earnings. In 2019, 80 percent of the working poor who usually worked full time suffered from at least one of these problems—typically low earnings, but often unemployment. And many of the working poor faced more than one of these obstacles. In the sections that follow, we provide a general background of these issues, emphasizing the role of education, gender, race, and ethnicity.

UNEMPLOYMENT

An individual is unemployed if they are available for work and have been actively seeking work in the previous four weeks. In a study of the widening socioeconomic divergence in US labor markets, Khatiwada and Sum (2016, pp. 201–205) find that the labor-market experience of workers varies substantially by skill and household income. For example, unemployment rates ranged from a high of 22.6 percent for high-school dropouts with household income less than $20,000 to a low of 1.4 percent for the best educated and most affluent households, those with a master's degree or better and $150,000 or more of household income. Furthermore, between 1999–2000 and 2013–2014, the unemployment rates of least educated, poorest workers grew at nearly twice the percentage points of the wealthiest, most educated workers. Education and household income aren't the only important determinants. A persistent regularity in US labor markets is the nearly constant differential between unemployment rates for white and non-white workers. Lang and Lehmann (2012) suggest this differential is higher for men than for women and is highest among low-skill workers. In a recent study of racial gaps in labor-market outcomes, researchers suggest that observable characteristics such as age, gender, education, and state of residence explain little of the black-white unemployment differential. The Hispanic-white unemployment gap is comparatively smaller and can largely be explained by the lower educational attainment of (mostly foreign-born) Hispanics (Cajner et al., 2017).

Black and Hispanic unemployment rates are also more sensitive to cyclical changes in GDP than are white unemployment rates, and these unemployment differentials are driven largely by a comparatively higher risk of job loss for blacks, and to a lesser extent Hispanics (Cajner et al., 2017). This is consistent with evidence from Couch and Fairlie (2010) who find that blacks are the first fired as business cycles weaken; and furthermore, the narrowing of the black-white unemployment gap near the peak of business cycles is driven largely by a reduction in the rate of job loss for blacks. Using data from US manufacturing sector, Borowczyk-Martins and his co-authors (2018) find that a model combining employer taste-based discrimination, search frictions, and skill complementarities can explain differences in the black-white wage and unemployment gaps; discrimination is quantitatively more important for understanding these gaps for low-skilled workers, whereas skill differences are the main driver of these gaps for high-skilled workers.

Securing a job does not end the relative labor-market difficulties of low-skilled, poor workers particularly black and Hispanic workers. Even when employed, these workers are often underemployed and suffer from higher rates of IPTW, sometimes referred to as part-time work for economic reasons

(PTER). As with unemployment, differences in education, income, race, and ethnicity are distinguishing factors.

INVOLUNTARY PART-TIME WORK

IPTW is an important source of labor underutilization not captured by the official unemployment or labor force participation rates; workers are involuntarily employed if they work part time but are available and would like to work full time. Khatiwada and Sum (2016) analyze IPTW work and find substantial overall increases from 2.4 percent of the labor force in 1999–2000 to 5.2 percent in 2013–2014. When both education and household income are jointly considered, the differential in IPTW is dramatic. Poor high-school dropouts with household income less than $20,000 had an involuntary part-time employment rate of 17.7 percent, compared to high-school graduates in households with income between $20,000–$40,000, where the rate was only 7.8 percent. Among educated high-income households, IPTW is rare: for those with bachelor's degrees and household income between $100,000 and $150,000 the rate was only 1.9 percent while the wealthiest, most educated had an involuntary part-time employment rate of only 1.1 percent. IPTW is clearly a problem of the most disadvantaged workers.

Since the mid-1980s, Hispanics have had the highest rate of IPTW. Compared to native-born whites, blacks had 51 percent higher odds of being underemployed, while native-born Hispanics had a 32 percent higher chance. However, foreign-born Hispanic citizens had IPTW rates 2.3 times as high as native-born whites; among the foreign-born, non-citizen Hispanics had IPTW rates nearly 3 times as high (Young and Mattingly, 2016).

The Great Recession increased these differences, particularly for Hispanic workers; between 2007 and 2009 the rate of IPTW for these workers tripled from 4.2 percent to 12.5 percent. Foreign-born Hispanics have had higher IPTW rates than native-born Hispanics every year since 1994 and their rate has been significantly higher since 2009, especially for non-citizen Hispanics. Young and Mattingly (2016) suggest that while foreign-born non-citizens often have higher IPTW rates than foreign-born citizens or native workers, over the last two decades this difference has only persisted among Hispanics. For example, during the last two recessions (2001 and 2007–2009), much of the increase in IPTW was concentrated among non-citizen Hispanics.

Both Young and Mattingly (2016) and Cajner et al. (2017) find that involuntary part-time employment is greatest among less-skilled jobs and workers with less education. Cajner et al. find that relative to whites of the same gender, differences in education and occupation explain some of the differences in IPTW rates among whites and Hispanics. Nevertheless, substantial unexplained gaps remain for black and Hispanic rates relative to whites even after controlling for these observables. Young and Mattingly suggest that because non-white workers are overrepresented in more volatile industries and occupations, this increases the risk of IPTW, especially during recessions. This is consistent with Valletta et al. (2015) who find that while IPTW is primarily cyclical, market-level factors, particularly shifting industry employment composition, largely explain sustained levels of IPTW since the Great Recession. They also find suggestive evidence linking rising levels of involuntary part-time work with informal work in the gig economy. Finally, in an analysis of worker movement in and out of the labor force, Cajner et al. find that rates of IPTW declined more slowly for black males than white males during the recent recovery, since the net movement for black males from part-time to full-time work was less stable over time, and non-existent from 2013 to 2016. Involuntary part-time work suggests that there are substantial structural issues in the economy that make it difficult for workers with low levels of education, particularly non-white workers, to work full time and decrease their probability of poverty.

Becoming employed is the first challenge poor workers face though it is not the only challenge: low wages for the work they perform is often the largest obstacle low-skilled workers face. The following section introduces the notion of poverty wages and then discusses wage gaps based on differences in education, gender, race, and ethnicity.

LOW WAGES/EARNINGS

While the share of workers earning poverty-level wages has declined over the past three decades, nevertheless in 2016 one in eight workers worked for poverty-level wages. A poverty-level wage is an hourly wage that would leave a full-time, year-round worker below the official poverty measure for their family size if they are the sole earner in the family. Figure 2.3 considers differences in poverty wages overall and by gender.

Women are more likely than men to earn poverty-level wages, and as figure 2.4 demonstrates, there are also important racial and ethnic differences. Black and Hispanic workers are far more likely to be paid poverty-level wages than white workers. While 9.6 percent of white workers were paid poverty wages in 2016, 15.4 percent of black and 21 percent of Hispanic workers earned such wages. Notably, black-white poverty wage gaps have remained relatively consistent over time, while Hispanic-white gaps have increased slightly.

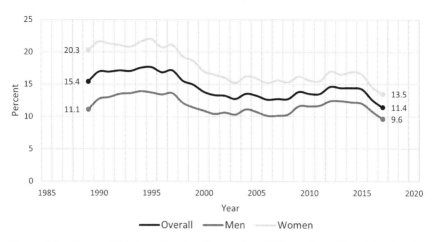

Figure 2.3 Share of Workers Earning Poverty-Level Wages Overall and by Gender, 1989–2017. *Source*: David Cooper, EPI Economic Snapshot, June 15, 2018a.

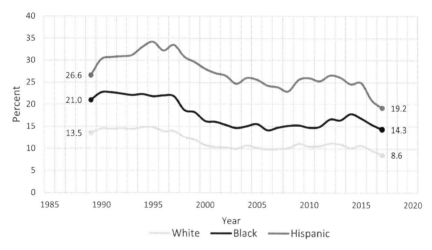

Figure 2.4 Share of Workers Earning Poverty-Level Wages, by Race and Ethnicity, 1986–2017. *Source*: David Cooper, EPI Economic Snapshot, June 21, 2018b.

A potential reason for a higher share of poverty-level wages among Hispanics could be their relatively larger family size, since a family's poverty threshold depends upon the size of the family. Cooper (2018b) finds that family size alone is not enough to explain this difference: over the same period, Hispanic family size has decreased at the same time the share of families earning poverty wages has increased. Furthermore, if the Hispanic poverty wage rate was recalculated with family sizes similar to white workers,

Table 2.4 Comparison of Real Median Hourly Earnings by Education, Gender, and Poverty Status, SPM Families with Children, Select Years 1995–2018 (2012 dollars)

Year	All	Less Than High School	High-School Graduate	More Than High School	All	Less Than High School	High-School Graduate	More Than High School
	Poor Men				**Poor Women**			
1995	$8.75	$8.51	$8.75	$9.92	$7.38	$6.92	$7.51	$8.19
2002	$9.16	$9.11	$9.16	$9.98	$7.94	$7.36	$7.94	$8.95
2006	$8.98	$8.57	$9.04	$10.03	$7.75	$7.15	$7.72	$8.79
2010	$9.02	$8.39	$9.28	$10.08	$8.00	$7.44	$7.93	$9.21
2018	$9.71	$9.46	$9.27	$10.32	$8.60	$7.74	$8.46	$9.17
	Non-Poor Men				**Non-Poor Women**			
1995	$20.21	$12.69	$17.50	$25.21	$13.41	$8.86	$11.67	$16.21
2002	$21.33	$13.06	$18.27	$27.04	$15.11	$9.64	$12.82	$18.32
2006	$21.03	$13.28	$17.71	$26.80	$15.20	$9.54	$12.52	$18.26
2010	$20.17	$12.82	$17.14	$25.78	$15.19	$9.44	$12.39	$18.35
2018	$21.51	$13.97	$17.20	$26.94	$16.77	$9.94	$12.69	$19.74
Difference in Non-Poor and Poor Real Median Hourly Earnings by Education and Gender (2012 dollars)								
	Men				**Women**			
1995	$11.46	$4.18	$8.75	$15.29	$6.03	$1.94	$4.16	$8.02
2002	$12.17	$3.95	$9.11	$17.05	$7.17	$2.28	$4.88	$9.36
2006	$12.05	$4.71	$8.67	$16.76	$7.45	$2.39	$4.80	$9.47
2010	$11.15	$4.43	$7.86	$15.69	$7.19	$2.00	$4.46	$9.14
2018	$11.80	$4.51	$7.93	$16.62	$8.17	$2.20	$4.23	$10.57

Source: Authors' calculations based on Current Population Survey: IPUMS-CPS, University of Minnesota and Historical SPM data, Columbia University.

poverty wages would still be significantly more common among Hispanic families than white families.

Table 2.4 shows that real median hourly earnings for each education level are higher for the non-poor than the poor for both men and women. Considering low-skill workers with a high-school education or less, the hourly earnings "premium" is larger for non-poor men than for non-poor women, and for workers with more than a high-school diploma, non-poor hourly wages are more than twice those of the poor for both men and women. In part, this reflects the different educational composition of the more than high-school category (some college, college graduate, graduate degree) for the poor and non-poor. Among the non-poor workers in 2018 with more than a high-school diploma, 52 percent completed college, 33 percent with a bachelor's degree only, and another 19 percent with a graduate degree. Among the poor workers in 2016 with more than a high-school diploma, 33 percent completed college, 25 percent with a bachelor's degree only, and only 8 percent with a graduate degree. Returns to education are much greater for the non-poor than the poor; non-poor men and women who have graduated from high school have median real hourly earnings a third or more higher than non-poor high-school dropouts. Among the poor, the advantage of high-school graduation is much smaller for both men and women.

Taken together, higher unemployment and involuntary part-time employment rates, low wages, and declining labor force participation suggest that low-skill workers, particularly non-white workers, face a very different labor market then better educated, more affluent workers of any race. We now turn to a comparison of work and wage gaps among poor and non-poor SPM families with children.

WORK AND WAGE GAPS: A COMPARISON OF NON-POOR VERSUS POOR ADULTS IN SPM FAMILIES WITH CHILDREN

We begin with a comparison of work effort for poor and non-poor adults in SPM families with children. The non-poor are nearly 30 percentage points more likely to work than their poor counterparts, regardless of gender. Though this work gap is substantial, both poor and non-poor labor force participation follow a similar trend with the exception of poor men: labor force participation for non-poor men and women and poor women fell before and during the Great Recession before rebounding by 2016. However, no group saw participation levels return to pre-recession levels. The Great Recession had a larger negative impact on the labor force participation of men than women, and that is especially true for poor men. What accounts for these differences in work effort? When asked why they are not working, poor men are more likely than non-poor men to claim that they are unemployed or unable to find work, or have home and family obligations, but they are less likely to be ill, disabled, retired, or in school. Consistent with the literature, over half of women who don't work at all say that their non-participation is due to home and family responsibilities, and this is true regardless of poverty status. Poor and non-poor women also have similar percentages who are either ill, disabled, retired, or in school. Poor women are somewhat more likely to be unemployed or unable to find work than are non-poor women.

UNDERSTANDING POOR SPM PARENTS
WHO WORK AND WHO DO NOT WORK

We begin with a comparison of the work effort of poor men and women in SPM families with children. We then investigate these gendered differences in work effort based on differences in education, race, and marital status.

Poor men are approximately 20 percentage points more likely to work than poor women, though basic trends over time are the same for both groups: increased work effort in 1990s, declining work effort in the twenty-first century which precedes and continues through the Great Recession, and increased work effort post-recession. However, the Great Recession appears to have had a larger negative impact on poor men than poor women, as the decline in the percentage of men who work was nearly three times as large (10.4 vs. 3.5 percentage points) as that of women.

Table 2.5 suggests that work effort differs significantly by race and ethnicity, particularly for men. Foreign-born Hispanic men are significantly more likely to work than are other men. Between 1995 and 2006, their work effort actually increased when all other men, but particularly native-born Hispanic men, decreased their work effort. Non-Hispanic black men are the least likely to work full-time and most likely to not work at all; their probability of working is nearly 20 percentage points lower than the average for all men, and nearly 30 percentage points lower than foreign-born Hispanic men. Non-Hispanic white and foreign-born Hispanics are most likely to be full-time workers. While the Great Recession significantly decreased the work effort of all men, Hispanic men, regardless of nativity, were particularly hard hit.

Across racial groups, poor women's work effort has become more similar over time. While nearly 60 percent of poor women regardless of race don't work, generally white and black women are more likely to work than Hispanic women (regardless of nativity), while native-born Hispanic women are slightly more likely to work than their foreign-born counterparts. For those who work, most women work less than year-round, full time; non-Hispanic

Table 2.5 Work Effort by Gender, Race, and Marital Status, SPM Poor Adults in Families with Children, Select Years, 1995–2018 (percent)

Year	All	Non-Hispanic White	Non-Hispanic Black	Native-Born Hispanic	Foreign-Born Hispanic	Married Couple	Cohabitating Couple	Single Parent
Men								
Works Year Round, Full Time								
1995	40.8	42.3	23.0	33.3	51.3	43.8	27.1	25.6
2002	43.1	43.2	23.4	31.8	56.0	48.6	39.3	26.2
2006	41.8	35.6	20.5	28.7	61.4	45.0	36.1	25.3
2010	28.2	27.7	14.8	18.3	39.0	29.9	29.3	19.4
2018	38.3	34.7	24.1	27.9	55.0	38.3	44.7	30.6
Works Less Than Year Round, Full Time								
1995	27.5	28.1	24.5	31.6	26.9	25.2	36.4	32.5
2002	22.2	23.5	20.7	24.3	20.8	20.8	28.5	24.2
2006	21.4	24.6	19.1	21.6	19.4	20.7	31.6	20.5
2010	24.6	23.5	17.4	20.8	30.5	25.2	27.2	19.7
2018	19.5	18.8	16.5	21.0	20.7	18.9	24.4	23.4
Does Not Work								
1995	31.7	29.6	52.5	35.1	21.8	30.0	36.5	41.9
2002	34.7	33.3	55.9	43.9	23.2	30.7	32.3	49.6
2006	36.8	39.7	60.4	49.7	19.2	34.2	32.3	54.2
2010	47.2	48.7	67.8	60.9	30.5	44.9	43.4	60.8
2018	42.3	46.5	59.4	51.1	24.3	42.8	30.9	46.0
Women								
Works Year Round, Full Time								
1995	13.8	13.0	15.3	11.2	14.5	12.9	13.3	16.1
2002	15.9	13.6	19.4	15.7	15.9	12.8	11.9	20.1
2006	15.7	13.5	18.2	13.8	17.0	14.9	13.6	18.2
2010	12.8	11.9	14.0	11.4	13.7	12.1	13.3	14.5
2018	15.6	13.3	17.7	14.8	17.1	13.5	12.8	22.2

(continued)

Table 2.5 (Continued)

Year	All	Non-Hispanic White	Non-Hispanic Black	Native-Born Hispanic	Foreign-Born Hispanic	Married Couple	Cohabiting Couple	Single Parent
Works Less than Year Round, Full Time								
1995	28.4	34.3	26.2	26.8	21.6	27.9	29.1	29.7
2002	25.7	32.1	25.5	23.9	18.3	23.0	28.5	28.4
2006	23.7	29.8	22.5	24.3	17.6	22.5	28.9	25.9
2010	23.1	26.8	20.6	22.4	20.9	22.3	25.1	24.5
2018	23.6	23.0	24.2	25.7	24.2	22.5	30.0	25.8
Does Not Work								
1995	57.8	52.7	58.5	62.0	63.9	59.2	57.6	54.2
2002	58.5	54.3	55.1	60.4	65.8	64.3	59.6	51.5
2006	60.6	56.7	59.3	61.9	65.5	62.7	57.5	55.9
2010	64.1	61.3	65.5	66.2	65.4	65.7	61.5	61.0
2018	60.8	63.7	58.1	59.5	60.3	64.0	57.2	52.0

Source: Authors' calculations based on Current Population Survey: IPUMS-CPS, University of Minnesota and Historical SPM data, Columbia University.

black women are slightly more likely to work year-round, full-time than are other women. While the Great Recession reduced the work effort of women across racial groups similarly, they were not affected as much as men were.

Table 2.5 also considers work effort by marital status. Women in single parent or cohabiting families are more likely to work, and if they work, more likely to work year-round full-time than women in married couples, also though these differences have become smaller over the years. In 1995, men in married couples were significantly more likely to work year-round full-time while men in cohabiting and single-parent families were more likely to work part-time or not at all. Over time men in cohabiting relationships have increased their work effort, while men in married couples have reduced theirs, so that by 2018, cohabiting men more closely resemble men in married couple families than men in single-parent families. While women in single-parent families are more likely to work and have higher rates of year-round full-time work, men in single-parent families are least likely to work and have the lowest rates of full-time work. While both men's and women's work effort declined during the Great Recession, in that workers were less likely to work year-round full-time and more likely to not work at all, men were particularly hard hit.

Table 2.6 presents data on real median hourly earnings for adults in SPM families by race and by marital status. Median hourly earnings of poor adults are very similar across racial/ethnic groups for both men and women. Median hourly earnings for non-Hispanic white workers of both genders recovered more rapidly after the Great Recession than did hourly earnings of other groups. Consistent with the literature discussed previously, foreign-born Hispanic men were particularly hard hit by the Great Recession; their hourly earnings fell more and recovered more slowly. Generally, men in married couples, and single mothers have higher hourly earnings than their counter-parts in other families, while women in cohabiting relationships earn less than other women.

The median wages in table 2.6 showed how the wages of typical workers differ among various groups. They do not tell us which groups are composed of workers with very low wage rates and which groups actually have a large number of workers with relatively high wage rates. Table 2.7 assigns each group to one of four "wage bins": those earning less than $9 per hour, those earning from $9 to $12 per hour, those earning between $12 and $15 per hour, and those earning at least $15 per hour. In addition to creating bins of comparable size, these wage levels are important because they are important milestones for state minimum wages. In 2018, the year represented in the table, only 12 states had a minimum wage level above $9 per hour, and no state had a minimum wage level above $12 per hour; just two years later, 21 states had minimum wages above $9 per hour, and 8 of those states had

Table 2.6 Real Median Hourly Earnings, by Gender, Race, and Marital Status, SPM Poor Adults in Families with Children, Select Years, 1995–2018 (2012 dollars)

Year	All	Non-Hispanic White	Non-Hispanic Black	Native-Born Hispanic	Foreign-Born Hispanic	Married Couple	Cohabitating Couple	Single Parent
Men								
1995	$8.75	$9.14	$8.51	$8.68	$8.57	$8.75	$9.45	$8.96
2002	$9.16	$9.31	$8.81	$9.52	$9.31	$9.31	$9.01	$8.48
2006	$8.98	$8.85	$8.49	$9.11	$9.19	$8.99	$8.37	$9.29
2010	$9.02	$9.62	$8.57	$8.92	$8.75	$9.07	$8.47	$8.82
2018	$9.71	$10.27	$9.18	$8.85	$9.84	$9.93	$9.18	$9.46
Women								
1995	$7.38	$7.58	$7.09	$7.38	$7.21	$7.38	$7.20	$7.58
2002	$7.94	$8.14	$8.04	$7.81	$7.81	$7.94	$7.20	$8.14
2006	$7.75	$7.82	$8.04	$7.82	$7.34	$7.75	$7.19	$7.83
2010	$8.00	$8.25	$8.00	$8.00	$7.81	$8.00	$7.44	$8.19
2018	$8.60	$8.60	$8.72	$8.82	$8.46	$8.46	$7.94	$8.64

Source: Authors' calculations based on Current Population Survey: IPUMS-CPS, University of Minnesota and Historical SPM data, Columbia University.

Table 2.7 Adults with Full-Time Jobs in SPM Poor Families with Children: Wages in 2018 by Gender, Race, Marital Status, and Education

	Men				Women			
	Share with Wage <$9	Share with Wage >= $9 & <$12	Share with Wage >= $12 & <$15	Share with Wage >= $15	Share with Wage <$9	Share with Wage >=$9 & <$12	Share with Wage >=$12 & <$15	Share with Wage >=$15
All:	26.9%	27.9%	29.2%	16.0%	33.7%	31.6%	23.9%	10.8%
By Race and Nativity								
Non-Hispanic White	**33.4%**	**28.3%**	27.9%	10.4%	**35.7%**	31.1%	23.9%	9.3%
Non-Hispanic Black	27.0%	**30.5%**	26.7%	15.7%	**36.2%**	29.1%	23.9%	10.8%
Native-Born Hispanic	24.8%	25.9%	**31.9%**	**22.4%**	28.8%	29.0%	**27.8%**	**14.4%**
Foreign-Born Hispanic	21.5%	27.9%	29.2%	**19.3%**	31.2%	**35.6%**	21.7%	**11.5%**
By Family Status								
Married Couple	25.6%	27.7%	**29.4%**	**17.3%**	29.2%	**32.1%**	**25.5%**	**13.3%**
Cohabiting Couple	**29.4%**	**28.8%**	**30.3%**	11.5%	**34.1%**	**33.7%**	**25.8%**	6.4%
Single Parent	**38.2%**	27.9%	23.0%	10.9%	**44.3%**	29.7%	19.3%	6.8%
By Educational Attainment								
Less than High School	25.9%	**30.2%**	27.7%	**16.2%**	**38.5%**	**36.6%**	17.8%	7.1%
High School, No College	24.5%	27.6%	**30.9%**	17.0%	35.1%	30.7%	24.3%	9.8%
Some College	**27.6%**	**28.0%**	25.9%	15.7%	29.1%	31.4%	**27.7%**	11.8%
College Graduate	**35.5%**	23.0%	29.2%	16.0%	34.3%	28.7%	23.9%	15.1%

Source: Authors' calculations based on Current Population Survey: IPUMS-CPS, University of Minnesota and Historical SPM data, Columbia University.

minimum wages of $12 per hour or more. At the federal level, the Congressional Budget Office (2019) study of the potential consequences of a higher federal minimum wage looked directly at wage rates of $12 and $15 per hour, though the actual federal minimum wage remains $7.25.

To make the results in table 2.7 more accessible, the shares of groups that exceed the overall share are indicated in bold type. The fact that over 25 percent of poor working men and over 33 percent of working women earn less than $9 per hour is not surprising, nor is it surprising that the group of poor workers with the highest percentage earning less than $9 per hour are single. It is more surprising that 16 percent of the poor working men and almost 11 percent of the poor working women earn more than $15 per hour and that the ethnic groups with the highest share of wages of $15 or more are Hispanics. Sullivan and Ziegert (2021) shows that the large number of poor Hispanic workers with relatively high wages is largely a consequence of the fact that poor Hispanic families have poverty thresholds that are several thousand dollars higher than other groups because their families are relatively large. Furthermore, they go on to show that in general, poor workers with relatively high wages have high thresholds that are associated with some mix of a large family and location in a metropolitan area with a high cost of living.

Up until this point, our analysis has focused on an individual adult's work effort or wages. Since poverty is measured at the family level, we now turn our focus to family work effort. Table 2.8 considers the number of workers and composition of work effort in poor SPM families by race and marital status.

Considering all SPM families together, the number of families with at least one full-time worker grew between 1995 and 2002, fell slightly by 2006 and more significantly during the Great Recession, and by 2018, had nearly recovered to pre-recession levels. Excluding the Great Recession, approximately 40 percent of poor families have at least one full-time worker, 30 percent have only part-time workers and remaining 30 percent have no workers at all. Compared to this overall average, non-Hispanic white families saw a larger decrease in families with at least one full-time worker, so that there are fewer such families in 2018 than 1995. Of all racial and ethnic groups, black non-Hispanic families are least likely to have a full-time worker and are most likely to have no workers at all. Native-born Hispanic families improved their work effort over the period; they were significantly more likely to have at least one full-time worker in 2018 than 1995 and are also less likely to have no workers at all. Finally, foreign-born Hispanic families have significantly higher work effort than other groups, with higher rates of full-time work and lower rates of non-work. With the exception of the Great Recession (2010), approximately 60 percent of foreign-born Hispanics have

Table 2.8   Composition, Poor SPM Family Work Effort by Race and Marital Status, Select Years 1995–2018 (percent)

	1995	2002	2006	2010	2018
All					
Households with two or more full-time workers*	4.6	4.6	5.0	3.9	5.3
Households with exactly one full-time worker*	33.6	38.5	37.0	30.4	38.2
Households with only part-time workers	32.1	30.5	28.8	31.5	27.3
Households with no workers	29.8	26.5	29.2	34.3	29.3
Non-Hispanic White					
Households with two or more full-time workers*	4.3	3.6	3.0	3.1	4.3
Households with exactly one full-time worker*	35.6	36.8	33.1	29.5	33.3
Households with only part-time workers	35.6	34.3	33.7	32.8	27.5
Households with no workers	24.6	25.3	30.3	34.7	34.9
Non-Hispanic Black					
Households with two or more full-time workers*	2.1	2.0	2.1	2.0	2.6
Households with exactly one full-time worker*	23.3	28.3	26.5	20.5	28.6
Households with only part-time workers	31.5	32.2	29.7	30.0	29.6
Households with no workers	43.2	37.5	41.8	47.5	39.2
Hispanic-Native Born					
Households with two or more full-time workers*	2.2	4.3	4.4	3.7	5.8
Households with exactly one full-time worker*	30.1	38.5	34.5	28.0	40.6
Households with only part-time workers	28.2	26.6	28.2	29.0	25.9
Households with no workers	39.5	30.7	32.9	39.3	27.8
Hispanic-Foreign Born					
Households with two or more full-time workers*	10.3	9.6	11.7	6.9	9.0
Households with exactly one full-time worker*	46.6	53.4	55.1	42.3	53.0
Households with only part-time workers	26.1	23.6	20.6	32.1	25.3
Households with no workers	17.0	13.4	12.7	18.7	12.6
Married Couple					
Households with two or more full-time workers*	8.5	8.6	9.3	6.6	9.1
Households with exactly one full-time worker*	50.8	54.3	54.2	41.9	49.0
Households with only part-time workers	28.3	24.3	22.5	30.7	23.6
Households with no workers	12.4	12.8	14.0	20.9	18.3
Cohabiting Couple					
Households with two or more full-time workers*	4.2	5.5	5.2	3.6	6.8
Households with exactly one full-time worker*	36.7	42.5	46.0	38.6	50.0
Households with only part-time workers	39.7	36.9	32.6	35.2	26.7
Households with no workers	19.4	15.1	16.1	22.6	16.5
Single Parent					
Households with two or more full-time workers*	1.8	1.7	2.3	2.0	1.9
Households with exactly one full-time worker*	21.1	26.6	24.5	20.9	26.9
Households with only part-time workers	34.2	34.2	32.4	31.3	30.3
Households with no workers	43.0	37.6	40.8	45.8	40.9

*May include additional part-time workers
Source: Authors' calculations based on Current Population Survey: IPUMS-CPS, University of Minnesota and Historical SPM data, Columbia University.

at least one full-time worker and they are the only group whose likelihood of full-time work increased between 2002 and 2006.

With the exception of the Great Recession (2010), nearly 60 percent of poor married couple families have at least one full-time worker and this percentage has remained relatively stable over time. Over the last two decades, cohabiting couple families have increased the probability of at least one full-time worker and reduced the probability of non-work; about half of cohabiting couples have a full-time worker. For cohabiting couples, the incidence of part-time work is less than married couple families and is more similar to that of single-parent families. Nearly a third of workers in cohabiting and single-parent families only work part-time. Only 25 percent of single-parent families have a full-time worker; and these families are significantly more likely to have no workers at all.

Poor SPM families who do not have a current worker are either available for work but cannot find a job, or do not work because they have family responsibilities or are a student, or do not work because they list illness, disability, or retirement as a reason for not working. For all families, nearly 15 percent of those who do not work say that they cannot find work; 55 percent don't work because of home responsibilities or studies; and nearly 30 percent are ill, disabled, or retired. Foreign-born Hispanics are unusual in that nearly three of four families cite family responsibilities or studies as a reason for not working. Nearly 30 percent of non-Hispanic white, non-Hispanic black, and native-born Hispanics list illness, disability, or retirement as a reason for non-work, while only 12 percent of foreign-born Hispanics families fall into this category.

Cohabiting couple families are most likely to have an adult seeking work, while single-parent families are the least likely; married couple families fall somewhere in between. For all family groups, family responsibilities and studies are the most likely reason given for not working. Compared to other families, single-parent families are more likely to have an ill, disabled, or retired adult member who cannot work.

Table 2.9 compares the work effort of adults in SPM families by displaying "hours of work per available adult." An "available adult" is any adult who worked at all in the last year, no matter how many hours per week and no matter how few weeks, as well as any adult who did not work because they were unable to find work. Those who say they are unable to find work include both those who were actively seeking work, meeting the technical definition of "unemployed," and those who were not actively seeking work, often called "discouraged workers." Table 2.9 contains both the number of available workers and hours per available worker for poor SPM families with children. There are substantial differences by race and family groups. Foreign-born Hispanics have more workers and work more hours

Table 2.9 Poor SPM Family, Average Weekly Hours per Available Worker, by Race and Marital Status, Select Years 1995–2018

	1995	1999	2002	2006	2010	2018
All						
Average Weekly Hours	23.1	25.7	24.8	23.9	20.1	21.3
Number of Available Workers*	1.22	1.23	1.17	1.17	1.30	1.00
Non-Hispanic White						
Average Weekly Hours	24.6	25.9	24.8	22.0	19.0	19.3
Number of Available Workers*	1.20	1.22	1.14	1.12	1.22	0.95
Non-Hispanic Black						
Average Weekly Hours	16.4	20.1	18.6	17.5	14.8	16.5
Number of Available Workers*	1.01	0.98	0.98	0.94	1.09	0.88
Native-Born Hispanic						
Average Weekly Hours	19.8	23.4	23.2	22.3	18.8	22.1
Number of Available Workers*	1.09	1.20	1.17	1.14	1.29	1.09
Foreign-Born Hispanic						
Average Weekly Hours	28.8	31.6	30.9	31.9	26.1	28.1
Number of Available Workers*	1.54	1.48	1.38	1.43	1.55	1.33
Married Couple						
Average Weekly Hours	28.0	29.9	29.2	28.8	23.3	26.3
Number of Available Workers*	1.50	1.47	1.38	1.40	1.50	1.28
Cohabiting Couple						
Average Weekly Hours	23.3	27.3	25.7	25.9	22.0	26.3
Number of Available Workers*	1.31	1.48	1.37	1.36	1.42	1.29
Single Parent						
Average Weekly Hours	17.2	20.5	19.5	18.2	16.2	16.1
Number of Available Workers*	0.87	0.91	0.90	0.90	1.04	0.82

*Available Workers include all adults who worked or were seeking work or indicated inability to find work as reason for not working.
Source: Authors' calculations based on Current Population Survey: IPUMS-CPS, University of Minnesota and Historical SPM data, Columbia University.

per worker, while non-Hispanic blacks have fewer workers and work fewer hours per worker. Married and cohabiting families are similar, while single-parent families have fewer available workers and work significantly fewer hours per worker. During the Great Recession (2006–2010) the number of available workers increased for every demographic group, perhaps due to "doubling up" of poor families, though over the entire period (1995–2018), nearly all racial and marital status groups show a decline in available workers.

CONCLUSION

For a family to escape poverty through work, two things must happen: first, the family must put forth sufficient work effort; and second, that work effort must generate sufficient earnings. This chapter has examined the broader social and economic trends that have affected both of these aspects. Some of these trends have made the escape from poverty more difficult. For example, there has been a decline in the labor-market opportunities for men with limited education, and the opportunities that remain have had stagnant real wages. The increased work effort of women that tended to reduce poverty in the 1990s has slowed down, and the wages of less educated women have also stagnated.

Since poverty is a family phenomenon, family work effort is partly a question of how many potential workers there are in the family. A family with only one adult or with a disabled adult has direct limits on its work effort, while a family with two or more able-bodied adults has greater earnings potential. Poor families typically have fewer potential workers than non-poor families. But even when a family has more than one potential worker, there are limits on the full-time opportunities available to persons with limited skills. The result is a large "work gap," as poor families with children typically work about 15 hours per week less than non-poor families with children. The potential benefits that might arise from reducing that work gap are limited by the low wages of the "working poor." The typical hourly earnings for the working poor in families with children is less than $9.50 for men and less than $8.50 for women.

The limits on the extent to which work effort can eliminate poverty are implicit in these numbers. If poverty families were to work the additional 15 hours per week that non-poor families work and earn $9 per hour for that work, their annual earnings would increase by $7020. As we will show in a later chapter, the amount of additional earnings that would allow a typical poor family to escape poverty through higher earnings alone, with no benefits from either tax credits or safety-net programs, is about $13,000 per year. In other words, higher earnings by themselves are not a panacea for poverty alleviation, and there are social and economic trends that further limit the potential benefits of increased work effort.

But earnings are not the only source of income for poor families. There are tax credits available to working families with children, and there are programs that supplement the purchasing power of needy families. On the other hand, there are also expenses that are associated with work effort, especially costs of child care. To understand the opportunities and limitations for poverty reduction through work effort, one must also understand the benefits and limitations of these other factors that affect family poverty. These are explored in the next chapter.

Chapter 3

From Work to SPM Family Poverty

We begin this chapter with a brief overview of welfare spending and the history of poverty policy in America. We then analyze the poverty status of our SPM families by studying the recipiency rates and mean benefit levels of various social safety net programs received by our families. We use a series of poverty thresholds to investigate the impact of this spending on the well-being of SPM families with children. Benefits from the social safety net not only improve current well-being but also have the potential to improve health and economic prospects of children throughout their lives (Hoynes and Schanzenbach, 2018).

ECONOMICS OF WELFARE SPENDING

Historically, federal welfare spending for poor and low-income families includes spending on nutrition, housing, and education programs; cash assistance; and health-care expenditures. Most spending is "means-tested," meaning that in order to receive these benefits, qualifying individuals or families have income and assets below prescribed eligibility thresholds. Between 1972 and 2012, inflation-adjusted spending by the federal government on these means-tested programs and tax credits increased more than tenfold, from $55 billion to $558 billion (Carrington, Dahl and Falk, 2013). Spending on health care includes spending on Medicaid, and the low-income subsidy for Medicare, part D; in 2012, health-care spending was nearly half of total spending, and Medicaid accounted for over 90 percent of health care expenditures. Cash assistance includes the refundable portions of Earned Income Tax Credit (EITC) and the Child Tax Credit (CTC), spending on Supplemental Security Income (SSI), and Temporary Assistance for Needy

Families (TANF) (and its predecessor, Aid to Families with Dependent Children, [AFDC]). In 2012, refundable tax credits accounted for more than half of this category, while TANF was just over 10 percent. Finally, nutrition, housing, and education category include spending on Supplemental Nutrition Assistance Program (SNAP, formerly known as Food Stamps), child nutrition programs (Women, Infant and Children (WIC), school breakfast and lunch programs), housing expenditures (section 8 housing vouchers, public housing and several smaller programs), and expenditures on Pell grants. In 2012, expenditures on nutrition programs accounted for nearly 60 percent of spending in this category, the remainder being evenly divided between spending on housing and education. Under current law, the Congressional Budget Office projects spending on these means-tested programs and tax credits will increase to $877 billion by 2023. Nearly 60 percent of this projected spending is driven by health-care spending, primarily Medicaid. The cost of benefits differs substantially among groups of Medicaid recipients. In 2010, average spending per enrollee was $10,200 for people under age 65 with disabilities, $9,500 for people age 65 or older, $2,400 for non-disabled adults under 65, and $1,800 for non-disabled children.

Changes in spending over time depend upon the number of participants, and changes in spending per participant. Both factors have increased in the last four decades. Changes in eligibility rules and the addition of new programs determine the number of participants; nearly half of the programs in existence today were developed after 1972. The number of participants also depends upon economic conditions and population changes. As documented in chapter 1 of this volume, the population of the United States is almost 50 percent larger today than it was in 1972. Total spending also depends upon spending per participant, which in turn depends upon changes in the level of benefits and their cost of provision. Over the last four decades, changes in federal spending for Medicaid, EITC, and SNAP, the largest programs in each of their respective categories, depended upon both increases in the number of participants and increases in spending per participant (Carrington et al., 2013).

Ellwood (1988) suggests that the history of poverty policy is complicated because of conflicts among basic American values of individual autonomy, the virtue of work, the primacy of the family, and a desire for a sense of community. These values guide poverty policy: people should be held responsible for their actions, families should provide for themselves, and as a community we should treat the poor among us with compassion, dignity, and fairness (p. 17). Ellwood suggests conflicts among these goals give rise to three "Helping Conundrums," awkward compromises in poverty policy which often result in unintended consequences: the security-work conundrum, the assistance-family structure conundrum, and the targeting-isolation conundrum.

The first conundrum, the security-work conundrum, is fundamental to most poverty spending: if compassionate policy makers give the poor money, food, or medical care, they may inadvertently undermine incentives for the poor to work and provide for themselves. Consequently, poverty spending is not overly generous or has complicated eligibility conditions to minimize work disincentives.

Economists have long been concerned with potential work disincentives of welfare spending. For example, theoretically cash welfare benefits can impact a recipient's decision to work or not, or adversely reduce hours of work. As with any social insurance program, the benefits of raising the living standards of the poor come with these potentially costly unintended consequences. Consider an example. Suppose a welfare program has an annual cash benefit guarantee of $10,000: individuals with earnings above this amount receive nothing while individuals with earnings less than $10,000 receive a subsidy equal to $10,000 minus their current earnings. The benefit reduction rate, or the marginal tax rate at which benefits are reduced for an additional dollar of income is 100 percent. Because potential recipients lose $1 of benefits for each additional $1 of earnings, this provides a substantial work disincentive for individuals with incomes below and even those slightly above $10,000. To reduce these work disincentives, policy makers could reduce the benefit reduction rate to 50 percent so that for each additional $1 earned, only 50 cents of benefits are lost. Unfortunately, this significantly increases program eligibility and costs since individuals with incomes up to $20,000 could participate in the program (The benefit to any individual, B can be expressed as a function of the guaranteed benefit, G and the benefit reduction rate (or implicit tax), t, and an individual's income, I: $B = G - t(I)$). This example illustrates the "iron triangle," of redistributive programs: it is nearly impossible to adjust the guaranteed benefit and the benefit reduction rate to simultaneously provide a socially reasonable guarantee, preserve participant work incentives, and contain program costs at politically acceptable levels. This problem is further complicated by the fact that poor individuals participate in multiple programs, each with their own benefit reduction rates. So instead of facing one marginal tax rate, an individual who receives multiple program benefits may face multiple rates which compound the disincentive effects (Carrington, Dahl, and Falk, 2013; Kosar and Moffitt, 2017). However, researchers Ben-Shalom, Moffitt, and Scholz (2012, p. 709) find that "the disincentive effects of antipoverty programs on the overall poverty-reducing impact of the social safety net are negligible."

A snapshot of families with children who have received at least one means-tested benefit in 2012, suggests that families with less educated adults and without a worker or with only a part-time worker, are more likely to receive benefits and when they do, they receive more benefits than families with better educated adults or more workers. Furthermore, Hispanic and black families and those with single heads or more children are more likely to receive benefits and higher benefit levels than Asian or non-Hispanic white families and those with fewer children. There is also evidence of the problems of the "iron-triangle": in order to preserve work incentives and provide benefits to families most in need, benefits are extended to better-off families whose resources are two and even three times their official poverty thresholds (Falk et al., 2015).

Policy makers have dealt with this potential work disincentives of poverty spending in a number of ways, most of which seek to reduce the pool of potential recipients. First, program eligibility could be based on participant characteristics associated with low incomes that are easy to verify, but difficult to change. For example, social insurance programs focus on the aged, blind, and disabled, while welfare and tax subsidy programs focus on families with children. Second, policy makers could make applying for assistance difficult or unattractive, so that only the neediest apply; work requirements or lifetime limitations on program recipiency, or frequent re-certification are prominent examples. Finally, policy makers can make welfare dependency less attractive by supporting programs such as job training and childcare which emphasize self-sufficiency.

The second conundrum, the assistance-family structure conundrum, has led to some of the most bitter debates among poverty policy makers. Poverty policy in the US has developed in a way that supports the most vulnerable in our society, the so called "deserving poor," the elderly, disabled, and families with young children, but provides little support to working age, childless couples, and single individuals. For example, Falk and co-authors (2015, p. 21) show relative spending levels by family type for select programs. They find that in 2012 the government spent $91.6 billion on working families with children, $89.5 billion on families with a disabled member and $38. 5 billion on families with an aged member, while spending only $11.3 billion on households without aged or disabled individuals or children. Furthermore, because single parents are eligible for benefits, conservatives like Charles Murray (1984) have argued that poverty spending has led to weakening of family ties and increases in non-marital births and single parenthood. While the needs of poor families with children are real, so theoretically are these negative unintended consequences.

Ellwood argues that the last conundrum, the target-isolation conundrum is the least discussed but might be the most important of the three conundrums. A goal of poverty policy is to target services to those who need them the most, which often means the poorest among us. While this may be economically efficient, it has the unintended consequence of stigmatizing the poor as somehow different from society, or as individuals who do not hold American values of individual autonomy, and the primacy of work and family. Consequently, such targeting can isolate the poor politically and erode compassion and empathy from better-off members of society. This can result in a "blaming the victim," mentality that makes serious progress against poverty difficult. Alesina, Glaeser and Glaeser (2004) argue that US spending on the poor is less generous than European countries because of racial heterogeneity in the United States. Racial animosity makes spending on the poor, who are disproportionately non-white, unappealing to many. The poor may be different from the rest of society, or they may have the same dreams and values as the rest of us but may not have been as fortunate in matters of health, work, and family origins.

A BRIEF HISTORY OF US SOCIAL SAFETY NET SPENDING

Table 3.1 summarizes key events in the history of the US poverty policy. Changes in welfare spending reflect the changing values and circumstances of American society. When women were more likely to raise children and maintain a home rather than join the paid labor force, early poverty spending goals emphasized income support for women and children whose male breadwinner was absent through death or abandonment. In the 1970s and 1980s as more mothers went to work, goals slowly changed to a system which by the late 1990s encouraged and supported work of poor mothers. The Personal Responsibility and Work Opportunity Reconciliation Act of 1996 (PRWORA) introduced work requirements and time limits on benefit receipt. And the form of spending has changed. Initially most spending took the form of cash benefits, but as concerns for fraud and abuse increased, and policy makers became more concerned about unintended consequences of cash benefits, increasingly benefits were in-kind, providing recipients access to specified goods and services, such as food stamps and health care rather than cash.

More recently, spending on poverty programs during the Great Recession deserves note. As described in chapter 2 in this volume, the Great Recession was one of the most severe economic downturns in our nation's recent history. Perhaps because of its severity, policy makers took the unusual step of making temporary increases in poverty programs to support poor and low-income families. In particular, they raised maximum SNAP benefits by 13 percent, increased EITC benefits for large families, provided additional funds for TANF, increased the CTC, provided a one-time reduction in payroll and income taxes for poor and low-income families (Making Work Pay Tax Credit), provided a one-time increase in benefits for Old Age and Survivors'

Table 3.1   Key Events in the History of the US Social Safety Net

Date	Event
Beginnings:	
1935	Creation of Aid to Families with Dependent Children (AFDC), Old Age, Survivors, and Disability Insurance program (OASDI), and Unemployment Insurance (UI)
1956	Creation of the Social Security Disability Insurance (SSDI) program
1962	Michael Harrington publishes *The Other America*
Great Expansion of the War on Poverty (1964–1975):	
1964	Formation of Food Stamp program
1965	Creation of Medicare and Medicaid programs
1965	Creation of Head Start program
1966	School Breakfast and National School Lunch programs formalized
1972	Congress creates the Supplemental Security Income (SSI) program
1975	Creation of the Women's Infants and Children (WIC) nutritional program
1975	Congress legislates the Earned Income Tax Credit (EITC)
Re-Assessing Early Antipoverty Efforts (Late 1970s–2000):	
Late 1970s	President Carter's expansionary welfare reform (public jobs component) fails
1980	Ronald Reagan elected president after campaign proposing retrenchment
1984	Charles Murry publishes *Losing Ground*
1988	Family Support Act passes in 1988 modifies AFDC to emphasize work, child support, and family benefits but is later judged as a failure
1990	President H. W. Bush expands EITC which contributes to increased employment of poor single mothers in the 1990s
1996	President Clinton oversees the most contractionary welfare reform in modern history, the Personal Responsibility and Work Opportunity Reconciliation Act, creates Temporary Assistance for Needy Families (TANF), and welfare caseloads fall from over 5 million in 1993 to less than 2.5 million in 2000
Late1990s	Increases in childcare subsidies and early childhood education (HeadStart)
1997	Children's Health Insurance Program (CHIP) passes to provide benefits for low-income families with children who do not qualify for Medicaid
Large Expansion, Little Reform (2000–2020):	
2001 and 2003	George W. Bush tax cuts increase the Child Tax Credit (CTC)
Great Recession -2009 Temporary Changes	Increases to Food Stamps (SNAP), expansion of unemployment insurance (UI), Making Work Pay Tax Credit, TANF expansion

(continued)

Table 3.1 (Continued)

Date	Event
Great Recession -2009 Permanent Changes	EITC expansion for families with three or more children; expansion in the refundable portion of CTC
Affordable Care Act. 2010	Medicaid spending expanded to provide increased coverage and access for lower-income families
Significant Reform, Temporarily Introduced (2021)	
2021	American Rescue Plan introduces a one-year temporary expansion of the CTC, increasing the credit from $2,000 to $3,600 for children under 6; and to $3,000 for children 6–17; for poor and moderate-income families; the credit is fully refundable. This has the potential to cut child poverty rates in half.
2021	American Rescue Plan Act introduces a one-year temporary expansion of the EITC, to include younger parents, age 19–24, eliminates the upper age limit, and increases the income cap for childless workers and increases the maximum credit for childless workers to $1,500.
2021	American Rescue Plan introduces a one-year temporary expansion of the Child &Dependent Care Tax Credit (CDCTC) by expanding eligible qualifying expenses from $3,000 to $8,000 for one dependent, and from $6,000 to $16,000 for two or more dependents; families earning up to $125,000 would be eligible for the full 50 percent credit; the credit would be fully refundable

Source: Based on Moffit, 2015 Table 1 and Haveman et al., 2015; and Sawhill and Welch, 2021.

Insurance and SSI recipients, and extended Unemployment Insurance (UI) benefits from the typical 26 weeks to 99 weeks. While changes in the EITC and CTC were made permanent, most of the other increases in spending were phased out by 2013. In total, these changes to the safety net resulted in additional 200 billion dollars of spending.

The impact of this spending on child poverty and the economy was impressive. Bitler, Hoynes and Kuka (2017) find that social safety net during the Great Recession provided important protection for poor families as after tax and transfer poverty for children was much lower than their private income poverty rates in the absence of this spending. However, they find that the protective effect of this safety-net spending was not the same for all demographic groups. In particular, children living in single-parent families, or Hispanic families, particularly those with immigrant household heads, experienced larger poverty cyclicality during the Great Recession than non-Hispanic white families with children, married couple, and native-born families. This increase in safety-net spending was also highly effective in tempering the length and depth of the Great Recession. Schanzenbach and co-authors

(2016) find that each additional dollar spent on these programs led to more than a dollar of additional spending in the economy. Similarly, the American Rescue Plan temporarily increased several components of the social safety net during the current COVID-19 pandemic (see table 3.1).

Funding and eligibility criteria for poverty programs vary from program to program and state to state. Different poverty programs may define participant resources and eligibility thresholds differently. Some program benefits are federally funded, but the administrative costs are shared by federal and state governments (e.g., Medicaid). Eligibility might be established by the federal government for all participants nationwide (e.g., SNAP), while other programs depend upon state governments to establish eligibility and benefit levels within guidelines from the federal government (e.g., TANF). As a consequence, eligibility for assistance and level of support may depend upon a potential recipient's state of residence.

Just because a person is eligible for a program benefit or service doesn't mean they receive it. Whether an eligible recipient receives benefits often depends on how those benefits are financed. In government budgets some poverty programs are discretionary, which require annual appropriations (e.g., housing policy), some are mandatory, meaning funds must be made available for all eligible applicants (e.g., SNAP), and some are mandatory, but funding is capped (e.g., TANF/AFDC). Discretionary programs are often underfunded, and eligible recipients face long waiting lists. For example, in 2012, only 18 percent of eligible persons received subsidized housing. In recent years, TANF/AFDC has had declining recipiency rates and benefit levels. But even when funding is mandatory, not all eligible persons receive benefits, as 2012 recipiency estimates suggest SNAP (69.6 percent), SSI (66.6 percent), and WIC (65.3 percent) (Falk et al., 2015).

Eligibility for federal poverty programs also depends upon citizenship status. Many of the most important federal programs: non-emergency Medicaid, Medicare, SNAP, SSI, TANF/AFDC have been denied to undocumented immigrants since the inception of these programs. And while lawful, non-citizen, permanent residents could receive benefits in a manner similar to US citizens before welfare reform in 1996 PRWORA, most were barred from receiving benefits for a five-year period after reform. Subsequent legislation restored access for some, but not all, qualified immigrants. In 2010 the Affordable Care Act (ACA), while not altering immigrant eligibility for Medicaid or Child Health Insurance Program (CHIP), did provide new opportunities for lawfully present immigrants to purchase health insurance in the established insurance marketplaces. Despite these changes, foreign-born Hispanics are more than twice as likely to lack health insurance as native-born Hispanics. Krogstad and Lopez (2014) find that 39 percent of all foreign-born Hispanics do not have health-care coverage, and nearly half do not have insurance if non-citizen. This compares to 17 percent of US-born Hispanics and 14 percent of US citizens overall.

Finally, there are a handful of exceptions to these federal restrictions for programs deemed necessary to protect life or guarantee safety: immigrants regardless of legal status are eligible to emergency Medicaid services if they would otherwise qualify for Medicaid, and immigrant children regardless of immigration status qualify for school breakfast and lunch programs. In addition, every state has opted to provide Supplemental Nutrition Program for WIC regardless of immigration status.

The National Immigration Law Center (Broder, Moussavian and Blazer, 2015) notes that since reform, many immigrants who are eligible for benefits hesitated to apply due to the confusion about eligibility and fear caused by the laws' chilling effects. Consequently, participation in federal programs by documented immigrants decreased sharply after 1996. Many states have tried to fill gaps in coverage, either by electing federal options to cover more documented immigrants or by spending state funds to cover some of the immigrants who are ineligible for federal benefits. The result has been a confusing hodge-podge of regulations that vary from state to state. And to complicate matters even more, citizen children born in the United States to undocumented immigrants may qualify for, but not receive, federal benefits because of fear or confusion on the part of their parents; receipt of benefits by a child does not change their parents' or any family members' eligibility for those benefits.

Changes in society's definition of the "deserving poor" have led to a shift in the emphasis of poverty programs from income support for poor families to support for poor workers and their families. This in turn has led to shifting patterns of eligible poor population. In addition, the expansion of health-care benefits through CHIP and the ACA, and tax-based credits like the EITC and CTC have changed recipiency patterns as well, extending benefits to families whose incomes are above their official poverty thresholds. In a study of the trends and distribution of income support, Moffit and Scholz (2010) find:

> Very poor elderly, disabled, and childless families received greatly increased expenditures, mostly arising from Social Security, Social Security Disability Insurance, SSI and the health programs. Very poor single-parent and two-parent households experienced declines in expenditures, driven largely by lower recipiency rates, benefit receipt or both in Aid to Families with Dependent Children/ TANF and Food Stamp programs. . . . However, expenditures received by one-and two-parent households further up the income scale increased, largely because of expansions of the EITC. Thus, there was a redistribution of income from the very poor to the near-poor and non-poor for these one-and two-parent households, as well as an overall relative redistribution from them to the elderly, disabled and childless. (p. 111)

Hoynes and Schanzenbach (2018) find that because of these changes, all of the gains in the spending on the social safety net for children since 1990 have gone to families with earnings. This shift in poverty spending from income support to work support has important consequences for the very poorest families with children. Because these families are less likely to have a worker, they do not receive this work-conditioned support. Consequently, these children may be left behind and are at risk for a lifetime of long-lasting negative consequences. US Census Bureau data suggests that in 2018, over 5 million children lived in families with incomes less than half the official poverty measure.

With this brief overview of the poverty spending in the United States we now turn our attention to our SPM families with children. The following section details their receipt of government tax credits and benefits and the effect these programs have on household poverty.

SPM FAMILIES, GOVERNMENT
BENEFITS, AND POVERTY

This section explores the effectiveness of government antipoverty policies by studying the major tax and transfer programs. We organize our analysis around six measures of poverty as defined in table 3.2. These poverty measures enable us to explore the relative impact of private income, government taxes and transfers, and medical and work expenses on family poverty. We proceed as follows: first we introduce our six measures of poverty. Following a basic description of key component parts, we analyze recipiency rates for key demographic groups: four racial groups (non-Hispanic white, non-Hispanic black, native-born Hispanics, and foreign-born Hispanics) and three family structures (married couples, cohabiting couples, and single-parent families) for two samples of poor families, the Private Income Poor and SPM Poor. We provide mean values of benefits for families who receive a particular benefit. We then explored the antipoverty effects of the programs studied.

Table 3.2 defines the six measures of poverty displayed in figure 3.1. We include the official measure of poverty only for reference. We begin our discussion with Private income Poverty. The private income poor are families whose resources (wages, salaries and asset income, including private pensions) are insufficient to raise them over the SPM threshold, *before* considering the effects of government taxes and transfers, and of work and medical expenses. We then describe the key governmental programs received by these poor families. We first consider the impact of the tax code (After-Tax Private Income Poverty). We next consider cash government social insurance: Old Age, Survivors and Disability payments, unemployment and workers

Table 3.2   Alternative Measures of Poverty, SPM Families with Children, 1995–2018

Official Poverty (OPM)
A family is poor if their resources, as defined by the official measure of poverty, are
   less than their official poverty threshold for that family. **(POV 1)**

Private income Poverty
A family is poor if private income (wages, salaries; self-employed and farm
income, dividends, interest, rents, and pension income) is less than their SPM
threshold. **(POV 2)**

After-Tax Private Income
A family is poor if private income net of taxes (federal income tax and credits, federal
   payroll tax, and state income tax) is less than their SPM threshold. **(POV 3)**

After-Tax and Post-Cash Social Insurance Income
A family is poor if private income plus government cash social insurance transfers
   (Social Security, workers unemployment, and compensation benefits) net of taxes is
   less than their SPM threshold. **(POV 4)**

After-Tax and Post-Transfer Income
A family is poor if private income plus government cash transfers (Social Security,
   workers unemployment and compensation benefits, supplemental security income
   [SSI], and cash welfare [AFDC or TANF], plus non-cash transfers (food stamps
   [SNAP], school lunches, WIC, housing energy assistance, LIHEAP) net of taxes is
   less than their SPM threshold. **(POV 5)**

Historical SPM Anchored Poverty (SPMa)
A family is poor if after-tax, post-transfer income less the sum of out-of-pocket
   medical expenses [MOOP], work and childcare expenses and child support
   payments to other families is less than their SPM threshold. **(POV 6)**

Source: Authors' calculations based on Current Population Survey: IPUMS-CPS, University of Minnesota and
   Historical SPM data, Columbia University.

compensation payments (After-Tax and Post-Cash Social Insurance Income).
We then consider means-tested cash and in-kind benefits (After Tax-and Post
Transfer Poverty). And finally, we consider the SPM poor, families who are
poor *after* taxes, transfers and medical and work expenses are considered.

Private Income and After-Tax Private Income Poverty

Figure 3.1 provides trends in our six poverty measures for all SPM families
with children between 1995 and 2018. As one would expect, measures of Private Income Poverty (POV2) are generally higher than other measures which
include the effects of government transfers. The changing role of the tax code
as an antipoverty measure can be clearly seen: before the early 2000s the tax
code had either a negative or neutral impact on poor families, while measures
of After-tax Private Income Poverty (POV 3) either exceeded or were identical to measures of Private income Poverty. Afterward the tax code has played

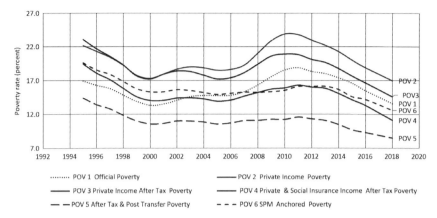

Figure 3.1   Poverty Rates, Various Poverty Measures, All SPM Families with Children Under 18, 1995–2018. *Source*: Authors' calculations based on Current Population Survey: IPUMS-CPS, University of Minnesota and Historical SPM data, Columbia University.

an increasingly important role in reducing Private income Poverty. Details of recent changes in the tax code, discussed below, help explain these effects.

Earned Income Tax Credit

Poor and low-income families typically pay some federal tax. The largest tax burden comes from the payroll tax, followed by excise taxes. Many of these families do not pay federal income taxes and instead have negative income-tax liabilities as a result of tax credits; that is, tax credits exceed their tax liability. The income tax includes some credits that are "refundable," and others that are not. While a non-refundable tax credit can reduce a family's tax liability to zero, a refundable tax credit which exceeds a taxpayer's liability can provide a cash payment to taxpayers who pay little or no taxes. Proponents of refundable credits argue that they help the families most in need of assistance only if the credits are refundable, while opponents of refundable credits argue that the tax code should be used to collect taxes, not redistribute income or carry out social policies. The Tax Policy Center (2020) estimates that in 2020, taxpayers in the lowest income quintile will, on average receive $860, primarily due to the EITC and the CTC.

The EITC was created in 1975 as a refundable tax credit to increase work incentives. Administered by the Internal Revenue Service, the EITC focuses on low- and moderate-income working families with or without children; it is designed to offset the regressive nature of Social Security payroll taxes for low-wage workers. The credit rises over a range of earnings (phase-in range), is constant over a range of incomes, and is gradually phased out as earnings increase. If the credit is greater than a family's tax liability, the balance is refunded. Table 3.3 provides program parameters for both single-parent and

Table 3.3 2018 Earned Income Tax Credit Parameters

	Phase in Rate (%)	Phase in Ends ($)	Maximum Credit Amount ($)	Phase Out Begins ($)	Phase Out Rate (%)	Phase Out Ends ($)
Single Filing Status						
Childless	7.65	6,780	519	8,490	7.65	15,270
One Child	34	10,180	3,461	18,660	15.98	40,320
Two Children	40	14,290	5,716	18,660	21.06	45,802
More than Two Children	45	14,290	6,431	18,660	21.06	49,194
Married Filing Jointly						
Childless	7.65	6,780	519	14,170	7.65	20,950
One Child	34	10,180	3,461	24,350	15.98	46,010
Two Children	40	14,290	5,716	24,350	21.06	51,492
More than Two Children	45	14,290	6,431	24,350	21.06	54,884

Source: IRS, 2018, http://www.irs.gov/credits-deductions/individuals/earned-income-tax-credit/eitc-income-limits-maximum-credit-amounts; and Center on Budget and Policy Priorities, 2018.

married couple families filing jointly. For tax year 2020, the maximum credit for a single-parent or married couple family with three or more children was $6,660 (US Internal Revenue Service, 2020).

The tax credit has been expanded over time: the Tax Reform Act of 1986 indexed policy parameters for inflation; the Omnibus Budget Acts of 1993 introduced a credit schedule for families without children and sharply increased the credit for families with two or more children; and the American Recovery and Reinvestment Act (ARRA) of 2009 introduced a new, more generous schedule for families with three or more children and substantially extended the married couple schedule in an effort to reduce marriage penalties for two-earner couples. These changes were crucial in helping low-income families navigate the Great Recession; they have since become a permanent fixture of the tax code. In FY2017 the program reached 27 million filing units and cost an estimated $61.9 billion. In response to the COVID-19 pandemic, the Biden administration introduced a number of changes: one-year temporary expansion of the EITC to include younger parents ages 19 to 24, eliminated the upper age limit for parents, and increased the maximum benefit for childless workers to $1,500. In addition, nearly half of the states have a supplemental state EITC program which typically adds a percentage to federal benefits.

One of the key research questions in the EITC literature concerns the work incentive effects of the EITC. Several researchers (Meyer and Rosenbaum, 2001; Holtz, Mullin, and Scholz, 2006) find the EITC explains much of the increase in labor-force participation for less educated, single mothers in the 1990s. However, this interpretation has been challenged by Kleven (2021), who provides evidence that the change in the 1990s was largely a consequence of the 1996 welfare reform and the contemporaneous macroeconomic expansion. Eissa and Hoynes (2004) found evidence that secondary workers in EITC families faced high marginal tax rates which act as a disincentive to work, and this effect may be mitigated by recent changes in the program. More recently, Hoynes and Rothstein (2016) find EITC quite successful in promoting work among poor families, while Hoynes and Patel (2018) show that the family earnings gains due to employment are as large as the government outlay from the EITC. Moulton, Graddy-Reed, and Lanahan (2016) find some evidence that these mothers leave the workforce when they lose the EITC benefit as their children age out of the program. Finally, Bitler, Hoynes, and Kuka (2017) find that the EITC does act as a safety net during economic downturns: higher unemployment leads to increased probability of EITC receipt and credits received for married couple families but has insignificant effects on single-parent families.

Several researchers suggest the EITC is an investment in poor children and their families. Hoynes, Miller and Simon (2015) find increases in after-tax income due to the EITC lead to fewer low birth weight births, while Evans and Garthwaite (2014) find that the EITC contributes to improvements in maternal health. Other researchers find that the EITC contributes to cognitive and human capital development including higher math and reading test scores (Dahl and Lochner, 2012, 2017; Chetty, Friedman and Rockoff, 2011). Bastian and Michelmore (2018) suggest larger EITC benefits during childhood lead to increased probability of completing high school, attending college, and higher employment as young adults.

Child Tax Credit

The EITC is not the only feature of the tax code designed to help families with children. Contemporaneous with welfare reform, Congress passed the Taxpayer Relief Act of 1997 which introduced the CTC, a measure designed to help working families offset the cost of raising children. The CTC reduces a family's tax liability by the amount of the qualifying credit. The CTC has a structure similar to the EITC (phase in, constant range, phase-out portions) but is more universal and not as well targeted to poor and low-income families as the EITC. Unlike the EITC, CTC parameters are not adjusted for inflation, and the credit initially was not refundable. In 2001, a refundable Additional Child Tax Credit (ACTC) was introduced and was significantly expanded in 2009 as part of the stimulus package. In 2017, Congress expanded the credit amount, more than tripling the income level at which the credit begins to phase out ($200,000 for single taxpayers, $400,000 for married filing jointly). Under 2018 tax provisions, families who qualify can receive a tax credit up to $2,000 per child under age 17. If the value of the credit exceeds taxes owed, a family may receive all or part of the difference in a refund check up to 15 percent of their earnings above $2,500; this refund can be worth up to $1,400 per child (US Internal Revenue Service, 2018). Finally, in response to the current pandemic, the American Rescue Plan introduced a one-year temporary expansion of the CTC, increasing the credit from $2,000 to $3,600 for children under 6 and up to $3,000 for children age six to 17 for poor and low-income families; the credit is fully refundable.

Together, the EITC and ACTC have become two of the most effective antipoverty programs. Hoynes and Patel (2018) found that the programs were initially well targeted, reaching families whose income after other taxes and transfers would otherwise be between 75 percent and 150 percent of the official poverty line. Using a SPM measure of poverty, Short (2014) found that income from refundable credits reduced the number of people in poverty by over 15 percent. In a series of simulations designed to explain increases in participation in EITC and ACTC over time, researchers Hardy, Smeeding and Ziliak (2018) find that EITC/ACTC use by different groups responds differently to economic, demographic, and policy changes: less educated family heads are roughly evenly affected by the economy, demographics, and policy; while for low-income families, policy is the most important. Finally, families headed by a single mother are more sensitive than married couple families to changes in EITC/ACTC participation caused by changes in the economy.

Table 3.4 provides recipiency rates and mean values received by recipients of private income and the EITC for two samples of the poor, private income poor, and SPM poor. The first horizontal panel provides data on all SPM families combined; succeeding panels break down this data into our four racial and ethnic groups and three marital status groups. When we consider all SPM families combined, we see recipiency rates of private income and the EITC are very similar for our two poverty samples. In both groups, the impact of the recession of 2001 and the Great Recession is clearly evident: recipiency of both private income and EITC falls with economic downturns. Perhaps more interesting is a comparison of our four racial and marital status groups.

As their higher labor-force participation discussed in chapter 2 would suggest, foreign-born Hispanics have the highest recipiency rates and values for both Private Income and EITC; this is true for both the Private Income Poor and SPM Poor families. Similarly, non-Hispanic blacks have the lowest recipiency rates and values due to their low earnings.

Table 3.4 also provides similar data based on marital status. As might be expected, married couples are most likely to receive private income and the EITC, single parents least likely; this is true for both poverty samples. For cohabiting couples, their receipt of private income most closely resembles that of married couples, which is reasonable since both family types potentially have two workers. However, cohabiting couple receipt of EITC more closely resembles that of the single-parent families since their legal status for tax purposes more closely resembles that of single-parent families.

While these differences are interesting, what is important is the impact of the tax code on private income poverty. Table 3.5 presents the difference between Private income Poverty and After-Tax Private Income Poverty rates, which illustrates the impact of the tax code on private income poverty for our demographic groups of interest. Negative numbers in the early years suggest the tax code contributed to poverty of a given group, since their after-tax poverty rates were higher than their pre-tax rates; in later years, a positive number suggests that the tax code had an antipoverty effect. Nonwhite families, particularly non-Hispanic black and foreign-born Hispanic families, benefited most from the impact of the tax code as did single-parent families (who are most likely black) after 2000. The antipoverty effects of the tax code were particularly important during the Great Recession for each demographic group.

Table 3.4 Recipiency Rates and Real Mean Benefits Received: Private Income and EITC by Race and Marital Status, SPM Families with Children, Select Years 1995–2018 (2012 dollars)

Year	Private Income Poor				SPM Poor			
	Private Income		Earned Income Tax Credit		Private Income		Earned Income Tax Credit	
	Percent Receiving	Mean Real Value of Recipients	Percent Receiving	Mean Real Benefit of Recipients	Percent Receiving	Mean Real Value of Recipients	Percent Receiving	Mean Real Benefit of Recipients
All SPM Families Combined								
1995	76.4	$10,346	60.3	$2,725	76.9	$14,899	59.6	$2,552
1999	81.0	$11,550	65.9	$3,152	82.0	$14,689	66.6	$2,922
2002	78.5	$10,750	61.2	$3,180	79.2	$13,361	59.9	$3,015
2006	77.7	$11,539	64.7	$3,157	77.4	$14,072	62.4	$2,967
2010	76.6	$11,208	65.0	$3,438	73.8	$12,962	59.3	$3,044
2018	81.2	$13,280	64.8	$3,562	80.9	$17,035	60.4	$3,142
Non-Hispanic White Families								
2018	79.7	$11,053	56.9	$3,319	80.5	$16,505	52.8	$2,852
Non-Hispanic Black Families								
2018	75.1	$11,620	60.8	$3,353	71.4	$13,304	53.4	$2,790
Native-Born Hispanic Families								
2018	81.5	$14,171	67.2	$3,577	81.2	$17,648	62.8	$3,126
Foreign-Born Hispanic Families								
2018	90.4	$17,793	81.1	$4,016	90.5	$20,333	76.9	$3,669
Married Couple Families								
2018	87.5	$16,283	75.4	$3,944	88.3	$21,947	72.2	$3,536
Cohabiting Couple Families								
2018	82.6	$13,535	61.9	$3,060	85.0	$18,232	55.6	$2,663
Single-Parent Families								
2018	76.5	$10,845	58.1	$3,343	73.9	$12,012	52.4	$2,859

Source: Authors' calculations based on Current Population Survey: IPUMS-CPS, University of Minnesota and Historical SPM data, Columbia University.

Table 3.5   Private Income Poverty Less After-Tax Private Income Poverty, Select Years 1995–2018

Year	All SPM Families	Non-Hispanic White Families	Non-Hispanic Black Families	Native-Born Hispanic Families	Foreign-Born Hispanic Families	Married-Couple Families	Cohabiting-Couple Families	Single-Parent Families
1995	−0.9	−0.9	−0.3	−0.3	−2.2	−1.3	−1.3	0.5
1999	0.1	0.1	0.9	0.0	−0.9	−0.3	−1.5	2.0
2002	0.3	0.0	1.0	0.2	0.7	−0.1	−0.4	1.8
2006	1.2	0.7	2.0	1.5	2.9	0.9	−0.7	3.0
2010	3.0	1.9	3.9	3.3	7.0	2.6	2.2	4.7
2018	2.4	1.3	4.2	2.4	5.3	1.9	0.8	5.0

Source: Authors' calculations based on Current Population Survey: IPUMS-CPS, University of Minnesota and Historical SPM data Columbia University.

Government Cash Transfers: Social Insurance Programs

Old Age, Survivors, and Disability Insurance

The phrase "Social Security" actually refers to a collection of insurance programs: Old Age, Survivors, and Disability Insurance (collectively known as OASDI) that are designed to protect individuals from uncertainties of everyday life. Originally a retirement program established with the Social Security Act of 1935, survivor benefits were added in 1939, and disability benefits in 1956. The Social Security Act also established the first national unemployment compensation program, UI and Aid to Dependent Children Program (a precursor to AFDC and TANF).

Social Security is a set of self-financed programs that provide monthly cash benefits to qualified retired or disabled workers and their families or to the survivors of deceased workers. There is no means-test for benefits; funding depends upon worker and employer contributions to a Social Security payroll or self-employed tax system; workers and employers in covered employment each pay 6.2 percent tax on earnings up to an annual earnings limit ($132,900 in 2020) while the self-employed pay the full 12.4 percent on net self-employment income (up to $132,900 in 2020). Social Security has a dual eligibility system; individuals may qualify either as workers or as family members of qualified workers. A worker is fully eligible for benefits if they have 40 "quarters of coverage" or credits. In 2019, the amount of earnings required for one credit was $1,360. Only four credits can be earned annually, regardless of earnings. To qualify for Social Security disability benefits, non-citizen workers must meet one of two additional requirements: they must have been assigned a Social Security number for work purposes on or after January 1, 2004, *or* they must have been admitted to the United States as a non-immigrant visitor for business (B-1 visa) or as an alien crewman (D-1 or D-2 visas) *and* they must be able to prove that they are in the United States lawfully in any given month for which benefits are paid. For all beneficiaries, OASDI benefit calculation depends upon a worker's age, employment history, and type of benefit. To protect beneficiaries from loss of purchasing power, OASDI benefits are annually adjusted for inflation using Bureau of Labor Statistics Consumer Price Index for Urban Wage Earners and Clerical Workers (Social Security Administration, 2018).

In August 2018, 62.6 million persons received benefits: 46.4 million were retired workers and their families, 10.2 million were disabled workers and their families, and 5.9 million were survivors of deceased workers. In December 2017, average monthly benefits were $1,404 for retired workers, $1,197 for disabled workers, and $1,151.71 for survivors. (Social Security Administration, table 5.a1 2018 stat abstract).

Though not designed as "poverty programs," the antipoverty effects of OASDI, particularly for the elderly, are well known: Social Security has reduced elderly cash income poverty rates from nearly 40 percent in the late 1950s to less than 10 percent today (Herd et al., 2018).

Unemployment Insurance

UI is a joint federal-state program designed as a temporary wage replacement for unemployed, eligible workers. While the Social Security Administration and Federal Unemployment Tax Act set broad standards to ensure conformity and compliance with state and federal laws, states design their own programs within this general framework to determine eligibility, and amount and duration of benefits. While there is wide variance within and among the states, most states provide up to 26 weeks of benefits. Benefits are not means-tested, and are available to unemployed workers who have demonstrated their labor-force attachment by a specified amount of recent work or earnings in covered employment. Within federally determined limits, weekly benefits vary with a worker's past wages; most states set benefits as a fraction of the past 12 months' wages. UI benefits are financed by payroll taxes paid by employers and collected by state and federal governments.

Unemployment benefits help to smooth fluctuations in the economy: during periods of prosperity, UI revenues grow while program spending falls, creating a surplus. During recession periods, revenues fall and program spending increases, mitigating the loss of earnings for the unemployed. In 1970, federal and state governments established the Extended Benefit Program which provides an additional 13 or 20 weeks of benefits for workers who exhaust their initial benefits during periods of particularly high unemployment. Finally, Congress can temporarily extend benefits even further, as was done in during the Great Recession in 2008. (Emergency Unemployment Compensation Program enacted June 30, 2008, expired January 1, 2014).

Gabe and Whittaker (2012) find that UI benefits significantly reduced poverty during recessions but had a markedly larger impact during the Great Recession than in the previous two recessions. This is in part due to the interaction of extended benefits with the ARRA of 2009: ARRA temporarily increased unemployment benefits by $25 per week for all recipients of any type of UI and excluded $2,400 of UI benefits from gross income calculations under federal tax provisions for 2009. In 2011, the poverty rate for persons in families receiving benefits was nearly 40 percent less than it otherwise would have been; UI benefits lifted an estimated 2.3 million persons out of poverty.

Perhaps because of this success, UI benefits have played an important role during the Covid-19 pandemic. The American Rescue Plan Act of 2021 provided supplemental federal unemployment benefits of $300 per week ($600/week early in the pandemic) in addition to state benefits while the Pandemic Unemployment Assistance Program extended eligibility to many workers who traditionally do not qualify for UI receipt including the self-employed, recent labor market entrants, and workers without sufficient earnings history. In addition, the first $10,200 of unemployment benefits will be nontaxable income for households with adjusted gross income of up to $150,000. Preliminary analysis by the National Employment Law Project (2021) finds that these unemployment benefits kept 4.7 million people, including 1.4 million children out of poverty in 2020.

Workers' Compensation

Workers Compensation program was the first social insurance program developed in the United States, predating the Social Security Act of 1935. First established by the federal government in 1908 to cover civilian employees engaged in hazardous work, by 1921 all but six states had compensation laws. Today all 50 states, the District of Columbia, Puerto Rico, and US Virgin Islands have their own programs. Workers Compensation is designed to provide cash benefits and medical care to employees who suffer work-related injuries or illnesses, and provides survivor benefits to dependents of workers who die on the job. In exchange for these benefits, recipients generally give up the right to sue their employers for damages of any kind. Benefits are paid for by employers as a cost of doing business; many employers use insurance from a private carrier or state fund. More than 138 million jobs were covered by worker's compensation plans in 2016 representing covered payroll of $7.4 trillion; $61.9 billion of benefits were paid out in 2016.

Table 3.6 provides recipiency rates and mean values received by recipients of UI and Workers' Compensation combined and OASDI benefits for private income poor and SPM poor families for our racial/ethnic and marital status groups. In our samples, poor families are about four times as likely to receive UI as Workers Compensation. The fact that 22 percent of private income poor families and 16 percent of SPM poor families have a household member aged 62 or older helps to explain the OASDI recipiency rates. The impact of business cycles on UI recipiency is clearly shown, as recipiency rises in years with higher unemployment rates for every racial/ethnic group and family group. The impact of the higher benefit levels provided by the ARRA of 2009

Table 3.6 Recipiency Rates and Real Benefits Received: Social Insurance Programs by Race and Marital Status, SPM Families with Children, Select Years 1995–2018 (2012 dollars)

Year	PRIVATE INCOME POOR				SPM POOR			
	Unemployment & Workers Compensation		Social Security, Old Age, Survivors & Disability		Unemployment & Workers Compensation		Social Security, Old Age, Survivors & Disability	
	Percent Receiving	Mean Real Value of Recipients	Percent Receiving	Mean Real Benefit of Recipients	Percent Receiving	Mean Real Value of Recipients	Percent Receiving	Mean Real Benefit of Recipients
All SPM Families Combined								
1995	18.9	$6,481	25.8	$15,235	14.7	$4,275	15.4	$10,876
1999	14.3	$6,466	26.0	$16,553	10.5	$4,067	14.6	$11,110
2002	22.3	$8,316	29.2	$17,549	15.74	$5,668	16.7	$12,470
2006	13.3	$7,140	29.8	$17,744	9.2	$4,976	17.9	$12,863
2010	25.7	$10,800	27.4	$17,756	18.6	$7,763	17.5	$13,378
2018	6.4	$5,998	28.7	$19,055	4.5	$4,771	16.7	$12,905
Non-Hispanic White Families								
2018	6.1	$5,881	37.0	$20,988	3.9	$4,839	20.6	$12,768
Non-Hispanic Black Families								
2018	6.6	$5,768	27.8	$16,281	4.9	$4,746	18.8	$13,439
Native-Born Hispanic Families								
2018	8.2	$5,981	25.4	$19,188	5.6	$5,195	14.9	$12,553
Foreign-Born Hispanic Families								
2018	5.8	$6,523	17.9	$17,378	4.4	$4,438	10.0	$12,621
Married Couple Families								
2018	7.2	$6,757	29.4	$22,164	5.7	$5,259	14.8	$14,217
Cohabiting Couple Families								
2018	6.4	$7,080	30.3	$19,159	3.3	$5,394	17.0	$14,020
Single-Parent Families								
2018	5.8	$5,061	27.7	$16,727	4.0	$4,061	18.1	$11,743

Source: Authors' calculations based on Current Population Survey: IPUMS-CPS, University of Minnesota and Historical SPM data, Columbia University.

is also clearly seen in the data for 2010. While the trends are similar for both groups, the private income poor have higher recipiency rates than do the SPM poor, as the programs pull some private income poor families out of poverty.

Among the private income poor, non-Hispanic whites and (to a lesser extent) native-born Hispanics are more likely to receive benefits and have higher benefit levels than the other groups. Among the SPM poor, whites and foreign-born Hispanics are similar in recipiency and mean values received, while blacks and native-born Hispanics are more similar. During the Great Recession, recipiency rates nearly doubled for both poverty samples and for all racial and ethnic groups.

Table 3.6 also contains information on OASDI benefits. Nearly 10 percent of our SPM families have either a head or family member over age 65. The first panel for all SPM units combined shows a modest upward trend in both percent received and mean value of benefits. In addition, recipiency rates and mean benefits received are higher for the private income poor than SPM poor. Non-Hispanic whites have the highest recipiency rates among the private income poor, while non-Hispanic blacks have the highest rates among the SPM poor; foreign-born Hispanics are the least likely to receive benefits for both samples of the poor.

Table 3.6 also considers UI and OASDI recipiency and benefit levels on the basis of marital status. For both poverty groups, recipiency trends are similar across marital status groups: cohabiting and married couples receive benefits at similar rates that are higher than those of single-parent families. This is consistent with the fact that these families have more potential workers on average than do single-parent families. Furthermore, benefit levels are higher for married couples than for other groups; this is consistent with the data from chapter 2 which suggest that married couples have higher educational attainment on average and are more likely to be employed at higher wages.

Recipiency of OASDI benefits exhibits a slight upward trend for all marital status groups for both poverty samples. The private income poor receive more benefits and at higher rates than do the SPM poor, consistent with the fact that these families have a slightly higher percentage of elderly members. Recipiency rates and benefit levels are similar across the three marital status groups in both poverty samples.

Table 3.7 provides evidence of the antipoverty effects of Social Security cash transfers for our demographic groups of interest. Increased recipiency of these programs, particularly of unemployment compensation during economic downturns, clearly helps to reduce poverty for all groups, as is evident in the 2002 and 2010 post-recession years. Non-white families and non-married parents benefit most. Recall that non-Hispanic whites and married couples have lower poverty rates than other groups; though their antipoverty effects of social insurance programs are smaller, they are nonetheless important.

Table 3.7   After-Tax Private Income Poverty Less After-Tax Private Income and Social Insurance Income Poverty, Select Years 1995–2018

Year	All SPM Families	Non-Hispanic White Families	Non-Hispanic Black Families	Native-Born Hispanic Families	Foreign-Born Hispanic Families	Married-Couple Families	Cohabiting-Couple Families	Single-Parent Families
1995	3.6	3.4	4.2	4.2	4.3	3.1	4.4	5.5
1999	3.1	2.4	4.8	4.2	3.9	2.5	3.6	5.3
2002	4.0	3.5	5.5	4.3	4.9	3.2	4.3	7.0
2006	3.3	2.8	4.6	4.2	4.0	2.5	4.6	5.9
2010	5.0	4.4	6.6	6.4	5.2	4.0	6.4	7.8
2018	3.5	2.7	5.5	4.4	4.0	2.4	4.1	6.7

Source: Authors' calculations based on Current Population Survey: IPUMS-CPS, University of Minnesota and Historical SPM data, Columbia University.

UI, Workers Compensation, and OASDI are government cash-transfer programs that do not require a means test: they are entitlements to eligible participants regardless of income. The next section examines government cash transfers that do require a means test. In particular, we turn our attention to SSI and to TANF (and its precursor AFDC).

Government Cash Transfers: Means Tested

Supplemental Security Income

Authorized by the Title XVI of the Social Security Act of 1972, SSI is a means-tested, federally administered, income assistance program for needy aged, blind, and disabled persons. When implemented in 1974, it replaced several smaller state and federal programs. Child participation increased after a 1990 ruling (Sullivan vs. Zebley) which made it easier for children to enroll. Eligibility is based on nationwide eligibility criteria; needy aged over 65 and blind must satisfy income and asset tests (assets less than $2,000 for singles, $3,000 for couples) while disabled children and adults must show an inability to work or commensurate disability through a process similar to that of Social Security Disability Insurance. A non-citizen may be eligible for SSI benefits if he or she meets program criteria, and is a "qualified alien." (See https://www.disability-benefits-help.org/faq/non-citizen-social-security-disability-benefits for the eight categories of qualifying aliens.) Income support is uniform for the needy aged, blind, and disabled. In December 2017, there were 8.2 million recipients, of which 27 percent were over age 65, 58 percent were between ages 18 and 65, and 14 percent were children under 18. Fourteen percent of recipients were needy aged, 85 percent were disabled, and less than 1 percent were blind. In 2019, maximum monthly grant is $771 for an eligible individual, $1,157 for a couple. Net benefit reduction rates are close to 100 percent of earnings, and eligibility is phased out at less than 200 percent of the official federal poverty line. SSI is administered by the Social Security Administration, but unlike OASDI, benefits are funded by general revenues of the US Treasury. All but four states, Arizona, Mississippi, North Dakota, and West Virginia, supplement federal SSI benefits.

Bound, Burkhauser and Nichols (2003) find that most adult recipients were not working for three years prior to applying for SSI benefits. Federal data suggests more than two-thirds of adult recipients are poor. In recent years, children's participation in SSI has increased as families see SSI as a preferred alternative to TANF. States also have an incentive to shift eligible children from their welfare rolls to SSI, as SSI benefits are fully federal-funded and are not time-limited. Schmidt (2013) finds that SSI caseloads increased the most in states with the most punitive welfare system, and Dugan and Kearney (2007) find reduced poverty for families with a child recipient.

Aid to Families with Dependent Children/ Temporary Assistance for Needy Families

AFDC was established by the Social Security Act of 1935 to provide cash assistance to single mothers who were the primary support for their children due to the death, disability, or absence of their spouse. In 1961, benefits were added for families with unemployed fathers. Jointly administered by the states and federal government, AFDC was an entitlement with limited funding; states set their own benefit levels. On the eve of welfare reform, the median state benefit level was 36 percent of the federal poverty level (US House of Representatives, 1996).

Due to increasing concerns about dependency and negative incentive effects of cash benefits on work and non-marital births, AFDC was terminated by the welfare reform known as the PRWORA of 1996. Its replacement, TANF, removed the federal cash entitlement and substituted nominally fixed block grants to states, Indian Tribes, and territories. TANF also includes work requirements, with cash fines for noncompliance, and a five-year lifetime limit on benefit receipt. Administered by the Department of Health and Human Services at the federal level, states were given broad flexibility to provide a range of benefits, services, and activities that promote work among low-income families with children. In FY2017, cash benefits represented only 23 percent of state and federal spending in the program (Committee on Ways and Means, 2018).

Since welfare reform, TANF has declined as a social safety net for families with children. Caseloads are at a historic low, even falling during the Great Recession. On the eve of welfare reform, 68 out of every 100 families with children in poverty received benefits; by 2018 that number had fallen to 22. Furthermore, benefits have declined in inflation-adjusted terms since 1996: TANF benefits are below two-thirds of the federal poverty line in all 50 states and the District of Columbia and at or below 20 percent of the poverty line in 18 states. In the median state in 2020, a family of three received $486 per month; in 13 states such a family received less than $300 (Center on Budget and Policy Priorities, 2020).

While there is evidence that welfare reform increased the work effort of single mothers, there has not been a significant reduction in their poverty. Matsudaira and Blank (2014) find that income gains from greater employment were largely offset by the loss of welfare benefits. Similarly, Grogger and Karoly (2009) provide evidence that lifetime limits on benefits do not lead to an increase in income or a decrease in poverty. While a large literature examines the impact of welfare reform on short-term family health, employment, and income outcomes (Grogger and Karoly, 2006; Ziliak, 2016), there is relative less evidence on the long-run impact of cash transfers. Duncan and co-authors (2011) find some evidence that such transfers can improve student achievement.

Table 3.8 provides data on SSI and TANF recipiency rates and mean value of benefits received by racial/ethnic groups and by marital status respectively. Given the near 100 percent net benefit reduction rates in SSI it is not surprising that recipiency rates and mean values of all racial groups are higher for the private income poor than the SPM poor. Recipiency rates for all groups are relatively stable over time. For both poverty groups, non-Hispanic blacks are slightly more likely to receive SSI benefits while foreign-born Hispanics are the least likely, presumably due to potential citizenship and eligibility issues. The decline in TANF recipiency is clearly seen in all demographic groups; TANF recipiency does not appear to be cyclical, as participation declined for all groups during the Great Recession. Non-Hispanic black and native-born Hispanics are more likely to receive benefits than non-Hispanic whites. Foreign-born Hispanics are least likely to receive TANF benefits due to the tightening of immigrant eligibility standards.

Table 3.8 also presents data on SSI and TANF recipiency for families with different marital demographics. For both poverty groups, married couples are the least likely to receive SSI benefits while single parents are most likely, though benefit levels for married couples are, as expected slightly higher. The decline in TANF enrollment is clearly visible for both poverty groups and all types of families; married couples are less likely to receive AFDC/TANF benefits; their participation rates are half that of single or cohabiting couples. While table 3.8 provides evidence of a decline in TANF recipiency, there is no evidence of an associated rise in SSI recipiency reported in the literature. Given the decline in means-tested cash benefits, we now turn our attention in the next section to means-tested in-kind benefits.

Government In-Kind Benefits: Nutrition, Housing, and Energy Assistance

*Supplemental Nutrition Assistance Program
(SNAP, formally known as Food Stamps)*

First started as a pilot program in 1961 and made permanent in 1964, all states were mandated to adopt the Food Stamp program by 1974. Renamed Supplemental Nutrition Assistance Program (SNAP) in 2008, SNAP is, with very few exceptions, the only universal safety-net program available to individuals of any age or family type. Benefit levels and eligibility standards are determined by the federal government, and benefits are fully funded by the federal

Table 3.8 Recipiency Rates and Real Benefits Received: Means-Tested Cash Benefits by Race and Marital Status, SPM Families with Children, Select Years 1995–2018 (2012 dollars)

| | Private Income Poor | | | | | SPM Poor | | | |
| | Supplemental Security Income | | Public Assistance Income (AFDC/TANF) | | | Supplemental Security Income | | Public Assistance Income (AFDC/TANF) | |
Year	Percent Receiving	Mean Real Benefit of Recipients	Percent Receiving	Mean Real Benefit of Recipients	Year	Percent Receiving	Mean Real Benefit of Recipients	Percent Receiving	Mean Real Benefit of Recipients
All SPM Families Combined									
1995	14.6	$8,238	42.9	$6,689	1995	10.2	$7,412	37.5	$6,115
1999	13.6	$8,213	26.6	$5,161	1999	9.3	$7,191	22.7	$4,611
2002	14.1	$8,283	19.9	$4,731	2002	9.4	$7,319	17.22	$4,204
2006	14.2	$8,687	16.9	$4,335	2006	10.3	$7,382	14.7	$4,059
2010	12.9	$8,901	15.2	$4,162	2010	9.4	$8,255	13.3	$4,083
2018	12.5	$8,842	9.8	$3,871	2018	7.6	$7,328	7.2	$3,426
Non-Hispanic White Families									
2018	13.9	$9,168	9.1	$3,913	2018	8.0	$7,354	6.1	$3,097
Non-Hispanic Black Families									
2018	15.6	$8,654	13.5	$3,538	2018	11.1	$7,358	10.9	$3,382
Native-Born Hispanic Families									
2018	13.8	$8,922	11.3	$4,125	2018	7.5	$7,491	8.5	$3,691
Foreign-Born Hispanic Families									
2018	5.7	$8,016	5.9	$4,380	2018	3.7	$6,999	4.7	$3,898
Married Couple Families									
2018	9.5	$9,491	5.8	$4,094	2018	4.8	$7,751	3.7	$3,446
Cohabiting Couple Families									
2018	15.1	$8,868	8.5	$4,694	2018	7.6	$7,611	5.9	$3,835
Single-Parent Families									
2018	13.9	$8,525	13.0	$3,674	2018	9.8	$7,100	10.4	$3,352

Source: Authors' calculations based on Current Population Survey: IPUMS-CPS, University of Minnesota and Historical SPM data, Columbia University.

government, while administrative expenses are shared by the states. With some exemptions, eligibility is restricted to those with net monthly income less than 100 percent of the federal poverty line, (gross monthly income less than 130 percent) with some limits on assets. Many states eliminated the asset test during and after the Great Recession. In FY2019, for the contiguous 48 States and District of Columbia, maximum monthly income for a family of three is $1,732, net or $2,252 gross. SNAP benefits are tied to the cost of US Department of Agriculture's "thrifty food plan"; in FY2019, maximum monthly benefits for a family of three was $505. In 2021, in the first update in more than 45 years, the US Department of Agriculture updated the thrifty food plan to better reflect current food prices, the current American diet, dietary guidance, and nutrients in food items. This modernization increased the cost of the plan by 21 percent. As a result, the average SNAP benefit will increase by $36.24 per person, per month or $1.19 per day for fiscal year 2022 (USDA, 2021).

While the welfare reform of 1996 left food-stamp rules relatively unaffected (Bitler, Hoynes, and Kuka, 2017), take-up rates plummeted from nearly 75 percent of eligible households to just more than 50 percent of eligible households five years later (Leftin et al., 2011). However, SNAP participation increased sharply during and after the Great Recession. In 2007, in an average month, fewer than 70 percent of 37 million people eligible participated; by 2016, 85 percent of 47 million eligible people participated. Total annual benefit cost in FY2016 were $66.5 billion. Ganong and Liebman (2018) find that loosening the asset rule, lengthening re-certification periods, and simplified reporting increased program participation.

SNAP benefits are well targeted: in 2016, the neediest individuals participate at higher rates than do other eligible individuals. For example, individuals with household incomes less than the poverty line participated at twice the rate of eligible households with low income (between 100–130 percent of the poverty line). Eligible children participate at rates close to 100 percent, while only 45 percent of eligible individuals over age 60 participate. In 2016, 75 percent of SNAP recipient households had earned income (USDA, table 2 Trends in SNAP participation 2010–2016).

The antipoverty effects of SNAP are well known. For example, using a SPM measure of poverty, Wheaton and Tran (2018) find that SNAP benefits removed 8.4 million people from poverty in 2015 and was particularly important for children, reducing the number of children in poverty by 28 percent. In addition to these short-term effects, researchers have long-term benefits as well. In particular, Almond, Hoynes, and Schanzenbach (2011) and East (2020) find evidence that SNAP receipt improves health outcomes at birth and in early childhood, while Hoynes, Schanzenbach, and Almond (2016) find direct evidence that childhood receipt of SNAP improves adult health status and economic outcomes.

Other Food Programs

SNAP is not the only nutrition program benefiting poor and low-income families. WIC and the National School Lunch Program (NSLP) and School Breakfast Program (SBP) are important sources of nutrition for poor families. WIC was introduced as a pilot program in 1972 and made permanent in 1974. The Food and Nutrition Service of the US Department of Agriculture provides grants to all 50 states, District of Columbia, Indian Tribal Organizations and US Territories. Total expenditures in FY2016 were $6.5 billion; average monthly food costs per participant were $42.77. The program provides supplemental foods, nutrition education, breastfeeding promotion and support, and referrals to other health, welfare, and social services for women, infants, and children under age five. To qualify, participants from these groups must have gross income less than 185 percent of the federal poverty line, and individually must be determined to be nutritionally at risk; participants may be automatically eligible through participation in SNAP, Medicaid, or TANF. In April 2016, 8.8 million women, infants, and children were enrolled in WIC. Most were infants and children (76 percent), 9.1 percent were pregnant women, 7.8 percent breastfeeding women, and 6.5 percent were postpartum women. Over half of pregnant WIC recipients enrolled during their first trimester. The program encourages breastfeeding, and since 2012 the portion of women who breastfeed exceeds the portion of postpartum women who do not. Vouchers or electronic benefit cards are used to purchase authorized foods such as fortified infant and adult cereals, fruits and vegetables, baby food and formula, peanut butter, dried/canned beans, and canned fish. In addition, WIC encourages proper child immunization. In a mega analysis of more than three dozen studies between 1979 and 2004, Fox et al. (2004) found that WIC increased average birth weight and reduced the incidence of low and very low birth weight infants.

Other important nutrition programs for children are the NSLP and SBP. The NSLP was established in 1946 and SBP in 1971. The goal of these programs is to increase child nutrition for eligible children to increase student learning. The Food and Nutrition Service of US Department of Agriculture provides cash subsidies and USDA Foods to State agencies which administer the program to public and nonprofit private schools and residential childcare institutions. Over 95 percent of the nation's schools participate. In exchange for these resources, schools must serve meals that meet federal nutritional requirements to eligible children at free or reduced prices. Children may be categorically eligible for free meals if their families qualify for SNAP, or based on their status as a homeless, migrant, runaway, or foster child. Or children may qualify based on family income and size; children from families with income at or below 130 percent of the official poverty line qualify for free meals; those from families with income between 130 and 185 percent of the official poverty line are eligible for reduced price meals. In 2016, 30.4 million children received school lunches and 14.6 million children received school breakfasts. Costs in FY2016 were $13.6 billion for NSLP and $4.2 billion for SBP.

Housing Assistance

The federal government has provided housing assistance to poor and low-income families since passage of the Housing Act of 1937. Over time the US Department of Housing and Urban Development (HUD) has administered three major programs to serve this purpose: publicly owned housing developments, privately owned, publicly subsidized project-based housing, and tenant-based system of housing vouchers. With publicly owned housing projects, local housing authorities receive allocations of HUD funding to build, operate, or make improvements. Families receive assistance only if they agree to live in a public housing project. The number of such units peaked in the 1990s at 1.4 million units. Because these projects concentrate poor families into separate neighborhoods, this type of housing subsidy has become increasingly disfavored by policy makers, yet by 2013 there were still over 1 million units available.

The second type of housing subsidy is privately owned place-based subsidies. While there have been a number of different programs over time, the current program is based on the Low-Income Housing Tax Credit (LIHTC) which was introduced as part of the Tax Reform Act of 1986. The LIHTC program is administered by state allocating agencies which determine priorities and award credits to developers to build or rehabilitate low-income rental housing. Credits are awarded for ten-year increments. Projects are eligible for credits if at least 20 percent of their tenants have incomes below 50 percent of area median income (AMI) or 40 percent have income below 60 percent of AMI. In practice, nearly all tenants qualify, since the number of credits available increases as the number of qualifying tenants increase. In addition, credits can also be used to pay the difference between tenant rent and total rental costs. Like public housing, subsidies are place-based; tenants receive the subsidy only if they live in the subsidized project. As of 2012, the program had supported the construction of nearly 2.5 million housing units at an annual cost of nearly $7 billion.

The third major type of rental assistance is a tenant-based rather than a place-based system. Low-income renters receive a housing voucher which they can use in private housing market. Currently called the Housing Choice Voucher program enacted in 1998, this program replaced Section 8 certificate and voucher programs created earlier. Currently the most prevalent of housing subsidies, tenants generally pay 30 percent of their income toward rent, and the voucher covers the difference between this payment and the rent up to a specified amount, generally based on fair market rents in an area. In 2013, 2.2 million tenant-based vouchers were provided. In 2018, Congress approved $22 billion for housing vouchers (Bell and Rice, 2018).

Housing assistance is not an entitlement. Assistance is provided based on eligibility and available funds. In 2016, HUD assisted near 4.7 million households, whose annual incomes on average were between $12,000 and $14,000. Roughly 38 percent of households have children, a third have an elderly head (or spouse), and additional third are headed by a disabled person. Nearly one-third identify as non-Hispanic white. While the number of households receiving rent assistance has increased over time, and those that receive aid are among the most disadvantaged, Kingsley (2017) estimates that of the 25.7 million households eligible for support, one in five receive support, another one in five are on waiting lists, and the remaining eligible households are not even in the queue as more than half of the waiting lists are closed. For those lucky enough to make it on a list, the average wait is more than two years.

Low-Income Home Energy Assistance Program (LIHEAP)

The purpose of the LIHEAP is to help the lowest income households meet their heating and cooling home energy needs. In addition, a small percentage of funds may be used for weatherization to reduce a household's vulnerability to the elements. Initially created by the Omnibus Budget Reconciliation Act of 1981, the program provides block grants to the states, recognized tribal organizations, and US territories. The size of a state's block grant depends upon a state's weather, fuel prices, and low-income population. The target population is low-income households with either elderly, disabled, or young children and incomes less than 150 percent of federal poverty guidelines or 60 percent of state median income. In FY2017, an estimated 5.4 million households received assistance at a cost of nearly $3.6 billion (LIHEAP Fact Sheet, 2018).

Table 3.9 provides data on government nutrition and housing program recipiency rates and mean benefit values for recipients based on our key demographic characteristics. Considering all SPM families combined (first panel in both tables), the private income poor are slightly more likely to receive SNAP benefits than the SPM poor, though benefit levels for both groups are very similar. Both poverty groups saw increases in participation rates and significantly higher benefits during the Great Recession, confirming the important antipoverty role SNAP played in this recession. Approximately three-fourths of both private income and SPM poor families received either WIC or School Lunch/Breakfast benefits. Finally, private income poor are

Table 3.9 Recipiency Rates and Real Benefits Received: Means-Tested, In-Kind Benefits by Race and Marital Status, SPM Families with Children, Select Years 1995–2018 (2012 dollars)

Year	Private Income Poor						SPM Poor					
	Food Stamps (SNAP)		WIC and School Lunch		Housing and Energy Assistance		Food Stamps (SNAP)		WIC and School Lunch		Housing and Energy Assistance	
	Percent Receiving	Mean Real Benefit of Recipients	Percent Receiving	Mean Real Value of Recipients	Percent Receiving	Mean Real Value of Recipients	Percent Receiving	Mean Real Benefit of Recipients	Percent Receiving	Mean Real Value of Recipients	Percent Receiving	Mean Real Value of Recipients
All SPM Families Combined												
1995	53.1	$3,427	84.2	$847	29.9	$3,523	47.8	$3,371	81.1	$832	26.3	$3,802
1999	41.7	$3,031	79.7	$835	28.2	$4,019	36.0	$3,022	77.0	$816	23.9	$4,416
2002	38.6	$3,132	74.8	$774	26.2	$4,207	34.4	$3,125	72.6	$773	22.4	$4,690
2006	43.5	$3,499	76.9	$779	25.7	$4,650	38.9	$3,490	74.0	$762	21.6	$5,137
2010	52.3	$4,287	78.6	$935	25.6	$4,782	44.3	$4,146	74.2	$885	19.1	$4,794
2018	49.1	$3,422	78.5	$1,033	25.6	$5,767	39.6	$3,303	73.1	$967	17.9	$5,651
Non-Hispanic White Families												
2018	47.3	$3,461	72.2	$920	22.4	$4,038	37.7	$3,368	65.4	$849	16.4	$4,172
Non-Hispanic Black Families												
2018	63.5	$3,386	80.6	$1,058	39.7	$6,662	54.3	$3,276	75.5	$1,005	28.8	$6,833
Native-Born Hispanic Families												
2018	47.9	$3,629	80.5	$1,091	27.1	$6,715	38.3	$3,495	74.0	$1,004	17.3	$6,048
Foreign-Born Hispanic Families												
2018	36.0	$3,254	85.2	$1,134	13.8	$6,353	29.1	$3,099	81.3	$1,053	9.9	$5,525
Married Couple Families												
2018	34.4	$3,533	76.1	$1,079	14.0	$5,128	25.4	$3,321	69.3	$978	8.4	$4,508
Cohabiting Couple Families												
2018	51.1	$3,676	77.0	$1,063	23.3	$5,344	40.7	$3,352	70.6	$1,015	15.8	$5,074
Single-Parent Families												
2018	58.9	$3,324	80.5	$997	34.3	$6,016	50.7	$3,284	76.8	$946	26.1	$6,047

Source: Authors' calculations based on Current Population Survey: IPUMS-CPS, University of Minnesota and Historical SPM data, Columbia University.

more likely to receive housing and energy benefits than the SPM Poor, consistent with the literature suggesting that these programs are targeted to the most disadvantaged. Furthermore, while the likelihood of receiving these benefits has been falling since the mid-1990s, the value of benefits received has been trending upward.

These general trends appear to hold true within each racial/ethnic and marital status group. Table 3.9 suggests that for both poverty groups, poor non-Hispanic blacks and native-born Hispanic families are more likely to receive SNAP benefits and have slightly higher benefit levels than non-Hispanic whites and foreign-born Hispanics. Both private income and SPM poor non-Hispanic white families are less likely to receive other nutritional benefits and have lower benefit levels than all other families. Finally, non-Hispanic blacks are significantly more likely to receive housing benefits, while foreign-born Hispanics are the least likely to receive these benefits. Benefit levels are similar for both native- and foreign-born Hispanics, reflecting the fact that both groups are likely to live in the same or similar neighborhoods. Benefits received by poor non-Hispanic white families are substantially lower.

For both poverty groups, married couples participate in SNAP at significantly lower rates than do cohabitating or single-parent families though their benefit levels are similar. Children's participation in WIC and school lunch and breakfast programs, on the other hand, does not vary by marital status of the adults. Finally, single-parent families participate in housing programs at higher rates and receive more benefits than do married or cohabiting families, suggesting that benefits do in fact reach the most disadvantaged.

Table 3.10 summarizes the impact of government means-tested cash and in-kind transfers on the poverty rates of our demographic groups of interest. Increased recipiency of these programs, especially during the Great Recession, clearly helped to reduce poverty for all groups. Families of color and non-married parents benefited most. Since non-Hispanic whites and married couples have lower poverty rates than other groups, their antipoverty effects of government transfers are smaller, but nonetheless important.

Work and Childcare Expenses and Out-of-Pocket Medical Expenses

In the final step of our analysis, we summarize the impact on poverty rates of work and childcare expenses and out-of-pocket medical expenses. Work and childcare expenses were discussed in more detail in chapter 2. The SPM records the value of out-of-pocket medical expenses (MOOP), as reported by survey respondents and then this amount is adjusted to reflect the cost of Medicare Part B premium for any Medicare recipients. Medical expenditures are calculated at the level of the family. These expenses are essential for work

Table 3.10 After-Tax Private Income and Social Insurance Income Poverty Less After-Tax and Transfer Private income Poverty, Select Years 1995–2018

Year	All SPM Families	Non-Hispanic White Families	Non-Hispanic Black Families	Native-Born Hispanic Families	Foreign-Born Hispanic Families	Married-Couple Families	Cohabiting-Couple Families	Non-Partnered Single Parents
1995	5.1	3.2	11.1	8.6	7.6	2.9	9.9	12.0
1999	3.6	2.1	8.3	6.1	5.4	1.8	6.3	9.9
2002	3.4	2.0	7.8	5.5	4.8	1.9	5.9	8.7
2006	3.4	2.0	8.5	5.0	4.1	1.6	5.2	9.4
2010	4.7	2.6	10.7	7.1	6.5	2.5	6.4	11.4
2018	2.6	1.3	6.0	3.3	4.2	1.3	3.3	6.7

Source: Authors' calculations based on Current Population Survey: IPUMS-CPS, University of Minnesota and Historical SPM data, Columbia University.

and family well-being, but are resources which cannot be used to cover other family expenses and are subtracted to obtain SPM poverty rates. Table 3.11 summarizes these expenses for our racial/ethnic groups and marital status groups respectively.

As one would expect, nearly all families have work and/or medical expenses; a comparison of SPM and private income poor suggests that there is little difference in the percentage of families who incur these expenses regardless of race, ethnicity, or marital status. Non-Hispanic black families and single-parent families are slightly less likely to report these expenses. SPM Poor have higher expenses than do the private income poor. This reflects the relatively small number of families who were not private income poor, but whose medical expenses push them below the SPM poverty threshold. For example, in 2016, 17 percent of the SPM Poor were not private

Table 3.11 Family Work and Childcare Expenses and Medical Out-of-Pocket and Medicare Part B Subsidy, SPM Families with Children by Race and Marital Status, Select Years 1995–2018 (2012 Dollars)

	PRIVATE Income Poor		SPM Poor	
Year	Percent Incurring	Mean Real Value of Expense	Percent Incurring	Mean Real Value of Expense
All SPM Families Combined				
1995	93.2	$3,381	93.5	$4,127
1999	94.7	$3,525	95.1	$4,225
2002	94.6	$3,701	94.9	$4,428
2006	93.7	$3,827	93.7	$4,612
2010	93.8	$3,240	92.5	$5,094
2018	95.5	$3,170	94.9	$5,795
Non-Hispanic White Families				
2018	96.1	$3,376	95.5	$7,796
Non-Hispanic Blaci Families				
2018	93.3	$2,775	91.5	$4,346
Native-Born Hispanic Families				
2018	95.2	$3,107	95.0	$4,951
Foreign-Born Hispanic Families				
2018	97.3	$3,307	97.1	$4,693
Married Couple Families				
2018	97.6	$3,925	97.2	$8,482
Cohabiting Couple Families				
2018	97.6	$3,925	97.2	$8,482
Single-Parent Families				
2018	93.6	$2,627	92.2	$3,819

Source: Authors' calculations based on Current Population Survey: IPUMS-CPS, University of Minnesota and Historical SPM data, Columbia University.

Table 3.12 After-Tax and Transfer Private income Poverty Less SPM Poverty, Select Years 1995–2018

Year	All SPM Families	Non-Hispanic White Families	Non-Hispanic Black Families	Native-Born Hispanic Families	Foreign-Born Hispanic Families	Married-Couple Families	Cohabiting-Couple Families	Single-Parent Families
1995	-5.2	-4.0	-7.4	-7.5	-9.9	-4.1	-6.0	-9.2
1999	-4.8	-3.2	-7.7	-6.2	-10.0	-3.5	-5.8	-9.3
2002	-4.7	-3.0	-7.6	-6.4	-9.3	-3.5	-6.3	-8.8
2006	-4.4	-2.8	-6.8	-6.1	-9.3	-3.2	-6.1	-8.4
2010	-4.3	-3.3	-5.6	-5.0	-7.4	-3.5	-5.8	-6.7
2016	-4.9	-3.5	-6.4	-5.8	-8.5	-4.1	-6.4	-7.1
2018	-4.1	-2.6	-6.1	-4.9	-8.2	-3.2	-5.1	-6.5

Source: Authors' calculations based on Current Population Survey: IPUMS-CPS, University of Minnesota and Historical SPM data, Columbia University.

income poor, but the median medical expenses of these families were nearly $9,000 and the mean over $15,000.

Table 3.12 summarizes the impact of work and medical expenses on the difference between After Tax and Transfer Poverty and SPM poverty. Recall that a negative number suggests that work and medical expenses contribute to a family's poverty since the number of families who are SPM poor exceeds the number who are below the After Tax and Transfer poverty threshold. Taken as a group, work and medical expenses increase the SPM poverty rate by 5 percentage points. The impact of these expenses on non-Hispanic white families and married couple families is substantially lesser than for other families and families with cohabiting and single parents. Foreign-born Hispanics are particularly hard hit; this is not surprising since they are less likely to have health insurance than other families and have higher work effort. For others, this may reflect the fact that these families are larger on average or that these families may have incomes clustered more closely to the poverty thresholds so that work and medical expenses are more likely to push them below their SPM poverty threshold.

Tables 3.13 and 3.14 summarize our analysis by unpacking private income and SPM poverty differences into their component parts. The first column in each table shows this difference for our demographic group of interest. The remaining four columns break this differential down by the respective poverty rates discussed in this chapter. For example, consider table 3.13 for all SPM families, Private income Poverty less SPM Anchored Poverty in 1995 was 2.6 percent. This difference is the sum of remaining poverty rate differentials in that row: $2.6 = -0.9 + 3.6 + 5.1 - 5.2$. These tables allow us to better understand the relative impact of different antipoverty policies on the poverty rates of different demographic groups.

Table 3.13 provides poverty rate differentials for our racial and ethnic groups. The difference between Private Income Poverty and SPM poverty (column one) is greatest for non-white families, especially non-Hispanic black families. Column two suggest that the tax code increased the poverty rate for all families in 1995, but after 2000 reduced family poverty, particularly in the aftermath of the Great Recession. Non-white families especially benefited. The social insurance programs, OASDI, and unemployment and workers compensation reduce poverty rates by 3 to 4 percentage points overall, slightly more for families of color. Government transfer programs, both cash and in-kind, have a large impact on poverty rates for all groups, but given their higher recipiency rates these programs are especially important for black and Hispanic families. Finally, accounting for work and medical expenses significantly increase the poverty of all groups, especially non-Hispanic black families whose incomes likely are clustered around the poverty thresholds, and foreign-born Hispanic families who are less likely to have health insurance.

Table 3.13 Poverty Rate Differentials Summary by Race, SPM Families with Children, Select Years 1995–2018

Year	Private income Poverty less SPM Anchored Poverty	Private income Poverty Less After-Tax Private Income Poverty	After-Tax Private Income Poverty Less After-Tax and Social Insurance Income Poverty	After-Tax Private Income and Social Insurance Income Poverty Less After-Tax and Transfer Private income Poverty	After-Tax and Transfer Private income Poverty less SPM Anchored Poverty
All SPM Families					
1995	2.6	-0.9	3.6	5.1	-5.2
1999	2.0	0.1	3.1	3.6	-4.8
2002	3.0	0.3	4.0	3.4	-4.7
2006	3.5	1.2	3.3	3.4	-4.4
2010	8.4	3.0	5.0	4.7	-4.3
2018	4.4	2.4	3.5	2.6	-4.1
Non-Hispanic White SPM Families					
1995	1.6	-0.9	3.4	3.2	-4.0
1999	1.4	0.1	2.4	2.1	-3.2
2002	2.5	0.0	3.5	2.0	-3.0
2006	2.7	0.7	2.8	2.0	-2.8
2010	5.5	1.9	4.4	2.6	-3.3
2018	2.8	1.3	2.7	1.3	-2.6
Non-Hispanic Black SPM Families					
1995	7.6	-0.3	4.2	11.1	-7.4
1999	6.3	0.9	4.8	8.3	-7.7
2002	6.8	1.0	5.5	7.8	-7.6
2006	8.3	2.0	4.6	8.5	-6.8
2010	15.6	3.9	6.6	10.7	-5.6
2018	9.8	4.2	5.5	6.0	-6.1

(continued)

Table 3.13 (Continued)

Year	Private income Poverty less SPM Anchored Poverty	Private income Poverty Less After-Tax Private Income Poverty	After-Tax Private Income Poverty Less After-Tax Private Income and Social Insurance Income Poverty	After-Tax Private Income and Social Insurance Income Poverty Less After-Tax and Transfer Private income Poverty	After-Tax and Transfer Private income Poverty less SPM Anchored Poverty
Native-Born Hispanic SPM Families					
1995	5.1	−0.3	4.2	8.6	−7.5
1999	4.1	0.0	4.2	6.1	−6.2
2002	3.6	0.2	4.3	5.5	−6.4
2006	4.6	1.5	4.2	5.0	−6.1
2010	11.8	3.3	6.4	7.1	−5.0
2018	5.2	2.4	4.4	3.3	−4.9
Foreign-Born Hispanic SPM Families					
1995	−0.1	−2.2	4.3	7.6	−9.9
1999	−1.6	−0.9	3.9	5.4	−10.0
2002	1.1	0.7	4.9	4.8	−9.3
2006	1.7	2.9	4.0	4.1	−9.3
2010	11.3	7.0	5.2	6.5	−7.4
2018	5.3	5.3	4.0	4.2	−8.2

Source: Authors' calculations based on Current Population Survey: IPUMS-CPS, University of Minnesota and Historical SPM data, Columbia University.

Table 3.14   Poverty Rate Differentials Summary by Marital Status, SPM Families with Children, Select Years 1995–2018

Year	Private income Poverty less SPM Anchored Poverty	Private income Poverty Less After-Tax Private Income Poverty	After-Tax Private Income Poverty Less After-Tax Private Income & Social Insurance Income Poverty	After-Tax Private Income & Social Insurance Income Poverty Less After-Tax and Transfer Private income Poverty	After-Tax and Transfer Private income Poverty less SPM Anchored Poverty
			All SPM Families		
1995	2.6	−0.9	3.6	5.1	−5.2
1999	2.0	0.1	3.1	3.6	−4.8
2002	3.0	0.3	4.0	3.4	−4.7
2006	3.5	1.2	3.3	3.4	−4.4
2010	8.4	3.0	5.0	4.7	−4.3
2018	4.4	2.4	3.5	2.6	−4.1
			Married Couple SPM Families		
1995	0.6	−1.3	3.1	2.9	−4.1
1999	0.4	−0.3	2.5	1.8	−3.5
2002	1.5	−0.1	3.2	1.9	−3.5
2006	1.8	0.9	2.5	1.6	−3.2
2010	5.6	2.6	4.0	2.5	−3.5
2018	2.4	1.9	2.4	1.3	−3.2
			Cohabiting Couple SPM Families		
1995	7.0	−1.3	4.4	9.9	−6.0
1999	2.6	−1.5	3.6	6.3	−5.8
2002	3.6	−0.4	4.3	5.9	−6.3
2006	3.0	−0.7	4.6	5.2	−6.1
2010	9.3	2.2	6.4	6.4	−5.8
2018	3.0	0.8	4.1	3.3	−5.1
			Single-Parent SPM Families		
1995	8.8	0.5	5.5	12.0	−9.2
1999	7.8	2.0	5.3	9.9	−9.3
2002	8.6	1.8	7.0	8.7	−8.8
2006	10.0	3.0	5.9	9.4	−8.4
2010	17.2	4.7	7.8	11.4	−6.7
2018	12.0	5.0	6.7	6.7	-6.5

Source: Authors' calculations based on Current Population Survey: IPUMS-CPS, University of Minnesota and Historical SPM data, Columbia University.

Table 3.14 conducts the same analysis by marital status. There are significant differences between Private Income Poverty and SPM poverty by marital status: married couple poverty differentials are generally small, cohabiting couples larger, and single parents larger still. The remaining poverty rate differentials help explain these differences. The tax code increases poverty or has very small positive effects on a couples' poverty rate before 2010 but has a larger impact after the Great Recession. The tax code has strong antipoverty effects for single-parent families throughout the period. Cohabiting and single-parent families benefit more from social insurance programs than do married couples, though social insurance programs have a greater antipoverty impact on the poverty rates of married couples than either taxes or government transfers. Means-tested transfers are the most important factor in reducing the poverty of families with cohabiting or single parents. Finally, MOOP and work expenses increase poverty rates for all families, but more so for cohabiting and single parents, whose family incomes are likely to be more closely clustered around the poverty thresholds.

CONCLUSION

This chapter has described the variety of antipoverty programs available to poor families. Over time, spending patterns for poor families with children have changed from income support to support for poor workers and from cash to in-kind benefits. Despite the increased work effort by these families and increased spending by the government, SPM poverty is still stubbornly high. Chapter 4 investigates what it will take to reduce poverty further.

Chapter 4

Wage Policies, Work Policies, and Other Policies—Which Policies Work?

The previous chapters have provided us with a comprehensive view of the last two decades of poverty among families with children. This chapter turns from analyzing how the past became the present to exploring policy combinations that can reduce poverty permanently. The goal is to answer a specific set of questions: What are the potential results of reducing the wage gap and/or work gap for poor families with unemployed adults? How much can these results be improved with programs like the EITC that complement work? How much can poverty be reduced by government programs that would relieve poor families of childcare or medical expenses? What might be the outcome of increasing benefits that support the unemployed or support children directly? By answering these questions, we expect to answer the questions that motivate this book: What are the options that might cut poverty in these families in half (or more)? How does the effectiveness of these options vary by family demographic characteristics? What are the possibilities and limitations of policies that focus primarily on the labor market? And what additional policies are best suited to reducing poverty in families for which labor-market policies are impractical?

Table 4.1 summarizes demographic characteristics of our poor SPM families. The panels involving marital status and educational attainment are particularly useful in understanding differences among race groups. Table 4.1 indicates that poor families with non-Hispanic black or native-born Hispanic heads are much more likely than average to have a single-parent family head, the family group most likely to be poor. Poor foreign-born Hispanics, on the other hand, are likely to be headed by a married-couple family, but Hispanics are held back by having relatively low educational

Table 4.1 Snapshot of Demographics and Median Poverty Gaps by Race and Marital Status of Poor SPM Families with Children Under 18, 2018

	All	Non-Hispanic White	Non-Hispanic Black	Native-Born Hispanic	Foreign-Born Hispanic	Married Couple	Cohabiting Couple	Single Parent
Family Size (Mean)								
Number of Adults	1.9	1.8	1.7	2.0	2.2	2.3	2.1	1.5
Number of Children	2.1	1.9	2.0	2.1	2.2	2.1	2.1	1.9
Identity of Other Adults (Percent)								
Adult Child	28.3	24.8	28.2	27.1	34.8	28.4	20.3	31.4
Parent of head	8.8	6.0	8.8	16.7	9.1	4.2	5.9	13.1
Other	13.1	10.7	12.9	15.4	15.9	8.9	11.1	18.3
Percent with any of the above	40.4	34.4	40.9	45.1	47.2	34.9	30.4	48.1
Percent with at Least One Adult Non-Citizen	33.2	14.3	16.2	20.4	85.4	46.3	33.8	21.0
Race								
All						39.6	10.8	49.6
Non-Hispanic White						43.7	11.3	45.0
Non-Hispanic Black						18.2	8.0	73.9
Native-Born Hispanic						35.0	11.3	53.8
Foreign-Born Hispanic						56.5	12.7	30.8
Marital Status (Percent)								
Marital Couple	40.7	44.9	19.6	34.1	58.2			
Cohabiting Couple	11.1	10.7	10.5	12.8	11.6			
Single Parent	48.2	44.4	69.9	53.1	30.2			

Education of Head and Spouse* (Percent)								
Less than High School	31.1	15.9	19.6	29.4	58.2	32.8	36.8	24.6
High-School Graduate	33.8	34.8	39.5	37.9	27.2	32.0	39.6	37.4
Some College	22.9	28.9	30.4	25.6	9.5	18.7	18.6	29.4
College Graduate	12.3	20.4	10.5	7.1	5.1	16.5	5.0	8.5
Baseline Poverty Rate (SPM Threshold Less Private Income)	**11.8**	**7.1**	**19.3**	**14.8**	**24.5**	**7.8**	**17.8**	**23.4**
Poverty Gaps								
Median Private Income Poverty Gap	$13,741	$13,300	$17,040	$15,506	$11,482	$11,119	$10,335	$16,420
Median SPM Poverty Gap	$7,273	$7,578	$6,603	$7,076	$7,470	$7,698	$7,257	$6,916
Median SPM Poverty Gap per Child	$3,886	$4,352	$3,702	$3,739	$3,479	$3,689	$3,943	$4,075

*Spouses include the partners of cohabiting heads.
Source: Authors' calculations based on Current Population Survey: IPUMS-CPS, University of Minnesota and Historical SPM data, Columbia University.

attainment, while foreign-born Hispanics face the challenge of low citizenship rates.

POVERTY GAPS

To understand what is required to reduce poverty among families with children in a substantial way, it is useful to begin by calculating "poverty gaps," the amount of money that would be required to lift a poor family above its SPM poverty threshold. The bottom panel of table 4.1 shows the median gap calculated in three different ways: (1) the gap between the SPM poverty threshold and the median value of private income; (2) the gap between the SPM poverty threshold and the median value of the SPM income definition that determines whether the family is or is not "SPM poor," as explained in chapter 3; and (3) the same gap restated on a per-child-basis. All three of these calculations are helpful in understanding how much money a "typical" poor family must receive to lift it above the poverty threshold. The first set of gaps displayed in table 4.1 shows that the median gap of private income is $13,741. The size of the gaps in private income are most easily understood by thinking of them in relation to annual earnings. For example, a full-year full-time job (40 hours per week for 52 weeks) at the federal minimum wage ($7.25) would provide annual earnings of $15,080. It would appear that for a family that lacks a full-time worker, the opportunity to find a full-time job could often be a ticket out of poverty, particularly if the job involves a wage above the federal minimum wage.

Table 4.2 summarizes key results from chapters 2 and 3 that help to explain why different groups have poverty gaps that vary across groups, especially racial groups, from less than $12,000 for foreign-born Hispanic families to over $17,000 for non-Hispanic black families. To understand why the gap is so much smaller for the foreign-born Hispanic group, table 4.2 shows that about 60 percent of poor foreign-born Hispanic families have at least one full-time worker and less than 15 percent have no worker at all, while for the other race groups only 30–45 percent of the poor families have a full-time worker and over 25 percent have no worker at all. Table 4.2 also makes a similar point about why single parent families have a relatively large poverty gap: less than 30 percent of them have a full-time worker, and 41 percent have no worker at all, compared to the married or cohabiting families that have over 50 percent with at least one full-time worker and approximately 16 percent with no worker at all.

Table 4.2 A Snapshot of Work, Government Benefits, and Work Expenses by Race and Marital Status, Poor SPM Families with Children, 2018

	All	Non-Hispanic White	Non-Hispanic Black	Native-Born Hispanic	Foreign-Born Hispanic	Married Couple	Cohabiting Couple	Single Parent
Work Effort by Gender (Percent)								
Men								
Works Year-Round, Full time	38.2	34.7	24.1	27.9	55.0	33.3	44.7	30.6
Works Less Than Year Round, Full time	19.5	18.8	16.5	21.0	20.7	18.9	24.4	23.4
Does Not Work	42.3	46.5	59.4	51.1	24.3	42.8	30.9	46.0
Women								
Works Year-Round, Full time	15.6	13.3	17.7	14.8	17.1	13.5	12.8	22.2
Works Less Than Year Round, Full time	23.6	23.0	24.2	25.7	24.2	22.5	30.0	25.8
Does Not Work	60.8	63.7	58.1	59.5	60.3	64.0	57.2	52.0
*Composition, Family Work Effort (Percent)**								
Families with two or more year-round, full-time workers	5.3	4.3	2.6	5.8	9.0	9.1	6.8	1.9
Families with exactly one year-round, full-time worker	38.2	33.3	28.6	40.6	53.0	49.0	50.0	26.9
Families with only part-year and/or part-time workers	27.3	27.5	29.6	25.9	25.3	23.6	26.7	30.3
Families with no workers	29.3	34.9	39.2	27.8	12.6	18.3	16.5	40.9
*Composition of Families with No Workers (Percent)***								
At least one adult seeking work	13.9	10.2	17.3	18.1	13.5	15.7	19.4	13.7
At least one adult family worker or student	53.8	51.6	51.2	55.3	68.2	60.8	57.8	54.8
All adults retired or disabled	32.3	38.1	31.5	26.6	18.3	23.5	22.8	31.5

(continued)

Table 4.2 (Continued)

	All	Non-Hispanic White	Non-Hispanic Black	Native-Born Hispanic	Foreign-Born Hispanic	Married Couple	Cohabiting Couple	Single Parent
Real Median Hourly Earnings (2012 dollars)								
Men	$9.71	$10.27	$9.18	$8.85	$9.84	$9.93	$9.18	$9.41
Women	$8.60	$8.60	$8.72	$8.82	$8.46	$8.46	$7.94	$8.24
Private Income								
Percent Receiving	80.9	80.5	71.4	81.2	90.5	88.3	85.0	73.9
Mean Real Private Income of Recipients (2012 dollars)	$17,035	$16,505	$13,304	$17,648	$20,333	$21,947	$18,232	$12,012
Earned Income Tax Credit (EITC)								
Percent Receiving	62.1	57.3	54.8	59.9	78.2	73.2	59.0	53.3
Mean Real Benefit of Recipients (2012 dollars)	$3,134	$2,907	$2,649	$3,142	$3,735	$3,582	$2,442	$2,791
Percentage Point Change in Poverty due to Tax Credits*	-2.2	-1.3	-3.2	-2.8	-4.9	-1.9	-0.6	-4.1
Food Stamps (SNAP)								
Percent Receiving	44.2	40.2	55.7	46.3	38.2	29.4	50.1	55.3
Mean Real Benefit of Recipients (2012 dollars)	$3,546	$3,572	$3,608	$3,787	$3,254	$3,502	$3,690	$3,536
Percentage Point Change in Poverty due to In-kind Transfers**	-4.0	-2.2	-8.5	-5.7	-6.0	-2.1	-5.6	-9.8
Family Work and Childcare Expense & MOOP (2012 dollars)								
Percent Incurring	95.4	97.1	92.3	93.9	96.7	97.9	97.3	92.9
Mean Real Value of Expense (2012 dollars)	$6,569	$8,736	$5,068	$5,329	$5,093	$9,818	$4,839	$4,093
Percentage Point Increase in Poverty due to Family Work Expenses & MOOP	4.9	3.5	6.4	5.8	8.5	4.1	6.4	7.1

*May also include additional part-time workers.

**Includes adults who indicate inability to find work as reason for not working.

***Due to data limitations, this includes both the EITC and CTCs.

****Includes SNAP, WIC & School Lunch & Housing programs.

Source: Authors' calculations based on Current Population Survey: IPUMS-CPS, University of Minnesota and Historical SPM data, Columbia University.

Families that have no worker or do not earn enough to escape poverty often rely on government benefits. These benefits are necessary for any serious program to reduce child poverty because, as table 4.2 shows, only about 14 percent of the families with no worker contain a person seeking full-time employment, while about 30 percent lack candidates for any job at all because the adult members of the family are either disabled or retired.

As we saw in chapter 3, private income poor families frequently receive various tax credits and government benefits, often adding up to several thousand dollars, that ought to be included in their income before calculating the poverty gap, while expenses for work and medical care should be subtracted. The lower panel of table 4.2 shows recipiency rates and average dollar amounts for the most important tax credit (the EITC) and the most important means-tested transfer program (SNAP) and also the extent to which tax credits and in-kind transfers reduce poverty. However, it also shows that the average private income poor family faces over $6,000 of expenses for work and child-care expenses and for out-of-pocket medical costs. Returning to the poverty gaps in table 4.1, we find that the median SPM poverty gap of $7,273 is much smaller than the private income gap and has less variation across groups.

The final row of table 4.1 recalculates the SPM Income Poverty Gaps on a per-child basis. The principal purpose of this calculation is to provide an approximate magnitude of the gap that might be covered by a benefit that directly supports children, such as a refundable CTC or some form of Child Allowance (CA). Because this is a median value, it would seem that it predicts that distributing $3,886 per child would cut the poverty rate in half, though that is not exactly correct because the CA would affect other components of the poverty calculation, partly because it might alter work incentives and partly because it would lead to a reduction in other means-tested benefits. It is nevertheless a useful baseline in thinking about approximately how generous a child benefit would have to be in order to have a major anti-poverty impact.

POLICY SIMULATIONS

The remainder of this chapter investigates the potential for reducing poverty through several different mechanisms and does so through a set of "policy simulations." Each of these simulations represents a different approach to addressing poverty with an initial focus on work opportunities for the unemployed and higher wages for the employed, then complemented by other options that either increase family income or reduce family expenses. These policy simulations estimate the effects of five different changes to the current situation: (1) providing work opportunities for potential workers who are not currently employed full time; (2) increasing the federal minimum wage; (3)

enhancing the generosity of the EITC for low-income workers; (4) alleviating the financial burden of childcare and MOOP; and (5) implementing a CA that distributes a per-child sum of money. While each change would have an independent impact on poverty, they could also be interactive. For example, more work at higher wages would impact both the amount a family would receive from EITC and the childcare expenses it would expect to incur. One of the principal purposes of the policy simulations is to compare the effects of options taken in isolation with options taken together.

Each simulation involves a specific change in the economic situation of the poor families in 2018. The first simulation assigns a full-time job offer at each state's minimum wage to every family member who is unemployed, and the results are calculated with different assumptions about how likely the potential workers are to accept the offer. In one case, it is assumed that the offer is universally accepted by all of the poor unemployed and in another case the offer is rejected by half of the potential workers selected at random. An additional pair of simulations adds half-time job offers for adult students and for homemakers who do not have a preschool child, again with take-up rates of 100 percent or 50 percent. The earnings from accepting these jobs will inevitably depend on the wages the jobs offer. The simulations are repeated with a federal minimum wage of $10, $12, or $15 per hour replacing the state minimum wages, including the case in which no one accepts the job offer, but all current workers with wage rates below the new minimum receive the wage increase.

The initial result of these work and wage simulations is higher earnings. In turn, the higher earnings generate changes in taxes (Social Security taxes and state taxes) and also tax credits (the EITC and in some cases the Child Care Tax Credit), so the simulation calculates a revised level of income after taxes for every family with higher earnings. If those families are recipients of means-tested transfers (TANF, SSI, SNAP or housing subsidies), the benefit amounts are adjusted appropriately. And since taking a job potentially affects work expenses, childcare expenses and out-of-pocket medical costs, those values are adjusted to be typical of current workers with similar earnings and demographics. The result is that the change in earnings becomes the basis for an adjusted level of SPM Resources to be compared to each family's SPM poverty threshold.

In addition to the simulations based on reducing the work and wage gaps, four additional sets of simulations are undertaken: (1) increasing the generosity of the EITC; (2) eliminating childcare costs (whether through a more generous tax credit or universal preschool); (3) introducing a universal CA or refundable CTC; and (4) eliminating MOOP for low-income families. Since each of these policy changes can be combined with policies designed to increase earnings, there are also a set of simulations that combine these four simulations with specific changes in work (50 percent uptake of full-time job offers for the U6 unemployed), the minimum wage ($12 per hour), or both.

The results of the simulations should be viewed as estimating the potential of various treatments, not as predicting their most likely outcomes. The incentives of any policy change may cause some families to alter their work effort. Broadly speaking, there are two different incentives involved. One of these arises because, as discussed in chapter 3, some benefits are reduced when a family increases its earnings. In particular, means-tested programs such as SSI, TANF, SNAP, and housing vouchers are designed so that benefits are phased out as family income rises. The other incentive factor is that higher family income generates alternatives with a variety of potential consequences. For example, a reduction of childcare expenses could induce a single parent to seek a full-time job, further increasing the family's resources. On the other hand, a well-paid full-time job for an unemployed family member in a family with more than one adult might induce some other adult family member to "spend" some of the increased income by reducing work hours. In fact, however, work disincentives are often offset by the EITC and other tax credits, and the bulk of the evidence shows that "workers in poverty typically have a greater incentive to work more hours or at higher wages than other workers do" (Shapiro et al., 2016). Because of these ambiguities, changes in work incentives are not directly incorporated into the simulations in this chapter, though they are discussed when they arise.

Addressing the Work Gap

This book focuses attention on the opportunities and limitations of family work as a solution to family poverty. For that reason, our initial simulations estimate the reduction in family poverty that would arise from reducing the "work gap" by employing unemployed adults in poor families. Chapter 2 identified three components of the work gap: persons who are actively seeking work, but unable to find it ("unemployed" by the usual definition); persons who have given up actively seeking work because they can't find work opportunities (usually known as "discouraged workers"); and persons who are working part-time because they have been unable to find full-time work ("involuntarily part time"). The Bureau of Labor Statistics uses the combination of these three to calculate an unemployment rate known as "U6," so they will be described here as "U6 unemployed."

In 2018, over 25 percent of all poor SPM families contained at least one person who was U6 unemployed. For this reason, the initial policy simulation is this: Every person who is unemployed by the U6 measure of unemployment is offered a full-time job that pays the minimum wage in the worker's state of residence. The assumption is that everyone is offered a job at a skill and experience level suitable for that person or a paid training period that develops the necessary skills.

Even if job qualifications are suitable, however, some persons might reject a minimum wage job. Chapter 2 suggested that jobs are often declined because the potential worker expects a job offer that exceeds a "reservation wage," frequently based on the past experience of the worker. Another possible reason for declining a job offer is a lack of job flexibility that is consistent with the potential worker's family responsibilities. The policy simulation therefore employs two different take-up rates. In one case every poor U6 unemployed adult accepts the job offer. One can think of the 100 percent take-up results as the maximum potential impact on poverty. In the other case, only half of them accept, which is perhaps more realistic.

The results of increasing work effort with jobs for the unemployed are shown in the upper panel of table 4.3. In the case where everyone accepts the job offer, the SPM poverty rate is reduced by 4.3 percentage points; when only half of the persons accept, the poverty rate is still reduced by 3.1 percentage points.

The poverty impacts differ substantially across race and family status groups. As chapter 2 showed, black and Hispanic workers have substantially higher unemployment rates than non-Hispanic whites. With 100 percent take-up non-Hispanic black families and foreign-born Hispanic families have their poverty rates reduced by approximately 10 percentage points, much more than non-Hispanic white families. Likewise, families with a single parent as family head benefit more than cohabiting families, and the married-couple families benefit least. The poverty reduction is smaller in every group when there is only 50 percent take-up, typically by 1 to 2 percentage points, but the pattern across race and family groups is the same regardless of the take-up.

The third and fourth lines in the in the bottom panel of table 4.3 push the work-gap policy simulation a step further by providing half-time work opportunities to homemakers and adult students who are neither working nor actively looking for work. In principle such work opportunities have considerable potential, since 40 percent of nonworking men and 65 percent of nonworking women fall in one of these two categories. The results show that the additional anti-poverty effect (above and beyond full-time work for the U6 unemployed) is typically from 1–3 percentage points (depending on take-up), except that the impact on poverty among foreign-born Hispanics is particularly large when take-up rates are high.

Making Work Pay by Increasing the Minimum Wage

Chapter 2 documented the fact that the real wages of low-wage workers (at the 10th percentile) have scarcely grown in the last four decades, and we thoroughly discussed the "working poor" phenomenon that is caused by

Table 4.3 Effect of Increasing Minimum Wage on SPM Poverty Rates by Race and Marital Status, for Persons in SPM Families with Children, 2018

	All	Non-Hispanic White	Non-Hispanic Black	Native-Born Hispanic	Foreign-Born Hispanic	Married Couple	Cohabiting Couple	Single Parent
Baseline Poverty Rate:	**11.8**	**7.1**	**18.3**	**14.8**	**24.5**	**7.8**	**17.8**	**23.4**
Percentage Point Reduction in Poverty Rates due to Specific Policy								
*Work Alternatives at Current Minimum Wage**								
Full-Time Work for U6	4.3	2.2	9.2	7.4	11.1	2.6	9.2	12.3
Unemployed—100% Take-up Full-Time Work for U6	3.1	1.4	7.2	5.8	9.6	1.9	7.4	10.4
Unemployed—50% Take-up Full-Time Work for U6 +Half-time 100% Take-up	7.4	3.8	12.5	10.6	17.6	5.0	12.5	16.6
Full-Time Work for U6 +Half-time 50% Take-up	4.9	2.4	9.0	8.2	13.4	3.4	9.3	13.0
Percentage Point Reduction in Poverty Rates due to Specific Policy								
Increase Federal Minimum Wage								
Federal Minimum=$10	3.1	1.3	7.0	5.7	9.8	1.9	7.3	10.3
Federal Minimum=$12	4.7	2.3	9.1	7.4	12.9	3.1	9.8	12.6
Federal Minimum=$15	7.1	3.6	11.6	9.9	17.8	4.8	13.1	15.9

* "U6 unemployed" may be unemployed or a discouraged worker or involuntarily part-time;
"Take-up" is the % of those offered a job who accept the offer at the stated wage;
"Half-time adds half-time work for all adult students and for homemakers from families with no pre-school children.
Source: Authors' calculations based on Current Population Survey; IPUMS-CPS, University of Minnesota and Historical SPM data, Columbia University.

real wage stagnation. We found that part of the problem is the prevalence of "poverty wages," which are far more common among black and Hispanic workers than non-Hispanic whites. Table 4.2 shows the actual level of the typical wages (median earnings per hour) of workers in poor families: $9.71 for men and $8.60 for women.

One reason for this long period of wage stagnation is that the real federal minimum wage (in 2018 dollars) has remained in the range of $6–8 per hour after having been above $8 per hour throughout the 1970s. The current federal minimum wage, which has been constant for a decade, is $7.25 per hour. As of 2021, 30 states and the District of Columbia have a minimum wage above the federal minimum, though only 20 of those states (plus DC) have a minimum wage of $10 or more.

The policy simulations involve increasing the federal minimum wage to a level that raises the earnings of many of the working poor. The three rows in the lower panel of table 4.3 estimate the effects of increasing the federal minimum wage to three different levels: $10 per hour, $12 per hour, and $15 per hour, the same values employed in the recent study by the Congressional Budget Office (2019).

Based on these basic policy simulations, an increase in the federal minimum wage to $10 would have effects that are neither negligible nor dramatic, reducing the overall SPM poverty rate by 3.1 percentage points, from 11.8 percent to 8.7 percent. However, the large difference in wages across race and marital status that was displayed in chapter 2 suggests that some groups will differentially benefit from increases in the minimum wage. The breakdowns by race and family status in table 4.3 show that an increase in the minimum wage has the potential to reduce poverty among the groups with the highest poverty rates by larger amounts, just as the data about wages suggest. The $10 minimum wage has the potential to reduce the poverty rate for black families by 7 percentage points, for native-born Hispanics by almost 6 percentage points, and for foreign-born Hispanics by almost 10 percentage points. Families without a married couple likewise have a potential poverty reduction of 7 to 10 percentage points. These are very substantial improvements for these groups.

A higher minimum wage alters incentives in ways that affect the labor market for low-wage workers. One of these incentives is that a higher minimum wage might also drive up the wages of workers whose wages are somewhat higher than the legislated minimum, but still not high enough to raise their families out of poverty. Another possible response is that the higher wages could cause some persons who did not find it attractive to work for the current minimum wage to find it appealing to work at the higher wage. Yet a third possible response is that some employers might lay off workers rather than pay the higher wage.

The concern that higher minimum wages might reduce employment has generated a large and contentious history of professional debate. Many studies of the employment effect of higher minimum wages find estimated effects to be small ("concentrated around zero") (Krueger, 2015). Regardless of methods and details, it seems to be a settled fact that a higher minimum wage reliably increases the earnings of low-wage workers as a group. Consistent with this conclusion, the Congressional Budget Office (2019) estimates that an increase in the minimum wage to the $12–$15 range would increase the earnings of 15 times as many workers as would have reduced earnings due to job loss. The debate is about the size of the poverty impact, not whether there is one.

Summing up this set of policy simulations, it is clear that universal availability of suitable work could generate large reductions in poverty rates, especially for groups that have high poverty rates to begin with. Even with 50 percent take-up the poverty rates for non-white groups and groups with unmarried heads could be cut almost in half. Would the benefits of reducing the work gap be even larger if the wage gap is reduced as well?

More Jobs at Higher Wages

A straightforward comparison can be drawn between the increase in the minimum wage to $10 and the job guarantee program for the U6 unemployed with 50 percent take-up: they reduce the estimated overall poverty rate by 3.1 percentage points, and the results of both simulations are similar for every subgroup. The next set of policy simulations combines the two treatments. The results are shown in table 4.4.

One can frame the results either by asking how much of the anti-poverty benefit comes from adding higher minimum wages to more work opportunities or how much additional benefit comes from adding additional work opportunities to higher minimum wages. Looking at the effect of higher minimum wages when there are jobs for every U6 unemployed adult with 100 percent take-up, we see that increasing the minimum wage to $10 further decreases poverty by 1.3 percentage points, and each additional $1 increase in the minimum wage beyond $10 decreases poverty by about an additional 0.7 percentage points. The one group that receives an obviously greater benefit than the others is foreign-born Hispanics. When there is only 50 percent take-up of the offered jobs, the foreign-born Hispanics again receive a greater benefit from the minimum wage increase. The differential benefit to foreign-born Hispanics can be interpreted in two different ways that arise from the same basic fact: this group often has job-market handicaps generated by low educational attainment, limited command of English and variable visa status,

Table 4.4 Effect of Increasing Work on SPM Poverty Rates by Race and Marital Status for Persons in SPM Families with Children, 2018

	All	Non-Hispanic White	Non-Hispanic Black	Native-Born Hispanic	Foreign-Born Hispanic	Married Couple	Cohabiting Couple	Single Parent
Baseline Poverty Rate:	**11.8**	**7.1**	**19.3**	**14.8**	**24.5**	**7.8**	**17.8**	**23.4**
Full-Time Work for U6 Unemployed—100%	4.3	2.2	9.2	7.4	11.1	2.6	9.2	12.3
Take-up								
Federal Minimum=$10	5.6	2.9	11.5	8.7	13.2	3.5	10.9	14.4
Federal Minimum=$12	7.0	3.8	13.2	10.0	15.9	4.5	12.8	16.3
Federal Minimum=$15	9.0	4.9	15.3	12.0	19.9	6.1	15.4	19.0
Full-Time Work for U6 Unemployed—50%	3.1	1.4	7.2	5.8	9.6	1.9	7.4	10.4
Take-up								
Federal Minimum=$10	4.4	2.2	9.3	7.3	11.8	2.8	9.1	12.5
Federal Minimum=$12	6.0	3.1	11.4	8.9	14.6	3.9	11.5	14.6
Federal Minimum=$15	8.1	4.3	13.7	11.0	18.8	5.4	14.4	17.6
Full-Time Work for U6+Half-time* 100%	7.4	3.8	12.5	10.6	17.6	5	12.5	16.6
Take-up								
Federal Minimum=$10	8.6	4.5	14.8	11.8	19.5	5.8	14.0	18.8
Federal Minimum=$12	9.8	5.3	16.4	13.0	21.1	6.5	15.3	20.5
Federal Minimum=$15	11.2	6.3	18.2	14.3	23.3	7.5	17.1	22.6
Full-Time Work for U6+Half-time* 50%	4.9	2.4	9	8.2	13.4	3.4	9.3	13.0
Take-up								
Federal Minimum=$10	6.2	3.1	11.3	9.2	15.5	4.1	11.0	15.1
Federal Minimum=$12	7.6	4.0	13.2	10.4	18.0	5.1	13.2	17.0
Federal Minimum=$15	9.5	5.2	15.5	12.4	21.1	6.3	15.6	19.9
Add $150 Stipend for Those Still Unemployed	2.4	1.8	2.4	2.3	3.5	2.2	2.4	2.5
To Full-Time Work for U6 Unemployed—50% Take-up	5.1	3.1	10.2	7.9	11.6	3.4	9.7	13.2
To Full-Time Work at $12 Minimum Wage—50% Take-up	6.7	4.1	12.7	9.5	15.1	4.5	12.3	15.6

Source: Authors' calculations based on Current Population Survey: IPUMS-CPS, University of Minnesota and Historical SPM data, Columbia University.

all leading to low wages. On the one hand, a higher minimum wage may remedy some of the poverty impact of those job-market handicaps. On the other hand, a higher minimum wage for foreign-born Hispanics could cause those workers to be displaced by workers whose productivity is better matched to the higher wage. A combination of higher wages and job opportunities that are suitable for immigrants would prove especially effective for the foreign-born Hispanic group.

The other way to interpret the effects of combining more work with higher wages is to consider the impact of greater work at any given minimum wage. At current wage levels, we estimated that full-time work for the U6 unemployed could potentially reduce poverty by 3 to 4 percentage points (depending on take-up) overall and 6 to 10 points for families with a non-white or unmarried head. At higher minimum wages, the potential poverty impact of greater work is smaller, about 1 to 2 percentage points overall and about 3 to 4 percent for families with a non-white or unmarried head.

Since some the simulations assume that only 50 percent of the U6 unemployed accept the job offer, we also add to two of the simulations a supplementary stipend for the unemployed of $150 per week to be added to any unemployment insurance that the family may be receiving, a mechanism that could be employed more generally during periods of rising unemployment. The supplementary stipend could be implemented in a wide variety of ways. Staying within the structure of this policy simulation, our particular implementation looks back at the weeks that the worker was unemployed during the previous year and adds $150 per week to the family income of those who did not take up the job offer. The income is assumed to be non-taxable but means-tested benefits would be reduced accordingly. The size of the benefit is chosen to be approximately half of what a person could earn from a full-time job at the federal minimum wage. The results are shown on the bottom panel of table 4.4. Because the benefit only goes to the unemployed, it does not have a dramatic effect on poverty rates, which decrease by an additional 1 to 2 percentage points, but it is particularly beneficial to the single-parent families that often struggle to find suitable work opportunities.

Whichever way one interprets the results of these simulations, it is clear that closing the work gap and closing the wage gap are both effective means of reducing poverty and that they complement each other. It is true that closing the work gap is less impactful when wages are higher, but if, as seems likely, higher wages would increase take-up, the anti-poverty effect could prove to be even larger than the policy simulations with reduced take-up suggest.

Combining Work and Wages with a More Generous EITC

One of the basic conclusions of chapter 3 was that the EITC plays a major role in enhancing the resources of low-income families with children, showing that 65 percent of private income poor families received the credit, and the average credit of the recipient families was more than $3,000. A Center for Budget and Policy Priorities (CBPP) analysis (2019) showed that the EITC benefited nearly 10 million children and pulled more than 3 million of them out of SPM poverty. These observations suggest that enhancing the EITC could reduce poverty substantially.

Enhancing the EITC is an especially appealing policy because it targets families with children, and especially single-parent families, as the credit substantially increases the reward to a jobless single parent who takes a low-wage job. For an unemployed person taking a job at the federal minimum wage of $7.25, the credit in 2018 would have added $2.18 per hour (with one child), $2.90 per hour (with two children), and $3.27 per hour up to 37 hours per week (with three or more children). The tax credit for a single parent working a full-year full-time job would have added $3,526 to the spendable income of the one-child family, $5,828 for the two-child family, and $6,557 for the three-child family. One might infer that the EITC would provide a strong incentive for single parents to seek full-time employment. As discussed in chapter 3, there is historical evidence that this is so, though the recent research by Kleven (2021) raises doubts about whether that history is a reliable guide for current policy. Regardless of its incentive effects the EITC can provide a substantial supplement to family income, though not always enough to raise the family out of poverty.

There are several different ways that the EITC could be expanded to enhance its impact on family poverty. The phase-in rates and maximum credits vary by the number of children (up to a maximum of three), but not by marital status, while the earnings level that begins the phase-out is determined by marital status, but not by the number of children (as long as there are any children at all). The policy simulations in table 4.5 are not based on specific changes in the tax credit parameters. Rather, the calculated EITC, both before and after other components of the simulation, is increased by 50 percent. The principal purpose of this simulation is to show how an enhanced EITC does or does not interact with other alternatives for closing the wage and work gaps.

To keep the table of results manageable, table 4.5 combines the enhanced EITC with three of the alternatives already discussed, namely: an increase in the federal minimum wage to $12; a full-time job for the U6 unemployed with 50 percent take-up; and a combination of those two. It shows that increasing the EITC by half without doing anything else is estimated to reduce the overall poverty rate by 3.8 percentage points, but for the non-white and

Table 4.5 Effect of Changing EITC or Eliminating Child Care Costs on SPM Poverty Rates by Race and Marital Status for Persons in SPM Families with Children, 2018

	All	Non-Hispanic White	Non-Hispanic Black	Native-Born Hispanic	Foreign-Born Hispanic	Married Couple	Cohabiting Couple	Single Parent
Baseline Poverty Rate:	**11.8**	**7.1**	**19.3**	**14.8**	**24.5**	**7.8**	**17.8**	**23.4**
	Percentage Point Reduction in Poverty Rates due to Specific Policy							
Baseline Reductions from Tables 4.2 and 4.3								
Increase Federal Minimum to $12	4.7	2.3	9.1	7.4	12.9	3.1	9.8	12.6
Full-Time Work for U6 Unemployed—50% Take-up	3.1	1.4	7.2	5.8	9.6	1.9	7.4	10.4
Full-Time Work at $12 Minimum Wage—50% Take-up	6.0	3.1	11.4	8.9	14.6	3.9	11.5	14.6
Increase EITC by half	3.8	1.5	7.4	6.7	12.3	2.6	7.2	11.0
& Increase Federal Minimum to $12	6.1	2.9	10.6	8.9	16.0	4.2	10.9	14.5
& Full-Time Work for U5 Unemployed—50% Take-up	5.1	2.4	9.7	8.3	13.8	3.5	9.1	13.5
& Full-Time Work at $12 Minimum Wage—50% Take-up	7.3	3.8	12.9	10.3	17.2	4.9	12.5	16.5
Universal Child Care	2.5	1.1	6.0	5.2	8.5	1.8	5.9	9.1
& Increase Federal Minimum to $12	6.3	3.3	11.0	9.1	15.9	4.3	11.8	14.8
& Full-Time Work for U6 Unemployed—50% Take-up	5.4	2.8	10.1	8.2	13.5	3.6	9.9	13.7
& Full-Time Work at $12 Minimum Wage—50% Take-up	7.5	4.1	13.1	10.5	17.2	5.1	13.3	16.7

(continued)

Table 4.5 (Continued)

Effect of Introducing Child Allowance or Eliminating Medical Expenses on SPM Poverty Rates by Race and Marital Status for Persons in SPM Families with Children, 2018

	All	Non-Hispanic White	Non-Hispanic Black	Native-Born Hispanic	Foreign-Born Hispanic	Married Couple	Cohabiting Couple	Single Parent
	Percentage Point Reduction in Poverty Rates due to Specific Policy							
$3,500 per child Child Allowance	4.9	3.0	9.2	7.8	11.9	3.2	9.6	13.1
& Increase Federal Minimum to $12	8.5	5.1	13.4	11.3	19.0	6.3	14.1	17.4
& Full-Time Work for U6 Unemployed—50% Take-up	8.3	5.0	13.2	11.5	18.0	6.1	13.6	17.2
& Full-Time Work at $12 Minimum Wage—50% Take-up	9.4	5.7	14.9	12.1	20.1	6.8	15.3	18.8
Eliminate MOOP	3.2	2.3	6.8	5.5	8.6	2.8	6.5	9.5
& Increase Federal Minimum to $12	6.3	3.3	11.0	9.1	15.9	4.3	11.8	14.8
& Full-Time Work for U6 Unemployed—50% Take-up	5.3	2.8	10.2	8.2	13.5	3.6	9.6	13.7
& Full-Time Work at $12 Minimum Wage—50% Take-up	7.5	4.0	13.2	10.3	17.4	5.0	13.3	16.7

Source: Authors' calculations based on Current Population Survey: IPUMS-CPS, University of Minnesota and Historical SPM data, Columbia University.

unmarried groups the poverty reduction is much larger, approximately 7 percentage points for black, Native-born Hispanic and cohabiting families and
more than 10 percentage points for foreign-born Hispanic and single-parent
families. This is somewhat less than the effect of increasing the minimum
wage to $12, but somewhat more than a $10 minimum wage, suggesting that
from a poverty alleviation perspective a more generous EITC might serve as
an alternative way to address the poverty associated with the wage gap.

Two additional policy simulations in table 4.5 focus on the work gap by
combining the enhanced EITC with the program described earlier that provides work for the U6 unemployed with a 50 percent take-up. Done by itself,
without an enhanced EITC, that job program was estimated to reduce poverty
by 3.1 percentage points. Adding the enhanced EITC would increase the
poverty reduction from 3.1 percentage points to 5.1 percentage points if the
jobs are at the state minimum wage or 7.3 percentage points if also combined
with the $12 minimum wage. Comparing the rows labeled "Full-Time Work
at $12 minimum wage" one sees that the additional anti-poverty effect of
enhancing the EITC is not very large, typically 1 to 2 additional percentage
points, as the work and wages have already lifted many families with potential workers out of poverty.

Eliminating Childcare Costs

The evidence in chapter 2 showed that childcare can be a very expensive component of a family's budget, averaging $143 to $189 per week (preschoolers
cost more). Herbst (2018) found that families in the bottom 25 percent
of the income distribution are more frugal, spending $52–$83 per week, but
even that represents 7 to 12 hours of work per week at a minimum wage job.
As chapter 3 pointed out, the Child and Dependent Care Tax Credit, which
can reduce a taxpaying family's tax bill by as much as 35 percent of these
expenses, is not refundable, so poor families who owe no federal income tax
derive no benefit from it. Childcare expenses are subtracted from a family's
After Tax and Transfer Income in the SPM poverty calculation, so they affect
poverty directly, and they also serve as a disincentive for work (Morrisey,
2017).

For those reasons, it is useful to embark on a policy simulation involving
childcare costs. For the purpose of understanding the anti-poverty potential
of removing childcare cost that would otherwise be an impediment to work,
we consider an alternative that could potentially eliminate childcare costs
for many families. This policy choice is generally known as "universal child
care" and is provided by many countries. There is already a developing interest in government-funded preschools, especially for children ages 3 to 4. In
addition to existing federally funded programs like Head Start, state-funded

preschools are now found in 44 states (and the District of Columbia), though only 8 of those states currently have programs that are substantially universal (Parker et al., 2018).

The results in table 4.5 suggest that a coordinated program that provides work opportunities at relatively high wages and with highly subsidized childcare has the potential to reduce poverty dramatically. Simply relieving poor families from the cost of childcare would reduce poverty by 2.5 percentage points, but the effects on high-poverty groups are much larger: 5 to 8 percentage points for non-white and cohabiting families and 9 percentage points for single parents. One of the likely benefits of universal child care is greater work effort; the reviews by Blau (2003) and Blau and Tekin (2007) suggest that this effect can be quite large, especially for single mothers. Consequently, it is especially useful to look at the combined effect of full-time work for the U6 unemployed combined with universal childcare. Universal childcare generally adds 2 to 3 percentage points to the impact of the jobs program and another 2 to 4 percentage points if combined with a minimum wage increase to $12. As with the case of policy combinations involving an enhanced EITC, it is possible to cut poverty by more than 7 percentage points by combining more jobs, higher wages and free child care, but it would require a coordinated effort to do so.

All of the policy simulations so far have involved increasing family resources by closing the work gap or wage gap directly and enhancing the anti-poverty effects through support of working families. There are, however, many families for which increased full-time work is unrealistic for reasons like poor health and others for which even full-time work at higher wages is insufficient to escape poverty. The next set of simulations take a different approach that includes such families. The first provides a CA to families simply because they have children, and the second eliminates the MOOP that often drive the working poor into poverty.

Combining Work and Wages with a Child Allowance

The previous policy simulations have shown that sufficiently aggressive policies for providing suitable work opportunities can reduce poverty in families with children, especially if matched with policies that "make work pay" through some mix of higher wage rates and a more generous EITC. However, if the real goal is to reduce poverty in families with children, including families with limited work potential due to the age or health of the adults, the most straightforward policy would be to subsidize families with a Child Allowance (CA). CA benefits are not exotic. More than a dozen countries have them, including the Nordic countries, the Benelux countries, Germany, the UK, and Canada. The only form of CA in the United States as of 2018 was the $2,000

CTC, up to $1,400 of which was refundable to families with at least $2,500 of earned income. A key difference from other countries is that the CTC benefits are unavailable to those with very low earnings or very high incomes.

The per-child poverty gaps shown in table 4.1 suggest an approximate sum of $3,000–$4,000 per child as an amount that could cut the poverty rate substantially. The policy simulation here looks at the potential effects of a $3,500 CA, both by itself and in conjunction with labor market interventions. The assumption throughout is that the CA would be treated as "income" for the purpose of calculating both the eligibility and the amount of means-tested transfer payments (TANF, SNAP, etc.), so the $3,500 CA would not add a full $3,500 to the resources available to families currently claiming those benefits.

The results in table 4.5 show that adding a $3,500 CA would reduce overall poverty by 4.9 percentage points, but with much larger impacts for some groups: 8 to 9 percentage points for non-Hispanic blacks and native-born Hispanics and 12 to 13 percentage points for foreign-born Hispanics and single-parent families. A CA has considerable potential to reduce poverty even after labor market interventions are implemented because it would address the needs of families that do not have an unemployed adult for whom there is a satisfactory job available. For example, a program offering a full-time job at the current minimum wage to all U6 unemployed with a 50 percent uptake would reduce the poverty rate by 3 percentage points. Would it also reduce the poverty gap for the remaining families? The answer is "almost not at all"—the poverty gap per child for the median poor family would fall from $3,886 to $3,519, so a $3,500 CA would still have great potential for poverty alleviation. Table 4.5 shows that in this case the combination of the full-time job with 50 percent take-up and the $3,500 CA would reduce poverty by 8.3 percentage points, cutting the poverty rate more than in half for every race group and every family status group in spite of the reductions in means-tested transfer payments.

An impediment to a CA is that a truly universal allowance would be very costly unless it replaces other programs. The basic idea of a universal CA is that, unlike means-tested programs, the benefits will not be "clawed back" if the family increases its earnings. However, cost considerations may require a deviation from that basic principle, in which case a family might find itself losing some portion of its CA as its earnings increase. It is also reasonable to expect that some families may choose to "spend" a portion of the allowance by trading work time for family time, with a typical estimate being that a 10 percent increase in income reduces the likelihood of parental employment by less than 1 percent for fathers and less than 2 percent for mothers. Another potential issue is that the details of current programs often reflect an aversion to subsidizing large families, though that could be addressed by reducing the additional CA for children beyond the first and/or reducing the child-related components of the EITC.

Perhaps the most substantial impediment to a CA, however, is political acceptance of the idea that reducing the poverty of families with children should be directly accomplished through targeted aid to the families rather than focusing on work incentives for the adults in the family, though our policy simulations suggest that a CA and a work program would have complementary effects.

Eliminate MOOP

The SPM poverty definition provides an opportunity to undertake an additional policy simulation: What would happen to SPM poverty among families with children if medical care were to become costless? This could happen in many different ways, whether through a universal program or a targeted program that covers not only those with inadequate cash incomes but also those at risk of being moved into poverty by their medical bills. For the purpose of the policy simulation, it is assumed that there would be no copays or deductibles.

The results are shown on the bottom panel of table 4.5. By itself the elimination of MOOP would reduce poverty by 3.2 percentage points. Since over 10 percent of poor families have no MOOP at all and over 50 percent have MOOP less than $1,000 per year, eliminating MOOP is a targeted policy. The idea that it can reduce poverty by more than 3 percentage points shows that large medical bills create poverty for many families who would not otherwise be poor and have few alternatives for covering those bills. A characteristic that makes the elimination of MOOP a distinctive option is that it reduces poverty by a quarter to a third in every race and family status group.

In addition, there are some families who could benefit from eliminating MOOP even if they are also beneficiaries of policies that reduce the work gap or wage gap. Eliminating MOOP would increase the poverty reduction of full-time work at a $12 minimum wage by an additional 1.5 percentage points (from 6.0 to 7.5), which is far from negligible.

CONCLUSION

As chapter 3 showed, the anti-poverty policy apparatus has generally become more work- centered. The primary purpose of the policy simulations has been to explore the limits of further expansions of a work-centered policy structure, the extent to which other policy changes could complement any of those expansions, and the policy combinations that have the potential to reduce poverty rates among various groups.

The exploration of mechanisms to close the wage gap, the work gap, or both suggests that it is possible to reduce poverty by a few percentage points with either a relatively modest increase in the minimum wage or the creation of appropriate jobs taken up by half of the persons to whom the jobs are offered. While a few percentage points may seem like a small achievement, the potential poverty reduction for the groups with the highest poverty rates are much larger. Substantial reductions in U6 unemployment may be overly optimistic, however, as more than 50 percent of those who are offered jobs may find the wages or working conditions unsuitable. A realistic program for reducing poverty by half will require a combination of policies that go beyond reducing work gaps.

Two of the policy options serve the dual purpose of reducing poverty and complementing parental work. One of these is an expansion of the EITC. Its potential impact as a stand-alone option is similar to that of a $10 minimum wage and is in that sense a substitute for it. However, a more generous EITC would also have the capacity to enhance the poverty impact of either (or both) of a job program or a higher minimum wage by supplementing the increased earnings. A jobs program that reduces U6 unemployment by half pays a $12 minimum wage and is supplemented by the more generous EITC would reduce poverty by half for every subgroup.

Another option that would complement parental work is some form of "universal child care," shifting much of the cost of childcare to programs sponsored or subsidized by governments. One of the benefits of the SPM poverty measure is that it accounts for childcare costs and thereby reveals the anti-poverty potential of subsidized childcare in a work-centered policy mix. By itself, the reduction of childcare expenses would decrease the poverty rate by 2.5 percentage points, but it could be combined with additional work opportunities at higher wages to reduce poverty by much more, as the outcomes are almost identical to those from expanding the EITC.

Two policy simulations involved policies that are not focused on work or the incentive to work and therefore address the poverty of families for whom full-time work is not a practical alternative. One of these simulations involved a CA program, which could be implemented through a refundable tax credit. A $3,500 per CA could reduce poverty by more than a third and by more than half in families headed by a single parent. The other simulation considers the effect of eliminating MOOP, a targeted policy that would reduce poverty in families with expenses that are often very large and preclude participation in the job market.

Some of the simulated results are particularly beneficial to specific groups. For example, foreign-born Hispanic families often contain low-wage

Table 4.6　Eight Policy Simulations that Reduce Poverty by>7 Percentage Points for Persons in All SPM Families and Effect of Alternative Policy Packages on SPM Poverty Rates, by Race and Marital Status for Persons in SPM Families with Children, 2018

	All	Non-Hispanic White	Non-Hispanic Black	Native-Born Hispanic	Foreign-Born Hispanic	Married Couple	Cohabiting Couple	Single Parent
		Percentage Point Reduction in Poverty Rates due to Specific Policy						
1. FT Work for U6+Half-time*, 100% Take-up	7.4	3.8	12.5	10.6	17.6	5.0	12.5	16.6
2. Federal Minimum Wage Increased to $15	7.1	3.6	11.6	9.9	17.8	4.8	13.1	15.9
3. FT Work for U6+Half-Time* @ $12 Minimum Wage, 50% Take-up	7.6	4.0	13.2	10.4	18.0	5.1	13.2	17.0
4. Increase EITC+FT Work for U6 @ $12 Minimum Wage, 50% Take-up	7.3	3.8	12.9	10.3	17.2	4.9	12.5	16.5
5. Universal Child Care+FT Work @ $12 Minimum Wage, 50% Take-up	7.5	4.1	13.1	10.5	17.2	5.1	13.3	16.7
6. $3,500 Child Allowance+FT Work for U6, 50% Take-up	8.3	5.0	13.2	11.5	18.0	6.1	13.6	17.2
7. $3,500 Child Allowance+$12 Minimum Wage	8.5	5.1	13.4	11.3	19.0	6.3	14.1	17.4
8. Eliminate MOOP+FT Work for U6 @ $12 Minimum Wage, 50% Take-up	7.5	4.0	13.2	10.3	17.4	5.0	13.3	16.7

*Half-Time Work for Students and Homemakers

Source: Authors' calculations based on Current Population Survey: IPUMS-CPS, University of Minnesota and Historical SPM data, Columbia University.

workers, so higher wages or an increase in the EITC are especially beneficial to that group. Non-Hispanic black families and native-born Hispanic families derive similar benefits from almost every simulation, with slightly larger poverty reductions for the black families because their poverty rate is higher to begin with.

Family status groups are also differentially affected. A program that provides jobs suitable to unmarried parents, with or without a cohabiting partner, could reduce the poverty rates of those high-poverty groups by very substantial amounts. Highly successful options require reducing either the work gap or the wage gap, usually both, but most of them also incorporate other policies that support or supplement increased earnings.

Table 4.6 provides a summary of eight policy packages for which the simulations achieve the goal of reducing poverty in families with children by more than 7 percentage points. All of them involve reducing the work gap, the wage gap, or both, but five of the eight also incorporate other policies that support or supplement increased earnings. The task of comparing specific policy packages requires a more detailed consideration of the details of specific policy proposals and their costs. The next chapter will apply a set of specific criteria to a variety of specific policy proposals using our policy simulations as a guide, ultimately leading to an evaluation of alternative packages based on different weightings of the criteria.

Chapter 5

Detailed Proposals and Their Cost

The previous chapter reported the results of a series of simulations estimating the extent to which poverty in families with children can be reduced by employing the unemployed, by increasing the minimum wage, by increasing the generosity of the EITC, by instituting a child allowance, and by reducing family expenditures on childcare expenses and medical expenses. These options address the needs of a wide variety of poor families: those with potential workers who are unemployed or underemployed and need a full-time job; those who are fully employed, but inadequately paid; those whose incentive to become employed is reduced because their earnings would be eaten up by childcare expenses and reduced benefits; or those with apparently adequate earnings that are cast into poverty by unreimbursed medical expenses.

While such a variety of challenges can be found in every race and marital status group, they are found in different proportions within those groups. If the goal is to reduce family poverty in ways that are both effective in reducing poverty for all groups and equitable to groups with particularly high poverty rates, such as unmarried parents or black and Hispanic families, specific policies will need to be combined to achieve that goal. Chapter 4 estimated the effect of a diverse list of policy combinations, including several with the potential of meeting the baseline goal of reducing by half the SPM poverty rate among families with children.

What chapter 4 did not do, however, was delineate the details or estimate the costs of specific policy implementations. Within the last few years, economists have advanced a variety of specific proposals for reducing poverty that are direct implementations of the general policy options explored in our simulations. Several of these proposals are derived from one of two sources.

First, the Russell Sage Foundation *Journal of the Social Sciences* devoted two consecutive issues in 2018 to the topic of "Anti-Poverty Initiatives for the

United States." Of the 15 proposals published there, 5 are closely related to the topics of this book and will be discussed in this chapter. Second, in 2019, The National Academies of Sciences, Engineering and Medicine produced a report entitled "A Roadmap for Reducing Child Poverty." This report was developed as a response to a 2015 Congressional mandate to propose options for reducing child poverty by half (6.5 percentage points) over the course of a decade. The task was undertaken by a committee of 15 scholars from multiple fields of study and various political preferences. Several of the policy implementations discussed in this chapter can also be found in the Biden administration's "American Families Plan," and we summarize the similarities and differences.

The policy proposals will be described in detail and evaluated by four criteria. The first is the proposal's capacity for reducing poverty in families with children. The second is equitable treatment of the poorest groups. These are the two criteria by which we judged the policy options represented in the policy simulations in the previous chapter. Though the authors of the proposals generally provide an estimate of the poverty impact, in many cases we rely on our estimates to focus on families with children and to compare the relative effect on different groups. The third criterion is the extent to which the policy is likely to increase or decrease poor families' incentives to become more self-sufficient by increasing family employment and earnings. As discussed in chapter 4, these incentives may arise for two different reasons. First, additional earnings can lead to higher childcare and work-related expenses or reduced benefits from means-tested programs, reducing the amount by which higher after-tax earnings increase expendable income. Second, higher family income may induce changes in how families balance work and family responsibilities. The final criterion is cost-effectiveness, measured as poverty reduction per dollar expended.

The understanding of poor families with children developed in the last four chapters can be combined with the proposals discussed in this chapter to provide a more nuanced assessment of policies that reduce poverty in families with children. After examining the policy proposals individually, we outline policy packages that may be more or less attractive based on the weight given to each criterion.

SPECIFIC PROPOSALS THAT FOCUS ON WORK GAPS

Work Requirements

We begin by examining three proposals that focus on the work gap. One of these proposals depends on an expansion of work requirements for benefits, a second proposes a universal work guarantee, and the third involves a work program directly targeted on the unemployed and underemployed.

The policy proposal focusing on work requirements was created by the Council of Economic Advisers in 2018. It aims to increase the labor market attachment of poor adults and reduce expenditures on means-tested programs by increasing poor adults' work effort in the current labor market. The proposal would require work or "work-related activity" by non-disabled (not receiving any disability benefit) working-age adults (ages 18 to 64) who receive benefits from one or more of three programs: Medicaid, SNAP, or federally subsidized housing. The proposal does not state precisely what the work requirement would be, but it appears to be modeled on the TANF work requirement of at least 30 hours per week for a one-parent family (20 hours if the youngest child is less than six years old) or 35 hours per week for a two-parent family (55 hours per week if the family receives federally subsidized childcare). "Work-related activities" may include unpaid community service programs, training programs, and some educational programs. Persons who do not comply would be ineligible for benefits.

The argument for the efficacy of work requirements was originally based on the results of the 1996 TANF welfare reforms that mandated work requirements and was, as we showed in chapter 2, associated with a substantial increase in full-time work by low-income adults with children, especially women in single-parent families. As we discussed in chapter 3, the design of SNAP and housing assistance policies creates a work disincentive, but the research base does not provide evidence that these disincentives have a large impact on the work effort of families with children. For example, the only strong evidence for substantially reduced work effort due to SNAP recipiency is among the foreign-born (Hoynes and Schanzenbach, 2012), and subsequent research on the results of the TANF reform generally shows that it has had limited effect on poverty, as those who have left TANF in order to work often joined the ranks of the "working poor" (Ziliak, 2016). The National Academies report reviews the evidence from controlled trials imposing work requirements and concludes that "there is insufficient evidence to identify mandatory work policies that would reliably reduce child poverty." There is no question that introducing work requirements for the largest in-kind transfer programs would decrease expenditures on the programs and encourage some current recipients to work the additional hours required to maintain eligibility. There is, however, no direct evidence that there would be a reduction in poverty, and the enforcement mechanism is predicated on denying health care and food/housing subsidies to the children in poor families, not just the adults who fail to respond to the work incentive or are unable to find suitable job opportunities.

Job Guarantees

The second proposal (Paul et al., 2018) is in sharp contrast to the first, though it also relies on the labor market for its anti-poverty impact. This proposal is similar to the National Investment Employment Corps idea initially broached by Darity (2010) that provides a federal job guarantee, essentially eliminating involuntary unemployment. Though some of the jobs would be directly provided by the federal government, others would be provided by state and local governments (including Indian nations) using federal funds. The jobs would serve to provide both "physical and human infrastructure," the latter involving jobs in areas like childcare and elder care. The guarantee would provide a job with a wage of at least $11.56 per hour, a value calculated to prevent poverty (based on the Official Poverty Measure) for a family of four with one full-time worker. Every job would include a benefits package for retirement and health care that is modeled on the programs currently provided to federal employees. It is assumed that these positions would have promotion potential so that the average wage would be over $15 per hour. Since private-sector workers could, in principle, leave their jobs for the guaranteed jobs, the program would provide both a de facto minimum wage and a standard for private-sector benefits packages.

   The authors do not attempt to calculate the effect of this program on poverty, but our analysis in chapter 4 can approximate it. The estimates in table 4.6 showed that we would expect the poverty rate for our population to fall by approximately 7 percentage points if the program had 100 percent take-up by the U6 unemployed, and even more if some half-time jobs were added or the $15 average wage were eventually to become a de facto minimum wage. Our estimate is that the guarantee of an $11.56 wage would reduce the poverty rate by 6.9 percentage points, from 11.8 percent to 4.9 percent. Since this reduction in the poverty rate exceeds the 2015 Congressional request made to the National Academies, we can treat this proposal as a baseline for estimating the scope and cost of doing so by employing the unemployed. The authors make no explicit effort to determine which groups would most benefit from this program, but it is clearly focused on the needs of the groups with the highest U6 unemployment rates. Our results in table 4.6 also suggested that a successful job program would generally be expected to provide the greatest poverty reduction to the groups with the highest poverty, but the lower-poverty groups of non-Hispanic whites and married couples would also benefit substantially. In the long run, the reduction in poverty would arguably be even greater than the snapshot estimate, because the job guarantee would provide a career path for persons who have trouble building a career in the current labor market, particularly persons who may suffer from the long-term impacts of discrimination, inadequate schooling, or a criminal record.

If the jobs are truly to be "guaranteed," many of them are presumably jobs in the public sector, in part because additional jobs are most needed in periods of high unemployment when the private sector may be reducing employment. A potentially substantial problem is that the workers taking the guaranteed jobs may displace government employees or private contractors paying higher wages. Ellwood and Welty (2000) suggest that 20 to 25 percent of the new jobs will displace other employees and that the number can only be kept that low if the duration of the guaranteed job is restricted or if the jobs are different from those undertaken by current employees and contractors. Providing those characteristics requires that the jobs program assign training and supervisory personnel. As a result, Ellwood and Welty estimate that 40 to 60 percent of the cost of public-service employment programs would be spent on administrative expenses.

For the reasons we have stated, the costs associated with a job guarantee cannot be precisely estimated. Using 2016 as a base year the authors estimate a cost of approximately $654 billion per year, roughly 10 times the total expenditures on the Earned Income Tax Credit, and they accept that the cost would be much higher if a substantial number of workers quit their private-sector jobs to take up the guarantee. As they point out, however, the program would lead to a substantial reduction in expenses on other programs. Unemployment insurance expenses would be substantially reduced, of course, as would SNAP benefits. The largest potential saving would be a reduction in Medicaid expenses, as a health-care program for the entire family would already be included in the benefits package attached to the jobs.

A recent proposal (Dutta-Gupta, 2018) is designed to accomplish some of the goals of the work guarantee, but on a smaller and more targeted scale. The program would provide subsidies to employers that would defer both the wages and the training costs of a full-time (35 hours per week) job at the minimum wage in the worker's state. These jobs would not, however, be subsidized indefinitely nor made available to all unemployed persons. This approach follows the conclusion reached by Dickert-Conlon and Holtz-Eakin (2000) that a wage subsidy to employers must be carefully tailored to raise the employment levels of targeted groups. In this case, eligibility would be restricted to three groups: the long-term unemployed (at least 16 weeks), the involuntarily part-time, and "discouraged workers" who have become "detached" from the labor force after a failed job search. If an eligible person takes the job, the subsidy would last for only nine weeks unless renewed. Recipients would retain full eligibility for the earned income and childcare tax credits, which are crucial to the anti-poverty impact.

The program is estimated to reduce the overall SPM poverty rate by only 0.3 percentage points. That is, however, largely a consequence of the strict eligibility rules and the modest take-up rate, as shown by the estimate that the SPM poverty rate among the actual recipients would be reduced by 15 percentage points (from 35 percent to 20 percent). The program is targeted on populations with particularly high poverty rates, and for those recipients it would presumably be highly effective. The program would have to be more attractive to a less targeted population to have a major effect on the national poverty rate, however. Simulations based on the assumption of 20 percent take-up (Wimer et al., 2018) estimate the annual cost of the program at approximately $15.9 billion per year. That is about 2.5 percent of the estimated cost of the universal job guarantee described above, so one would expect the anti-poverty effects to be correspondingly small, and that expectation is correct.

In summary, a job guarantee could indeed generate a large reduction in poverty, just as our policy simulations suggested. It would achieve that poverty reduction at considerable expense, however, even with lower expenditures on unemployment insurance and means-tested transfers. The cost could be reduced by targeting the program and reducing its generosity at the expense of reducing the overall impact. The attraction of such a program hangs on two questions: (1) How important is it that poverty reduction be delivered through the labor market, even if the program costs far more than any reduction in means-tested benefits would save? (2) Are the additional goods and services that the program creates sufficiently beneficial that the poverty reduction can be considered a by-product of investments that would be desirable even if the expenses were not targeted on the unemployed? Heavy reliance on a large employment program funded by the federal government is a logical consequence of answering at least one of those questions (preferably both) with a "yes."

PROPOSALS FOR INCREASING THE
FEDERAL MINIMUM WAGE

In Chapter 4 we showed that a policy focused on increasing family earnings is unlikely to be highly effective unless it substantially reduces the wage gap. Since in 2018 half of all working poor working women made less than $8.60 per hour and half of all poor working men made less than $9.71 per hour, it would require a minimum wage in excess of $10 per hour to increase the earnings of a majority of poor recipients. We begin with three specific proposals for increasing the minimum wage. The first is the proposal in the National Academies report (2019) to increase the federal minimum wage to $10.25 over the course of three years. The second is a proposal by Romich and Hill (2018) to increase the federal minimum wage to $12 over the course of two years combined with a temporary hiring subsidy for employers. The third is an assessment by the Congressional Budget Office (2019) of increases in the federal minimum wage to $10 or $12 or $15, all to be implemented over the course of six years.

As a baseline for evaluating the overall poverty impact of these proposals, the results in table 4.5 estimated that a $10 minimum wage would reduce poverty in families with children by 3.1 percentage points, a $12 minimum wage by 4.7 percentage points, and a $15 minimum wage by 7.1 percentage points. The authors of the proposals are less optimistic about the effects of the higher minimum wage, even if implemented over the course of years. The National Academies report estimates that the $10.25 minimum wage would reduce child poverty by 1.5 percentage points, and Wimer et al. (2018) estimate that the $12 minimum wage proposal of Romich and Hill would reduce overall poverty (not just children or families with children) by 2.3 percentage points. The CBO estimates focus more on earnings than on poverty per se, but based solely on their results we infer that a $10 minimum wage would be predicted to have almost no effect on poverty, that a $12 minimum wage would reduce poverty by approximately 1 percentage point and a $15 minimum wage by approximately 3.2 percentage points.

It is typical of these estimates that they predict an effect that is no more than half as large as those in our policy simulations. The main difference is that our policy simulations assume that the higher minimum wage has no adverse effect on the employment of low-wage workers in families with children. The National Academies estimate of the effect of a $10.25 minimum wage is that 1.3 percent of adults who currently earn below the new minimum wage would lose their jobs (as would 4.7 percent of affected teenagers), and the estimated effect of the $12 minimum wage proposed by Romich and Hill (2018) is that 6.5 percent of the affected workers would lose their jobs in the absence of a job subsidy. The CBO analysis provides a set of potential results from a six-year phase-in of a higher minimum wage, ranging from a negligible net job loss from a $10 minimum wage to an 0.3 million net job loss from a $12 minimum wage to a 1.3 million net job loss from $15 minimum wage.

Our contention is that whatever the exact effect of an increase of the minimum wage on job loss, a higher minimum wage is certain to increase the earnings of most families with children, and that the reduction in the overall poverty rate of these families is likely to be larger than these models predict. The most recent results that focus directly on poverty (Dube, 2019) suggest that the $10 minimum wage would reduce child poverty in the "long run" (three years) by approximately 2.3 percentage points, a $12 minimum wage by approximately 3.5 percentage points, and a $15 minimum wage by approximately 5.1 percentage points.

The National Academies report includes a section that addresses differences in which groups of children would benefit most from a minimum wage increase to $10.25. They find that the group that stands to benefit most is children in families whose lack of citizenship reduces or eliminates access to benefits, as a higher wage would increase their families' income without regard to immigration status. Children in black families are also found to benefit differentially. Dube (2019) finds that minimum wage increases differentially reduce the poverty of black and Hispanic families, though not of single mothers, though our policy simulations suggest that minimum wage increases to $10 or $12 may differentially benefit the unmarried, whether cohabiting or not. Churchill and Sabia (2019) maintain that the minimum wage has lost most of its effectiveness as a policy tool for addressing poverty among immigrants due to recent changes in immigration policy and immigrant behavior, particularly the tendency of immigrant workers to work in the informal sector. Summing up, there seems to be a consensus that minimum wage increases are especially beneficial for black and native-born Hispanic workers, but there is less agreement about how well minimum wage legislation addresses the poverty of immigrants and single parents.

The third criterion is the extent to which the policy affects work incentives. For those who are not working because jobs fail to meet an unemployed person's reservation wage or fail to cover work and childcare expenses, a higher minimum wage is clearly an incentive to work. For persons like teenagers and immigrants, however, a higher minimum wage may deprive them of the opportunity to find a job at a wage that other workers might be reluctant to accept. Both of these effects would be more important for a relatively large increase, and that is the reason why the Romich and Hill proposal for a $12 minimum wage is matched with a job program that provides a temporary tax credit to employers hiring low-wage workers.

The final criterion is cost. An obvious advantage of increasing the minimum wage is that it increases tax payments overall (in spite of the EITC), and it also reduces expenditures on means-tested transfer payments. The resulting increase in taxes and reduction in transfer payments is how Romich and Hill (2018) propose to fund the tax credit component of their proposal.

The most optimistic interpretation of the policy options discussed so far is that it is potentially possible to reduce poverty among families with children to much lower levels if both the work gap and the wage gap are substantially and simultaneously reduced. The more pessimistic conclusion is that even the combination of a universal job program and a doubling of the federal minimum wage would leave many families in poverty, particularly single-parent families. Are there other policies that could reduce poverty while also improving incentives to work or removing disincentives? Our simulations in the previous chapter suggest two possibilities that have generated specific policy proposals: (1) increasing the generosity of the Earned Income Tax Credit, which would both incentivize work by enhancing the rewards and supplement increased earnings; and (2) reducing, or even eliminating, the childcare expenses that are both a disincentive for parental work and a direct cause of SPM poverty because they are subtracted from when calculating the net resources of the family.

A PROPOSAL FOR ENHANCING THE EITC

Given the potential of the EITC for reducing family poverty, it is not surprising that an expansion of the EITC is a component of the policy packages proposed by the National Academies (2019) to address child poverty. That proposal has two basic components. The first component is to increase the phase-in rates to 1.4 times their original values. For example, the 40 percent phase-in rate for a family with two children would be increased to 56 percent; and since the maximum earnings to which the credit applies would remain unchanged, the maximum credit would also increase to 1.4 times its previous value. Mindful of the impact on tax revenues, however, this proposal reduces the program cost by increasing the phase-out rates to 1.4 times their original size, reducing the work incentive for the second earner in a married-couple family.

The estimated overall reduction in SPM child poverty is 2.1 percentage points, especially benefiting black and single-parent families. Our policy simulation was more optimistic in estimating a poverty reduction of 3.8 percentage points. The difference in the estimated poverty reduction is partly because the National Academies' proposal is less generous (a 40 percent increase in the phase-in rate rather than a 50 percent increase). Also, the National Academies' simulation assumes that the EITC would induce some workers, especially second earners, to quit working, though the net effect on employment would be positive. This program achieves its goals at considerable expense in spite of the increased phase-out rate: the total amount of the EITC would increase by $21.8 billion, offset in part by a $2.5 billion reduction in expenditures on means-tested benefits. If the goal is to increase the rewards that unmarried parents receive from working, enhancing the EITC is potentially effective. However, the reduction in poverty comes at the price of a substantial increase in expenditures on "negative taxes," and any attempt to restrain this expense with high phase-out rates creates disincentives, especially for the second earner in a married-couple family, and would also increase the current disincentive for a cohabiting couple to marry.

A PROPOSAL FOR A REFUNDABLE
CHILDCARE CREDIT

A mechanism for reducing childcare expenses that builds on the current tax system is alteration of the Child and Dependent Care Tax Credit (CDCTC), which is calculated as a percentage of expenses paid to a service provider for the care of children under age 13 (and for other dependents who are unable to care for themselves). The percentage of the cost that is refunded through the credit can be as much as 35 percent for persons with incomes less than $15,000 and falls to 20 percent for persons with incomes over $43,000. This credit sounds as though it would be attractive to poor parents facing child-care expenses, but it has a defect in that regard: unlike the EITC, it is not refundable, so poor families whose *taxable* income is too low to generate a tax liability don't actually receive the credit. The National Academies report proposes to make the CDCTC a fully refundable credit so that it could be added on as an additional benefit for a family that owes no income tax or has negative taxes due to the EITC. They also propose expanding the percentage to be refunded to 100 percent of actual expenses on a preschool child up to a maximum of $4,000 ($6,000 for more than one child). If the child is age 5–12, the percentage to be refunded would be 70 percent up to a maximum of $3,000 ($6,000 for more than one child). The full credit would be applied for families with income of less than $25,000, then would phase out by reducing it as income rises until completely phased out at an income of $70,000.

The National Academies estimate is that this action alone would reduce child SPM poverty by 1.2 percentage points, and would particularly benefit black and single-parent families. That is only half of the 2.5 percentage point reduction that our policy simulation predicted from a truly universal childcare system, but the National Academies' proposal has the considerable advantage that it could be directly implemented by adjusting the existing tax system without generating complex interactions with state and local preschool systems. Based on our policy simulations, a policy that reduces or eliminates childcare costs is of lesser value to married-couple families, and the National Academies simulation also shows a differential benefit for single parents when the CDCTC is used as a policy lever.

The National Academies estimate of the annual budget for the enhanced CDCTC is $5.1 billion. The unsuccessful proposal of the Obama administration to extend free preschool to all children at age 4 in families below 200 percent of the poverty level and to extend Head Start for younger children involved an expenditure of approximately $6.6 billion per year for 10 years but was predicated on matching expenditures by states and localities.

The conclusion seems to be that the principal benefit of a more generous, high-quality childcare system, however implemented, is not so much a direct reduction in poverty as it is a response to a major reason why the adults in a family with children may be reluctant to take a job. If the goal is to enhance work incentives for low-income families, then focusing a refundable CDCTC on families with young children appears to be a relatively cost-effective approach. In addition, improvements in access to preschools focused on improving educational outcomes would have reduced poverty as a by-product. Later in this chapter we will examine very recent policy proposals that involve both the CDCTC and the availability of childcare and pre-kindergarten education.

PROPOSALS FOR CHILD ALLOWANCES

Recent suggestions for a CA in the United States include a proposal (with three variations) by Shaefer et al. (2018), one by Bitler et al. (2018), and two alternatives from the National Academies report. These proposals are closely related to each other. All of them propose replacing the CTC and ACTC with a universal CA paid to all children who are citizens by birthright or naturalization, without regard to the earnings or citizenship status of their parents. The various proposals differ, however, in both the generosity of the benefits and the mechanisms by which they try to reduce the potentially large cost of a universal benefit.

From the standpoint of the potential for poverty alleviation the key questions are: How much does the CA provide per child, and how much (if at all) does that amount vary based on either the number of children in the family and/or the age of the children in it? The tradeoffs are discussed in detail by Shaefer et al. (2018), who offer three options. The most straightforward option is a CA that is identical for all children without regard to either the number of children in the family or their age, the same as in the policy simulation in chapter 4. Their simulations employ a standard of $250 per month for each child. They then consider a somewhat more generous option that would add an additional $50 per month for children under age 6 and a less generous option that would gradually decrease the per-child payment for additional children (for example, a family with three children would receive $550 per month in CA rather than $750 under the standard benefit option). The amount of poverty reduction that these three options generate depends on which variant one chooses. The authors' simulations predict that the baseline program would reduce child poverty by 6.4 percentage points, the more generous version by 6.9 percentage points, and the less generous version by 5 percentage points. One of the National Academies options also involves a $250 per month CA, and they estimate that it would reduce child poverty by 5.3 percentage points. These estimates are slightly more optimistic than those derived from our policy simulation, which predicted a 4.9 percentage point reduction.

Recognizing the potential cost of such a generous program, Bitler et al. (2018) propose a smaller CA of $2,000 per child. They insist that a $2,000 benefit "would be more than enough to provide meaningful benefits" (p. 51), but it is clear that they also have the goal of devising a CA proposal that is practically self-funding. They accomplish this by eliminating not only the CTC and ACTC, but also by substantially reducing the EITC, which would have its phase-in rate reduced to 7.65 percent and a maximum benefit (for the entire family) of a little more than $500. As they point out, every low-income family would receive more from the $2,000 CA than they would lose from the EITC adjustment. However, the overall structure of benefits would be refocused from the working poor, who would receive little net benefit, to families with negligible earnings. As a result, the impact of the proposal on family poverty would probably be small, less than 1 percentage point according to Wimer et al. (2018).

The National Academies report also considers a $2,000 CA, but it provides only one mechanism for reducing the cost: phasing out the CA benefit on the same schedule as the current CTC. In particular, the EITC would not be affected. This proposal would have a more substantial impact on poverty, an estimated overall reduction of child poverty by 3.4 percentage points. Unlike the Bitler et al. proposal, however, this proposal has a substantial net cost, estimated at $32.9 billion.

Only the National Academies report directly addresses the question of which groups benefit most. Their analysis shows larger reductions for black children and children in single-parent families, similar to the policy simulation results in table 4.8. One can presume that the Bitler et al. proposal would also be favorable to those same groups, which have lower family work effort than the other groups, but not groups such as foreign-born Hispanics and married couples that have high work effort and reliance on the EITC. The Shaefer et al. proposals resemble our policy simulations closely enough that they would be likely to reach a similar conclusion: that a generous CA generally reduces poverty by a similar *proportion* (more than one-third, but usually less than one-half) in all groups.

The work incentive effects of a CA are complex. The basic idea of a "universal" CA is that, unlike tax credits and means-tested programs, the benefits will not be "clawed back" if the family increases its earnings, avoiding the work disincentive generated by a benefit reduction rate. However, cost considerations may require that some benefits be phased out, and it is also reasonable to expect that some families, particularly two-parent families, will choose to "spend" a portion of the allowance by trading work time for family time. The National Academies simulation of the basic $250/month

CA estimated that there would be some reduction in earnings so that child poverty would be reduced by only 5.3 percentage points rather than 6.4 percentage points if the CA had no effect on work incentives. The reduction in the EITC that is built into the Bitler et al. (2018) proposal would also reduce work incentives, especially if the CA is counted as income when calculating means-tested benefits.

Summarizing these results, instituting a CA would bring the American system for supporting the financial needs of children closer to systems in countries that have lower child poverty rates than the US. There are reasons to favor the CA mechanism. If the program is available to most families, it loses the stigma of being a "poverty program," though complete universality increases the amount of money flowing through the program budget. Perhaps the most substantial impediment to a CA is political acceptance of the idea that supporting children should be directly addressed through targeted expenditures rather than focusing on work incentives for the adults in the family. As the policy simulations in table 4.8 suggested, however, a CA and a work program could have complementary effects.

A POLICY ALTERNATIVE TO A CHILD ALLOWANCE: EXPAND MEANS-TESTED TRANSFERS

As chapter 3 showed, the principal means-tested programs do not distribute money: SNAP benefits can only be spent on food, and rental subsidies can only be spent on rent. It seems to be more politically attractive to help poor families to pay for necessities like food or housing than to give them money to spend as they please. Economists often question whether the restriction on SNAP expenses is relevant in that most recipient families spend more on food than their SNAP benefit and can therefore just use their SNAP benefit to free up cash for other purchases, though the importance of this phenomenon has been called into question (Hastings and Shapiro, 2018). That is the reason why SNAP and housing subsidies are treated as being "the same as cash" in calculating SPM poverty. Expanding SNAP and housing subsidies would employ existing bureaucratic structures to increase the resources available to those who are eligible.

Based on the size of the program and the fact that it is available everywhere, SNAP expansion is the obvious candidate for increasing family resources through transfer payments. To calibrate the amount by which SNAP benefits might be increased, it is useful to draw on the analysis by Gundersen et al. (2018), which focuses on family "food insecurity." Food insecurity is measured by the answers to questions like, "Were you ever hungry but did not eat because you couldn't afford enough food?" or "Did a child in the household ever not eat for a full day because you couldn't afford enough food?" Slightly more than half of all SNAP recipients report some degree of food insecurity during the previous year. Based on a set of questions about the extent of food insecurity, the authors find that the average amount of additional money that would alleviate food insecurity for families with children is $45.69 per week ($2,376 per year). In addition, the National Academies proposal suggests that the cost of food security for a teenager is about $30 per month larger than the amount built into the current SNAP benefit formula.

The National Academies (2019) proposal simulates the effect of two possible levels of additional generosity, increasing SNAP benefits by either 20 percent or 30 percent. The larger of these two is estimated to increase average benefits per family by approximately $1,900 per year. Both proposals also incorporate an additional $360 per year for each teenager and an additional $180 per year for each school-age child, the latter to be distributed during the summer months when school lunch programs are not available. The estimated child poverty reductions from these proposals are substantial: 1.7 percentage points for the 20 percent increase in benefits and 2.3 percentage points for the 30 percent increase in benefits. Since tables 3.14 and 3.15 showed that SNAP recipiency is much more common among poor unmarried families and somewhat more common among poor blacks and native-born Hispanics, these groups would differentially benefit from a SNAP expansion.

In the same vein as the SNAP proposals, the National Academies report also proposes an expansion of housing vouchers. Housing vouchers have considerable potential for poverty alleviation, as they typically serve to restrict housing costs to 30 percent of income. However, as we pointed out in chapter 3, housing vouchers, unlike SNAP, are not a genuine "entitlement," because the program is not funded to provide the benefit to most of those eligible to receive it. About 20 percent of eligible families actually receive vouchers, another 20 percent are on waitlists, and the remaining 60 percent of eligible families are excluded, either because the waitlists are closed or because there are no suitable rentals from landlords willing to accept the vouchers. According to HUD data, even if HUD vouchers were a fully funded entitlement, 30 percent of the recipients would not find suitable housing. Seeing underfunding as the basic problem, the National Academies report simulates the effects of funding vouchers to be used by 50 to 70 percent of the eligible families that are not currently receiving any form of subsidized housing. The estimated decrease in child poverty is 2.1 percentage points with 50 percent take-up and 3 percentage points for 70 percent take-up, slightly larger than the effect of the SNAP expansions. The National Academies' simulations suggest that the benefits would differentially reduce poverty among non-white and single-parent families, which chapter 3 showed to be the principal recipients of the current programs.

Because food and housing are essential expenditures, one would expect that subsidizing both of those expenditures simultaneously would have substantial effects on poverty, and the National Academies simulations suggest that this expectation is correct. At the lower levels of the two expansions the program expansions can be combined to reduce child poverty by 3.8 percentage points and at the higher levels by 5.3 percentage points. That is, just expanding these two in-kind programs in plausible ways would be expected to reduce child poverty substantially.

That said, expansion of SNAP and housing vouchers come at considerable cost. The estimated budget impact of the two SNAP proposals is $26.4 to $37.4 billion per year, larger than the National Academies' EITC proposal, which had a cost of $19.3 to $21.8 billion per year. For this reason, the EITC proposal would have a lower cost per child raised out of poverty than either of the SNAP proposals. The EITC and SNAP proposals could, however, be considered as complementary policies rather than substitutes. The projected costs of the housing voucher expansions would be in the range of $24.1 to $34.9 billion per year, somewhat smaller than the costs of the SNAP expansions despite having larger impacts on child poverty. A major benefit of a generous SNAP program, however, is that its relatively simple set of eligibility rules and its widespread administrative structure permit SNAP benefits to be quickly deployed in recessions (Hoynes and Schanzenbach, 2019), while housing vouchers may be viewed as more of a long-run solution, especially in areas with unusually high housing costs.

COMPARATIVE COST-EFFECTIVENESS

Table 5.1 summarizes the results from the principal alternatives described in this chapter. The second column indicates whether the benefits arise at least in part from an increase in family earnings or whether they arise in spite of a negative effect on family earnings. The third column gives the estimated poverty reduction, measured as percentage points of reduction in child poverty. The fourth column records approximate estimates of the annual cost that would be borne by the federal government budget. The final column is a measure of cost-effectiveness: the annual cost of each percentage point of poverty. One way to think about the size of these expenditures is to compare them to the National Academy estimate that child poverty costs $800 billion to $1.1 trillion per year due to increased crime, worsened health, and lower earnings when poor children become adults. This leads to the conclusion that each percentage point reduction in child poverty would reduce this long-run cost by roughly $60 billion per year.

Table 5.1   **Effect of Policies and Policy Packages on Child Poverty Rate**

	Effect on Earnings	Percentage Point Reduction in Child Poverty	Annual Cost ($ Billions)	Cost per 1% Reduction ($ Billions)
Proposal				
$10.25 Minimum Wage	Positive	1.5	3.7 Surplus	2.5 Surplus
$12 Minimum Wage + Employer Tax Credit	Positive	2.3	0.0	0.0
Increase Work Requirements	Positive	Small if any	Unknown Surplus	N/A
Job Guarantee	Positive	6.9	654	94.8
Targeted Wage Subsidy	Positive	0.3	16	53.3
Increase EITC Phase-In Rate	Positive	2.1	19.3	9.2
Increase Childcare Credit	Positive	1.2	5.1	4.3
$2,000 Child Allowance Replaces CTC	Negative	3.4	32.9	9.7
Expand SNAP	Negative	2.3	37.4	16.2
Expand Housing Vouchers	Negative	3.0	34.9	11.7

Since the cost estimates were not created with a common methodology, differences in cost-effectiveness are not precisely comparable. It is therefore useful to put the cost-effectiveness estimates into groups that differ substantially.

Three of the proposals are essentially costless. Work requirements would actually generate some net revenue, but the most likely outcome is that they would scarcely reduce poverty at all, so they are not really relevant to the topic of poverty reduction. Minimum wage increases are also essentially costless because the increase in the federal minimum wage would generate tax revenue (especially payroll tax revenue) in spite of some possible loss of low-wage jobs and some increases in EITC benefits. The Romich and Hill (2018) proposal uses the increased tax revenue from a $12 minimum wage to provide transition job opportunities for the unemployed, generating an estimated poverty reduction of 2.3 percentage points at zero net cost.

At the opposite end of the cost spectrum, the Paul et al. (2018) job guarantee would generate the largest reduction in poverty, but the cost per percentage point is estimated at more than $90 billion, by far the largest amount of any proposal. However, the job guarantee is not just a transfer of resources; it is a deployment of resources to produce goods and services, so its real cost-effectiveness depends on the value that society places on those goods and services, not just the benefits of poverty reduction. If the output has a value of 75 percent of the cost, as Ellwood and Welty (2000) suggest may be possible, then the remaining cost per percentage point would fall to $22.5 billion. The wage subsidy proposed by Dutta-Gupta (2018) is a much less expensive alternative but has a very small impact on poverty, so it is also relatively cost-inefficient at a cost exceeding $50 billion per percentage point of poverty reduction.

The two tax credit proposals have a relatively low cost for each percentage point of poverty reduction. Enhancing the childcare credit and making it fully refundable would be a relatively inexpensive way to offset an impediment to parental work, reducing poverty by 1.2 percentage points at the relatively low estimated cost of $4.3 billion per percentage point. Increasing the phase-in rate of the EITC would generate almost twice the poverty reduction (2.1 percentage points), but at almost 4 times the cost, so the estimated cost per percentage point is larger at $9.2 billion. Although these tax-credit proposals are relatively cost-effective, they have one obvious defect: they are of little or no benefit to families with adults who are unemployed, underemployed, or out of the labor force entirely.

Three of the policies listed in table 5.1 directly generate purchasing power for poor families. The largest poverty reduction and the lowest net cost is a $2,000 CA. It achieves a 3.4 percentage point reduction in poverty at a less than $10 billion cost per percentage point, the cost having been reduced by eliminating the CTC and phasing out the CA for high-income families. The last two proposals in table 5.1 involve expansion of SNAP and housing vouchers, the most important in-kind transfers. These proposals are slightly less cost-effective than the CA, with less poverty reduction for a higher cost. That they are less cost-effective than a CA is partly due to the work disincentive generated by high benefit reduction rates and partly by the fact that in-kind transfers, particularly housing vouchers, are not truly universal.

SUMMARIZING THE PROPOSALS

The only proposal covered in this chapter that approximates the goal of reducing poverty by half is the Job Guarantee proposal, which practically eliminates the work gap through public employment and reduces the wage gap by offering wages that would become de facto minimum wages. In principle such a program could be tailored to meet the needs of those who would ordinarily have trouble finding suitable work due to job-market liabilities such as disability, inadequate education, poor command of English, heavy family responsibilities, a criminal record, or prejudiced employers. However, combining payments to the workers with the managerial and administrative costs of the program leads to costs that only seem to be cost-effective if the goods and services produced by the workers are regarded as having considerable social value beyond the alleviation of poverty.

If the mass creation of publicly funded jobs is regarded as excessively costly or politically unpalatable, the proposed alternative is often to "make work pay." Whether this is best done through minimum wages or the EITC is partly a matter of how an increased minimum wage might affect certain industries, regions, or demographic groups and partly a matter of how tax credits affect the federal budget. Neither of the proposals is likely to generate a very large reduction in poverty by itself. However, higher wages often lead to a higher EITC benefit, especially for single parents, so the simultaneous implementation of higher wages and a more generous EITC could lead to a dramatic reduction in the prevalence of the "working poor." But what about poor families with little or no earnings?

The proposals on the last three lines of table 5.1 all address poverty directly by increasing the purchasing power of low-income families. While none of the proposals comes close to reducing poverty by half, increasing the CA to $3,000 per year or simultaneously expanding both SNAP and housing vouchers could reduce poverty by more than 5 percentage points. The principal concern in addition to cost seems to be that generous transfer payments reduce work incentives, so some of the anti-poverty effect of the transfer is offset by lower earnings.

In short, there does not seem to be a single policy change that would dramatically reduce poverty in a cost-effective way. Chapter 4 ended with a table (table 4.6) that suggested that reducing poverty dramatically would require a mix of policies, and the National Academies report arrived at the same conclusion.

ALTERNATIVE POLICY PACKAGES FOR REDUCING CHILD POVERTY BY HALF: THE NATIONAL ACADEMIES REPORT

Although the National Academies committee included scholars with diverse political preferences, the report arrived at a consensus that there is no plausible "silver bullet" policy that could successfully address the mandate to reduce child poverty by half (essentially the same conclusion that we reached in chapter 4). In earlier parts of this chapter, we have summarized their analysis of almost every program identified as likely to reduce child poverty by at least 1 percentage point.

To make the most successful proposals clearer, the National Academies report initially focuses on two policy packages that reduce child poverty substantially but fail to meet the goal. One of these is a "work-oriented" package that combines these components: roughly doubling the phase-in rate for the EITC and increasing the maximum credit by approximately $1,000; making the CDCTC fully refundable and increasing the share of expenses that are creditable, as described in the discussion earlier in the chapter; and an increase in the minimum wage to $10.25. This program would lead to a substantial increase in employment, but it would only decrease child poverty by 2.5 percentage points. It would cost about $8.7 billion, or $3.5 billion per percentage point. This combination is so cost-effective that some components of it are incorporated into the other policy packages. Our estimates in table 4.4 show that this policy package could be more effective if it were more generous, as the combination of a $12 minimum wage with a substantial EITC expansion could reduce poverty by more than 6 percentage points and by more than 10 percentage points among black and foreign-born Hispanic families and among unmarried families, whether partnered or not.

The other policy package in the National Academies report that does not succeed combines the same tax-credit changes as the first, but instead of increasing the minimum wage, it replaces the CTC with a $2,000 CA. This program combination would be more effective than the first, reducing child poverty by 4.3 percentage points, but also more expensive, with a projected annual cost of $44.5 billion, which is $10.3 billion per percentage point. This policy package could also be more effective if made more generous, as our estimates in table 4.5 suggest, though a more generous CA would be very costly unless it was targeted on the low-income population and phased out quickly as income rises.

The National Academies report finds just two policy packages that succeed in cutting child poverty in half. One of these combines the same tax-credit policies described in the previous paragraph with a 35 percent increase in SNAP benefits and full funding of housing vouchers. This package is estimated to decrease child poverty by 6.6 percentage points, and as tables 3.14 and 3.15 showed, these programs are especially beneficial to groups with high poverty rates. The work disincentives of the SNAP and housing expansions are more than offset by the work incentives of the tax credits, but the annual cost rises to $90.7 billion per year, a cost of $13.7 billion per percentage point.

The National Academies policy package with the largest poverty reduction expands the EITC by 40 percent. It also adopts the minimum wage increase to $10.25 from the "work-oriented" package and combines it with a $2,700 CA that replaces the CTC. In addition, it incorporates two smaller changes: a program to assure that families receiving child support receive at least $100 per month and restoring eligibility to legal immigrants for the CA and all existing means-tested programs. This combination is estimated to reduce child poverty by 6.8 percentage points. Because of the relatively generous EITC expansion and the minimum wage increase, this combination expands employment and earnings, while the more generous CA provides benefits to families that are not as directly connected to the labor market. Funding for the more generous EITC and CA drives the annual cost up to $108.8 billion, or $16 billion per percentage point.

BIDEN ADMINISTRATION PROPOSALS

Subsequent to the completion of this chapter, the Biden administration has released major policy proposals that have the potential to reduce poverty in families with children. Some of these policies are targeted directly on that goal, while in other cases reduced poverty is a plausible by-product of a policy with more general goals.

Broadly speaking, the policy proposals can be separated into three categories. First, there is a set of policies focused on generating employment opportunities. We know that increased employment opportunities for members of poor families could generate large reductions in family poverty. Second, there are proposals which can potentially reduce poverty by providing services that may make it easier for parents to maintain full-time employment, and in some cases these proposals may also provide additional job opportunities. And third, there are proposals to increase the resources available to families with children directly by altering the details of the federal income tax credit structure.

The principal policy component addressing job opportunities is the set of policies that came to be known as the Infrastructure Investment and Jobs Act. As we have emphasized, the value of such policies will ultimately be judged by the value of the infrastructure they fund, but as the name of the law implies, job creation is also a major goal of the legislation. The question here is whether those jobs are likely to be available to the unemployed in poor families with children. Carnevale and Smith (2021) and Kane (2021) provide approximate descriptions of the workforce that is likely to be required by the infrastructure projects that the legislation is designed to subsidize. They find that the occupational structure of infrastructure work does not require extraordinary educational attainment, with 37 percent of employees having only a high-school diploma and 17 percent of employees lacking even that, and these numbers suggest that there will be opportunities for poor adults. Moreover, the infrastructure occupations are relatively well-paid, about $3 per hour more than other occupations with a similar education profile. Unfortunately, 90 percent of all employees in the relevant occupations are men, so poor women in families with children are unlikely to find employment opportunities in these fields. Carnevale and Smith also show that while many of these occupations have limited educational requirements, about one-third of the jobs with limited educational requirements require at least six months of training. They conclude that successfully filling the infrastructure jobs is going to require a "ramping up" of training programs, and the corresponding analysis by Kane argues for the creation of an "infrastructure talent pipeline." Unfortunately, funding of the required training is not included in any of the current legislation, reducing the potential of the new infrastructure jobs to reduce family poverty.

A second set of policy components affect the services available to poor families, primarily the proposals to make pre-K education universal for students ages three and four to provide childcare centers for students age less than three that are free of charge for low-income families, and to reduce the long waiting line for in-home elder care paid for by Medicaid. Since table 1.3 suggested that over 6 percent of poor families with children have the head's parent in the home, the third component is not entirely irrelevant, but we will focus on the other two. The chapter 4 simulations suggested that universal childcare, whether provided entirely in centers or partly in pre-K schools for those who are old enough, could have a direct impact on family poverty (as much as 2.5 percentage points) and these impacts could increase by an additional 3 to 5 percentage points if the provision of childcare enables unemployed parents who have been serving as caretakers to find employment. Whether these programs would actually provide job opportunities for poor parents is less clear. The new jobs are potentially numerous, but many of them, particularly in pre-K schools, would require substantial educational prerequisites.

The third set of policy components involves tax credits. As we know from information provided in chapter 3, tax credits, especially the EITC, already have considerable power to reduce child poverty, and in subsequent chapters we have explored the potential benefits of expanding the EITC and other tax credits as well. The current proposals involve three tax credits: the EITC, the CDCTC, and the CTC. The proposed EITC expansion is focused on childless taxpayers and thus has no direct impact on child poverty, though it could enable some noncustodial parents to keep up with child support. The current proposals focus on the other two tax credits that can impact a poor family's purchasing power directly.

The proposed change in the CDCTC would make it much more beneficial to low-income families. The current tax credit for families with incomes under $15,000 is restricted to 35 percent of care expenses and decreases as income rises with a maximum total of $3,000 for one child under the age of

13 or $6,000 for two or more, and it is not refundable if the credit exceeds the family's tax liability. The proposal increases the share of expenses to 50 percent, increases the maximum to $4,000 for one child under the age of 13 or $8,000 for two or more, and is refundable if the credit exceeds the family's tax liability. Since the allowable expenses may include after-school and summer care, this proposal has the potential to allow working parents to expand hours, though Sawhill and Welch (2021) have pointed out that the needs of most working parents would be more effectively met by the universal childcare and pre-K proposals discussed above.

The most impactful proposal is to create a generous and fully refundable CTC. The current CTC begins to phase in at a rate of $0.15 per dollar earned after earned income reaches $2,500, a built-in work incentive. The maximum refundable credit is currently $1,400 per child (though up to $2,000 per child can be credited against tax liabilities), and the definition of a child ends at age 16. The proposal is to convert the CTC into a fully refundable tax credit of $3,600 for every child under age six and $3,000 for every child ages six to 17. This is an entirely different tax-credit design, essentially a CA distributed through the tax system, and it includes the possibility of monthly distribution, allowing the family to plan ahead. The most recent assessment by Marr et al. (2021) estimates that the expansion would cause child poverty to fall by about 5 percentage points, and by 8 to 9 percentage points for black and Hispanic children. These estimates are similar to the simulations in chapter 4 and the National Academies estimates, though those proposals are somewhat different in their generosity. The size of the reduction in child poverty has been challenged, however, because it does not account for the effect of eliminating the work incentives built into the current CTC. Corinth et al. (2021) estimate that the number of working parents who would leave the labor force after receiving the revised CTC would increase child poverty by almost half as much as the monthly payments would reduce child poverty. The CTC expansion has a cost of about $120 million per year (Sawhill and Welch, 2021). However, the expanded credit does not even begin to phase out until annual income reaches $75,000 for a single filer or $150,000 for a couple fling jointly, so it is not actually targeted on poor families. Consequently, the cost-effectiveness of the CTC in reducing poverty is partially decided by how much of the $120 million annual cost is expended on families with incomes far in excess of the poverty threshold.

Policy packages often pursue multiple goals that are not entirely compatible and generate tradeoffs. In pursuing the goal of addressing poverty among families with children the creation of a generous and fully refundable CTC is a very appealing alternative, but its expense and the loss of the work incentive built into the current CTC design suggest that, as Sawhill and Welch suggest, greater generosity of the EITC for families with children might have been an alternative emphasis. They also suggest that the package might better have considered whether a major expansion of the CDCTC would really be necessary if the childcare and pre-K components are fully funded and efficiently expanded. Despite those tradeoffs, however, the policy package as a whole would directly reduce child poverty and also address some of the common barriers to parental employment.

CONCLUSION: TRADEOFFS

The policy proposals reviewed in this chapter involve tradeoffs, and the National Academies report emphasizes that the overall goal of cutting child poverty in half can only be achieved at considerable cost whatever the specific components of the policy package. While this emphasis is accurate, we want to provide greater clarity about which goals are best met by which components.

If the fundamental goal is to meet the challenge that was set to the National Academies of cutting child poverty in half, the analysis in both this chapter and its predecessor suggest that the most straightforward policy is the initiation of a CA that is sufficiently generous to lift many families out of poverty regardless of the family's work effort, and the Biden administration's Child Credit proposal would accomplish that goal in a way that is compatible with the existing tax system. It is also one of the few policies (reducing out-of-pocket medical expenses is another) that reduces poverty in about the same proportion for every race and family status group. The problems with the CA and other programs that directly support poor families are that they do not provide a work incentive and also have a large impact on the federal budget.

Most of the policy packages we have studied operate on the assumption that a major goal is to incentivize poor families to escape poverty through increased family work effort, generally by policies that "make work pay." The principal policy tools are increases in the federal minimum wage and increased generosity of the EITC, though one might wish to treat an enhanced and fully refundable childcare credit as part of this same category. The most successful policy packages generally include a minimum wage increase, with the differences being a question of how far and how fast. Those who object to minimum wage increases often view enhancing the EITC as an alternative, but the results reported in both this chapter and its predecessor indicate that enhancing the EITC is actually more effective if combined with an increase in the minimum wage. The greatest impact on poverty through work effort would be achieved with a job guarantee that provides suitable work at living wages for the unemployed and underemployed, but even aside from the complexities of administering such a program, it would be very costly.

A third criterion that we have emphasized in this chapter is cost-effectiveness. An increase in the minimum wage is an attractive component of a policy package because it generates tax revenue that reduces the overall cost of the package. A CA can reduce child poverty directly, but its effectiveness would depend on its generosity, and generosity increases the cost. Some of the same benefits for needy children can be delivered through existing means-tested programs like SNAP and housing vouchers, but these programs are also costly and have adverse impacts on work incentives due to high benefit reduction rates.

There are two additional policy options that we discussed in chapter 4 that deserve consideration as part of potential policy packages. One of these is increased government support for high-quality preschool options that reduce or eliminate the need for working parents to bear that expense, a policy option that is built into the Biden administration proposals. The other is government policies that reduce or eliminate out-of-pocket medical expenses. Such programs are not necessarily targeted on poor families, but either of these programs could reduce their poverty rates as much as 2 to 3 percentage points even if that reduction is a by-product of programs evaluated on broader criteria.

The lesson seems to be that there are no policies that by themselves balance poverty reduction and work incentives in a highly cost-effective way. Programs that enhance work incentives are inherently limited in their capacity to decrease poverty because many families have limited ability to respond to the incentives unless accompanied by expensive programs that guarantee suitable employment opportunities and offset the expenses associated with parental work. The most straightforward means of achieving poverty goals generally reduce work incentives. Programs constrained by strict budgets are simply doomed to fail. There are policy packages that can be truly successful in reducing poverty among families with children, but they require policymakers to accept the tradeoffs involved.

Conclusion

The last chapter of a book like this should provide answers to the question: "So What?" We take for granted the proposition that reducing poverty among families with children is a desirable goal, whether the reasons are primarily moral or practical. In fact, as we pointed out from the start, reducing child poverty has the potential to be an excellent investment, as the children removed from poverty grow up to be more productive, to be less dependent on government safety-net programs in later life, and to be less likely to have poor children of their own that propel a cycle of poverty into a subsequent generation.

To create an understanding of poverty in families with children we devoted the first three chapters to describing trends in demography, in labor markets, and in government policies that have affected poverty rates among families with children over the course of the last 25 years. All of these trends have implications for future policy decisions. The succeeding two chapters explored various paths that future policies might take, first with a set of broad policy alternatives and then with a set of specific proposals put forward in recent years. We have evaluated these potential policies based on their effectiveness in reducing family poverty, especially among groups with especially high initial poverty rates.

Chapter 1 focused on three trends, the first two of which carry through the entire book as we explore differentials among demographic groups. The first trend is increased racial and ethnic diversity, especially due to the growth of the Hispanic population, both native-born and foreign-born. The second trend is the increasing share of families in which the family head is unmarried, partly a consequence of an increased share of families in which the head is cohabiting rather than married. Since these groups with rising shares of the population all have poverty rates above the national average, these trends all tend to increase the national poverty rate, and our analysis of policy options looks directly at how these different groups are affected. The third trend is the general improvement in the educational attainment of the adults in families with children. While it is true that the most rapidly growing groups have relatively low educational attainment, the proportion with both high-school diplomas and college degrees has risen in every group.

Although our policy chapters focus on policies affecting labor markets, government benefits, or both, these trends in demography have additional policy implications that involve family poverty. For example, policies that address the unique challenges facing immigrants and their children include the provision of paths to citizenship and the creation of programs that provide access to health care, training opportunities for adults, and educational opportunities for their children. As to the increasing share of families with an unmarried family head, effective policies could involve improved access to affordable family planning services as a mechanism for reducing non-marital births and the elimination of marriage penalties built into government programs such as the EITC. As to education, there would be many benefits to providing high-quality education that begins at age three as well as broader access to education after high school, particularly programs that provide a clear path to a rapidly evolving labor market.

Chapter 2 focused on labor markets, ultimately concluding that policies that would dramatically increase the number of families escaping poverty through higher earnings will require some mix of appropriate job opportunities, higher wage rates, or both, policies that are discussed in subsequent chapters. However, the background of labor-market trends has additional implications that need to be taken into account. While many of the problems in labor markets for workers with limited educational attainment have been generated by some mix of globalized supply chains and skill-biased technical change, there have also been institutional factors that have made labor markets more difficult for workers in families that are at risk of falling into poverty. Among the most important of these are inadequate labor-market protections due in part to the decline of unions, as well as licensing requirements and non-compete clauses that inhibit both economic and geographical mobility.

Perhaps the most important trend, however, has been the rapid convergence of the gender gap in labor-force participation and the failure of institutions to adapt to this trend. The decline in labor-force participation among men has been driven to a significant degree by aging, disability, the stigma attached to a criminal record, and the decline of some traditionally male occupations, some of which could be addressed by a training environment that is not exclusively focused on the young. Meanwhile, expanding opportunities for women have been inhibited by slow progress in developing workplaces that are genuinely family-friendly, a problem that could be addressed in part by regulations mandating paid family leave or advance work scheduling, but especially with childcare policies that support women who want to work, policies that are directly addressed in chapters 4 and 5. The other trend that is extensively explored in chapter 2 is actually the lack of a trend: the virtual stagnation of median real wages and the gradual diminution of the real minimum wage in many states. Policies involving the federal minimum wage and wage supplementation by the EITC are also discussed in chapters 4 and 5.

The trends described in chapter 3 show the advantages of the Supplemental Poverty Measure as a poverty standard. The increasing importance of tax credits and in-kind transfer payments has changed the way we look at a family's resources, the deduction of work and childcare expenses has provided a more realistic measure of the family's expendable earnings, and the deduction of MOOP has identified families that have been rendered poor by expenditures that are often unexpected and sometimes very large.

The potential for alleviating family poverty through the further expansion of tax credits and in-kind transfers and potential poverty reductions from subsidized childcare and medical care are all explored in chapter 4 or chapter 5 or both, but some other policy implications are not. In particular, social insurance payments remain important in reducing or eliminating poverty in families eligible for these benefits. For example, a more generous treatment of disability would address poverty in families who may have little or no earnings potential. Likewise, the shift of emphasis from income support to earnings supplements has weakened the safety net during periods of high unemployment. An unemployment system that is more carefully integrated with means-tested programs could dramatically reduce the impact of recessions on families who are suddenly cast into poverty by lost earnings, a policy that would be particularly beneficial for the non-white and single-parent families that are often among the first to be laid off.

While chapters 4 and 5 are informed by the trends laid out in chapters 1 through 3, the focus of the chapters is on the alternative futures that would arise from various policy approaches, separately and in combination. To address the question of whether a work-based policy is "enough," chapter 4 begins by setting an arbitrary target defining "enough": reducing poverty in our target populations by half. The initial policy simulations show that expanding employment at current minimum wage rates cannot achieve the target unless suitable full-time employment is found for *every* person who is unemployed (a U6 unemployment rate of zero) *and* new half-time jobs are accepted by *every* adult who is not currently seeking work due to family responsibilities or obligations as a student. Having even half of the job offers accepted would require a public employment program of unprecedented cost and complexity, yet would not come close to being "enough" unless the nationwide minimum wage is raised to at least $12. Because the "working poor" are numerous, a policy program that reduces the U6 unemployment rate by half *and* imposes a national minimum wage of $12 *and* increases the EITC by half can reduce the poverty rate by half for every group except non-Hispanic whites, but completely ignores families with adults who are unsuited for the jobs being offered or unable to accept them due to disability or family obligations. This leads to three major conclusions: (1) reducing the unemployment rate among adults in poor families would reduce poverty, but not "enough"; (2) "making work pay" with higher wages or a more generous EITC would also reduce poverty; and (3) these policies should be considered as complementary to each other, but even as a package they do not address the impediments that keep many families from escaping poverty.

The other policy alternatives explored in chapter 4 are of two kinds. One policy option is a universal CA that would provide additional income for all families with children, a policy that would be most easily implemented through a CTC distributed monthly. The others directly address two large expenditures that affect many poor families: childcare expenses and MOOP. An annual CA of $3,500 per child would by itself reduce poverty among families with children by at least one-third and in some groups, especially the unmarried, it would come close to reducing it by half. Unlike the CA, eliminating large expenditures on childcare or MOOP would only alleviate the poverty of particular segments of the poor population, but these are particularly vulnerable segments that are frequently unable to benefit from labor-market policies. Both of these policies would reduce poverty by one-fourth or more by themselves and could be combined with almost any labor-market policy (lower unemployment or higher wages or both) to reduce poverty by half. The ultimate conclusion of chapter 4 is that lower unemployment and higher wages can reduce poverty substantially if sufficiently generous, but a truly effective policy package must also include policies that increase income received from tax credits or transfer payments and reduce expenditures on childcare or medical care to be "enough" to reduce poverty rates by half, far less by some larger number.

Chapter 5 uses the information compiled in the previous chapters to review and assess specific policy proposals that have been put forth within the last few years. In addition to discussing specific details, we were able to add budgetary cost-effectiveness (cost of each percentage point of poverty reduction) as an additional standard of comparison. This added criterion has somewhat surprising consequences. For example, the most cost-effective policy is to increase the minimum wage, a policy that is likely to generate net revenue from increased payroll taxes. Another highly cost-effective policy is to increase the childcare credit and make it fully refundable, though politicians who express concern about cost-effectiveness are often skeptical of one or both of these inexpensive policies. Increasing the generosity of the EITC is also relatively cost-effective, as is an annual CA, the former being less effective and the latter more costly. Near the end of chapter 5 we review the proposals made by the Biden Administration that would have the effect of reducing child poverty, finding that several of them, including the creation of more generous and fully refundable child and childcare credits, are among the relatively cost-effective options. The only policy proposal that comes close to reducing poverty by half all by itself is a job guarantee proposal that comes close to achieving the results of the job-creation policy simulations in chapter 4, but it is by far the most expensive option.

The tradeoffs inherent in the individual policies suggest that there ought to be some consideration of policy packages that combine cost-effective options. Chapter 5 concludes with a review of policy combinations, some of which could be successful in reducing child poverty by half, proposals that succeed because they address the needs of families with varying connections to the labor market. One package combines an increase in both the minimum wage and the generosity of the EITC, and another also makes the CDCTC fully refundable, policies that are focused on reducing poverty among the working poor. Two of the packages address poverty among families with more limited attachment to the labor market, but in two different ways: in one case by increasing the generosity of the SNAP program and fully funding housing vouchers; in the other case by implementing a more generous and fully refundable CTC while adding changes in policy that would benefit legal immigrant families.

The importance of seeking policy packages that combine work incentives with more generous tax credits or transfer payments can be illustrated with a thought experiment involving a family of four. Depending on the exact family demographics, the SPM threshold for this family would be approximately $30,000. If there is one full-time worker in this family, the worker would need to earn a wage rate of about $15 per hour to reach this threshold (in this case the EITC is just about sufficient to cover taxes owed). As discussed in chapter 5, the provision of a sufficient number of family-friendly full-time jobs at that wage level would be prohibitively expensive. But simply filling the entire $30,000 gap with a CA plus SNAP benefits would also be very expensive, since the SNAP benefits for that family (approximately $10,000) would need to be supplemented by a CA of $6,700–$10,000 per child (depending on whether there are three children or only two), a level of generosity far in excess of anything that has ever been proposed. Yet a $3,000 CA added to the earnings of a single parent (with three children) who takes a half-time job at $15 per hour with no childcare cost would just about reach the poverty threshold, thanks largely to the EITC. That particular policy package is well within the range of those that we explored in chapter 5. The lesson of these thought experiments is that policy packages that reduce child poverty directly and also incentivize parental work take advantage of the fact that parental work and government generosity can be complementary and are more likely to be successful if they are designed in that way.

As successful as some policy packages combining work with tax credits and transfer payments might be, they do not incorporate some additional policies that the simulations in chapter 4 identified as desirable. First of all, they do not incorporate job programs targeted on unemployed persons who face obvious hurdles to employment such as a lack of a high-school diploma, poor language skills, a criminal record, or the need for flexible schedules for persons who have family responsibilities. Second, they often fail to address the needs of families facing extraordinary expenses on child and dependent care, which can be addressed by some combination of refundable tax credits that defray those expenses and high-quality childcare and pre-kindergarten schooling that provide the necessary care at little or no cost to the family. Yet a third cause of family poverty is the MOOP that could be addressed by making Medicaid nationwide. These policies do not have poverty reduction as their primary purpose, but nevertheless have the potential to reduce family poverty substantially, and that benefit deserves greater consideration when evaluating these policy options.

This entire book is built on the proposition that poverty among families with children is costly to society and that the alleviation of such poverty should be viewed as a fundamental government responsibility to be funded accordingly. A policy structure that perpetuates child poverty should be considered a failure to carry this responsibility, and what we have shown is that the current mix of jobs, wages, tax credits, and transfer payments has not been successful. That said, there are several programs that can be adjusted or expanded to improve outcomes, so it is not clear what policy package is "ideal." Parents want the best for their children, and policies that reward parents for supporting their families through work have been successful enough to suggest that expanding them is likely to reduce child poverty. But the job market does not provide sufficiently lucrative job opportunities to be consistently reliable, so successful policy packages will inevitably require the federal government to increase the generosity of tax credits and transfer payments enough to reduce child poverty in families for which work is simply "not enough."

Bibliography

Abraham, Katharine G., and Melissa Kearney. "Explaining the decline in the US employment-to-population ratio: A review of the evidence." *Journal of Economic Literature* 58 (Fall 2020): 585–643.

Akerlof, George A., Janet L. Yellen, and Michael L. Katz. "An analysis of out-of-wedlock childbearing in the United States." *The Quarterly Journal of Economics* 111, no. 2 (1996): 277–317.

Alesina, Alberto, Edward Glaeser, and Edward Ludwig Glaeser. *Fighting poverty in the US and Europe: A world of difference.* Oxford University Press, 2004.

Almond, Douglas, Hilary W. Hoynes, and Diane Whitmore Schanzenbach. "Inside the war on poverty: The impact of food stamps on birth outcomes." *Review of Economics and Statistics* 93, no. 2 (2011): 387–403.

Autor, David H. "Skills, education, and the rise of earnings inequality among the 'Other 99 percent.'" *Science*, 344, no. 6168 (2014): 843–851.

Autor, David H., and David Dorn. "The growth of low-skill service jobs and the polarization of the U.S. labor market." *American Economic Review* 103 (August 2013): 1553–1597.

Autor, David H., Claudia Goldin, and Lawrence F. Katz. "Extending the race between education and technology." *AEA Papers and Proceedings* 110 (May 2020): 347–351.

Autor, David H., David Dorn, and Gordon H. Hanson. "On the persistence of the China shock." NBER working paper no. 29401. October 2021.

Autor, David H., David Dorn, and Gordon H. Hanson. "The China syndrome: Local labor market effects of import competition in the United States." *American Economic Review* 103 (2013): 2121–2168.

Autor, David H., David Dorn, and Gordon H. Hanson. "When work disappears: Manufacturing decline and the falling marriage-market value of young men." *American Economic Review: Insights* 1, no. 2 (2019): 161–178.

Autor, David H., Lawrence F. Katz, and Melissa S. Kearney. "Trends in U.S. wage inequality: Revising the revisionists." *The Review of Economics and Statistics* 90 (May 2008): 300–323.

Baily, Martin Neil, and Barry P. Bosworth. "U.S. manufacturing: Understanding its past and its potential future." *Journal of Economic Perspective* 28 (Winter 2014): 3–26.

Baker, Bryan. *Estimates of the unauthorized immigrant population residing in the United States: January 2014.* Washington, DC: Department of Homeland Security, Office of Immigration Statistics, 2017.

Bastian, Jacob, and Katherine Michelmore. "The long-term impact of earned income tax credit on children's education and employment outcomes." *Journal of Labor Economics* 36, no. 4 (2018): 1127–1163.

Bauer, Lauren, Diane Whitmore Schanzenbach, and Jay Shambaugh. "Work requirements and safety net programs." *The Hamilton Project* (2018). Available at: https://www.hamiltonproject.org/assets/files/WorkRequirements_EA_web_1010_2.pdf.

Bauer, Lauren, Patrick Liu, Emily Moss, Ryan Nunn, and Jay Shambaugh. "All school and no work becoming the norm for American teens." *Up Front* (2019). https://www.brookings.edu/blog/up-front/2019/07/02/all-school-and-no-work-becoming-the-norm-for-american-teens/.

Bayer, Patrick, and Kerwin Kofi Charles. "Divergent paths: A new perspective on earnings differences between black and white men since 1940." *The Quarterly Journal of Economics* 130, no. 3 (2018): 1459–1501.

Becker, Gary. S. *A treatise on the family.* Enlarged edition. Cambridge, MA: Harvard University Press, 1991.

Bell, Alison, and Douglas Rice. *Congress prioritizes housing programs in 2018 finding Bill, rejects Trump administration proposals.* Washington, DC: Center on Budget and Policy Priorities. July 19, 2018.

Ben-Shalom, Yonatan, Robert Moffitt, and John Karl Scholz. "An assessment of the effectiveness of antipoverty programs in the United States." In *The Oxford handbook of the economics of poverty*, edited by Philip Jefferson, 2012.

Bitler, Marianne P., Annie Laurie Hines, and Marianne Page. "Cash for kids." *The Russell Sage Foundation Journal of the Social Sciences* 4, no. 2 (2018): 43–73.

Bitler, Marianne, Hilary Hoynes, and Elira Kuka. "Child poverty, the great recession, and the social safety net in the United States. *Journal of Policy Analysis and Management* 36, no. 2 (2017): 358–389.

Black, Sandra E., and Jesse Rothstein. "Policy brief 3: An expanded view of government's role in providing social insurance and investing in children." In *Economists for inclusive prosperity*, 2019. Available at: https://econfip.org/policy-briefs/an-expanded-view-of-governments-role-in-providing-social-insurance-and-investing-in-children.

Black, Sandra E., Diane Whitmore Schanzenbach, and Audrey Brietwieser. "The recent decline in women's labor force participation." The Hamilton Project, Brookings Institute. October 2017. https://www.brookings.edu/research/the-recent-decline-in-womens-labor-force-participation/.

Blank, Rebecca M. "Presidential address: How to improve poverty measurement in the United States." *Journal of the Association for Public Policy Analysis and Management* 27, no. 2 (2008): 233–254.

Blau, David, and Erdal Tekin. "The determinants and consequences of child care subsidies for single mothers in the USA." *Journal of Population Economics* 20, no. 4 (2007): 719–741.

Blau, David. "Child care subsidy programs." In *Means-tested programs in the United States*, edited by Robert A. Moffitt, 443–516. Chicago, IL: University of Chicago Press, 2003.

Blau, Francine D., and Lawrence M. Kahn. "Gender differences in pay." *Journal of Economic Perspectives* 14, no. 4 (2000): 75–99.

Blau, Francine, and Lawrence M. Kahn. "The gender wage gap: Extent, trends, and explanations." *Journal of Economic Literature* 55, no. 3 (2017): 789–865.

Borowczyk-Martins, Daniel, Jake Bradley, and Linas Tarasonis. "Racial discrimination in the U.S. labor market: Employment and wage differentials by skill." *Labour Economics* 50 (2018): 45–66.

Bound, John, Richard V. Burkhauser, and Austin Nichols. "Tracing the household income of SSDI and SSI applicants. *Research in Labor Economics* 22 (2003): 113–158.

Bressen, James. "Employers aren't just whining—the 'skills gap' is real." *Harvard Business Review*, August 25, 2014, https://hbr.org/2014/08/employers-arent-just-whining-the-skills-gap-is-real.

Broder, Tanya, Avideh Moussavian, and Jonathan Blazer. *Overview of immigrant eligibility for federal programs*. Washington, DC: National Immigration Law Center, 2015. https://www.nilc.org/issues/economic-support/overview-immeligfedprograms/.

Brown, Susan L., J. Bart Stykes, and Wendy D. Manning. "Trends in children's family instability." *Journal of Marriage and Family* 78, no. 5 (2016): 1173–1183.

Brown, Susan L., Wendy D. Manning, and J. Bart Stykes. "Family structure and child well-being: Integrating family complexity." *Journal of Marriage and Family* 77 no. 1 (2015): 177–190.

Budig, Michelle J. *The fatherhood bonus and the motherhood penalty: Parenthood and the gender gap in pay*. Washington, DC: The Third Way, 2014.

Budig, Michelle J., and Melissa J. Hodges. "Differences in disadvantage: Variation in the motherhood penalty across white women's earnings distribution." *American Sociological Review* 75, no. 5 (2010): 705–728.

Budig, Michelle J., and Melissa J. Hodges. "Statistical models and empirical evidence for differences in the motherhood penalty across the earnings distribution." *American Sociological Review* 79, no. 2 (2014): 358–364.

Budig, Michelle J., and Paula England. "The wage penalty for motherhood." *American Sociological Review* 66, no. 2 (2001): 204–225.

Cajner, Tomaz, Tyler Radler, David Ratner, and Ivan Vidangos. "Racial gaps in labor market outcomes in the last four decades and over the business cycle." Finance and Economics Discussion Series 2017-071. 2017. Washington, DC: Board of Governors of the Federal Reserve System. https://doi.org/10.17016/FEDS.2017-071.

Cappelli, Peter. "Skill gaps, skill shortages and skill mismatches: Evidence for the U.S." National Bureau of Economic Research, 2014, No. w20382.

Carnevale, Anthony P., and Nicole Smith. *15 million infrastructure jobs: An economic shot in the arm for the COVID-19 recession*. Washington, DC: Georgetown University Center on Education and the Workforce, 2021.

Carrington, William, Molly Dahl, and Justin Falk. *Growth in means-tested programs and tax credits for low-income households*. Congressional Budget Office, 2013.

Case, Ann, and Angus Deaton. "Mortality and morbidity in the 21st century." *Brookings Papers on Economic Activity* 2017 (2017): 397–476.

Cavanagh, Shannon E., and Aletha C. Huston. "The timing of family instability and children's social development." *Journal of Marriage and Family* 70, no. 5 (2008): 1258–1270.

Center on Budget and Policy Priorities. "Policy basics: The earned income tax credit," 2019. https://www.cbpp.org/research/federal-tax/the-earned-income-tax-credit.

Center on Budget and Policy Priorities. *Chart book: Temporary assistance for needy families*. Washington, DC, August 2020.

Charles, Kerwin Kofi, Erik Hurst, and Mariel Schwartz. "The Transformation of manufacturing and the decline in U.S. employment." NBER Working Paper No. 24468 (March 2018).

Cherlin, Andrew J. "American marriage in the early twenty-first century." *The Future of Children* 15, no. 2 (2005): 33–55.

Cherlin, Andrew J., Frank F. Furstenbert, Lindsay Chase-Lansdale, Kathleen E. Kiernan, Philip K Ronins, Dopnna Ruane Morrison, and Julien O. Teitler. "Longitudinal studies of effects of divorce on children in Great Britain and the United States." *Science* 252, no. 5011 (1991): 1386–1389.

Cherlin, Andrew, Erin Cumberworth, S. Philip Morgan, and Christopher Wimer. "The effects of the great recession on family structure and fertility." *Annals of the American Academy of Political and Social Science* 650, no. 1 (2013): 214–231.

Chester, Alisa, and Joan Alker. "Medicaid at 50: A look at the long-term benefits of childhood Medicaid." *Georgetown University Center for Children and Families* (July 2015). https://ccf.georgetown.edu/wp-content/uploads/2015/08/Medicaid-at-50_final.pdf.

Chetty, Raj, John Friedman, and Emmanuel Saez. "Using differences in knowledge across neighborhoods to uncover the impacts of the EITC on Earnings." *American Economic Review* 103, no. 7 (2013): 2683–2721.

Chetty, Raj, Nathaniel Hendren, Patrick Kline, and Emmanuel Saez. "Where is the land of opportunity? The geography of intergenerational mobility in the United States. *The Quarterly Journal of Economics* 129, no. 4 (2014): 1553–1623.

Chien, Nina. *Factsheet: Estimates of child care eligibility & receipt for fiscal year 2018*. Washington, DC: US Department of Health and Human Services, Office of the Assistant Secretary for Planning and Evaluation, 2021.

Child Trends, Data Bank. *Births to unmarried women, appendix 1*, September 2018.

Churchill, Brandon F., and Joseph J. Sabia. "The effects of minimum wages on low-skilled immigrants' wages, employment, and poverty." *Industrial Relations* 58, no. 2 (2019): 275–314.

Committee on Ways and Means, US House of Representatives. *Green book*. Washington, DC, 2018. https://greenbook-waysandmeans.house.gov/.

Congress of the United States, Congressional Budget Office. *The effects on employment and family income of increasing the federal minimum wage*. Washington, DC: The Congressional Budget Office, 2019.

Cooper, David. "One in nine U.S. workers are paid wages that can leave them in poverty, even when working full time." *Economic Snapshot* June 15, 2018. Washington, DC: Economic Policy Institute. https://www.epi.org/publication/one-in-nine-u-s-workers-are-paid-wages-that-can-leave-them-in-poverty-even-when-working-full-time/.

Cooper, David. "Workers of color are far more likely to be paid poverty-level wages than white workers." *Working Economics Blog* June 21, 2018. Washington, DC: Economic Policy Institute. https://www.epi.org/blog/workers-of-color-are-far-more-likely-to-be-paid-poverty-level-wages-than-white-workers/.

Copen, Casey E., Kimberly Daniels, and William D. Mosher. *First premarital cohabitation in the United States: 2006–2010 national survey of family growth.* No. 64. US Department of Health and Human Services, Centers for Disease Control and Prevention, National Center for Health Statistics, 2013.

Corinth, Kevin, Bruce D. Meyer, Matthew Stadnicki, and Derek Wu. "The anti-poverty, targeting, and labor supply effects of the proposed child tax credit expansion." National Bureau of Economic Research, no. 29366, 2021.

Couch, Kenneth A., and Robert Fairlie. "Last hired, first fired? Black-white unemployment and the business cycle." *Demography* 47, no. 1 (2010): 227–247.

Council of Economic Advisors. *Expanding work requirements in non-cash welfare programs.* Washington, DC: Executive Office of the President, July 2018. https://www.whitehouse.gov/wp-content/uploads/2018/07/Expanding-Work-Requirements-in-Non-Cash-Welfare-Programs.pdf.

Council of Economic Advisors. *Expanding work requirements in non-cash welfare programs.* Washington, DC: Executive Office of the President, July 2018. https://www.whitehouse.gov/wp-content/uploads/2018/07/Expanding-Work-Requirements-in-Non-Cash-Welfare-Programs.pdf.

Council of Economic Advisors. *The labor force participation rate since 2007: Causes and policy implications.* Washington, DC: Executive Office of the President, July 2014. https://obamawhitehouse.archives.gov/sites/default/files/docs/labor_force_participation_report.pdf.

Council of Economic Advisors. *The long-term decline in prime-age male labor force participation.* Washington, DC: Executive Office of the President, June 2016. https://obamawhitehouse.archives.gov/sites/default/files/pag/files/20160620_cea_primeage_male_lfp.pdf.

Craigie, Terry-Ann, Samuel L. Myers, Jr., and William A. Darity. "Racial differences in the effect of marriageable males on female family headship." *Journal of Demographic Economics* 84, no. 3 (2018): 231–256.

Curtin, Sally C., Stephanie J. Ventura, and Gladys M. Martinez. *Recent declines in nonmarital childbearing in the United States.* Washington, DC: US Department of Health and Human Services, Centers for Disease Control and Prevention, 2014. *National Center for Health Statistics (NCHS Data Brief No 162).* htttp://s3.documentcloud.org/documents/1273985/births.pdf.

Dahl, Gordon B., and Lance Lochner. "The impact of family income on child achievement: Evidence from the earned income tax credit." *American Economic Review* 102, no. 5 (2012): 1927–1956.

Dahl, Gordon B., and Lance Lochner. "The impact of family income on child achievement: Evidence from the earned income tax credit: Reply," *American Economic Review* 107, no. 2 (2017): 629–631.

Daly, Mary C., Bart Hobijn, and Joseph H. Pedtke. Disappointing facts about the black-white wage gap. *FRBSF Economic Letter* 26 (2017): 1–5.

Darity, William A., Jr. "A direct route to full employment." *Review of Black Political Economy* 37, no. 3 (2010): 179–181.

Davis, Elizabeth E., Caroline Carlin, Caroline Krafft, and Nicole D. Forry. "Do child care subsidies increase employment among low-income parent?" *Journal of Family and Economic Issues* 39, no. 4 (2018): 662–682.

De, Kuhelika, Ryan A. Compton, Daniel C. Giedeman. "Macroeconomic shocks and racial labor market differences." *Southern Economic Journal* 88, no. 2 (2021): 680–704.

Dickert-Conlin, Stacy, and Douglas Holtz-Eakin. "Employee-based versus employer-based subsidies to low-wage workers: A public finance perspective." In *Finding jobs: Work and welfare reform*, edited by David E. Card, and Rebecca M. Blank, 262–295. New York: Russell Sage Foundation, 2000.

Dube, Arindrajit. "Minimum wages and the distribution of family incomes." *American Economic Journal: Applied Economics* 11, no. 4 (2019): 268–304.

Duggan, Mark G., and Melissa Schettini Kearney. "The impact of child SSI enrollment on household outcomes." *Journal of Policy Analysis and Management* 26, no. 4 (2007): 861–886.

Duncan, Greg J., Pamela A. Morris, and Chris Rodrigues. "Does money really matter? Estimating impacts of family income on young children's achievement with data from random-assignment experiments. *Developmental Psychology* 47, no. 5 (2011): 1263–1279.

Dutta-Gupta, Indivar, Kali Grant, Julie Kerksick, Dan Bloom, and Ajay Chaudry. "Working to reduce poverty: A national subsidized employment proposal." *The Russell Sage Foundation Journal of the Social Sciences* 4, no. 3 (2018): 64–83.

East, Chloe N. "The effect of food stamps on children's health evidence from immigrants' changing eligibility." *Journal of Human Resources* 55, no. 2 (2020): 387–427.

Eberstadt, Nicholas. 2016. *Men without work: America's invisible crisis.* West Conshohocken, PA: Templeton Press.

Edin, Kathryn, and Maria J. Kefalas. *Promises I can keep: Why poor women put motherhood before marriage.* University of California Press, 2011.

Edin, Kathryn, Maria J. Kefalas, and Joanna M Reed. "A peek inside the black box: What marriage means for poor unmarried parents." *Journal of Marriage and Family* 66, no. 4 (2004): 1007–1014.

Eissa, Nada, and Hilary Williamson Hoynes. "Taxes and the labor market participation of married couples: the earned income tax credit." *Journal of Public Economics* 88, no. 9–10 (2004): 1931–1958.

Ellwood, David T. *Poor support: Poverty in the American family.* Basic Books, 1988.

Ellwood, David T., and Elisabeth D. Welty. "Public service employment and mandatory work: A policy whose time has come and gone and come again?" In *Finding jobs: Work and welfare reform*, edited by David E. Card, and Rebecca M. Blank, 299–372. New York: Russell Sage Foundation, 2000.

Evans, William N., and Craig L. Garthwaite. "Giving mom a break: The impact of higher EITC payments on maternal health." *American Economic Journal: Economic Policy* 6, no. 2 (2014): 258–290.

Falk, Gene, Alison Mitchell, Karen E. Lynch, Maggie McCarty, William R. Morton, and Margot L. Crandall-Hollick. *Need-tested benefits: Estimated eligibility and benefit by families and individuals* (CRS Report No. R44327) Congressional Research Service, 2015. https://crsreports.congress.gov/product/pdf/R/R44327.

Fisher, Gordon M. "The development and history of the US poverty thresholds—A brief overview." *GSS/SSS Newsletter*, 6–7 (1997).

Flores, Antonio. "How the US Hispanic population is changing." *Pew Research Center* 18 (2017).

Folbre, Nancy. "Children as public goods." *The American Economic Review* 84, no. 2 (1994): 86–90.

Fomby, Paula, and Andrew J. Cherlin. "Family instability and child well-being." *American Sociological Review* 72, no. 2 (2007): 181–204.

Fox, Liana, Christopher Wimer, Irwin Garfinkel, Neeraj Kaushal, and Jane Waldfogel. "Waging war on poverty: Poverty trends using a historical supplemental poverty measure." *Journal of Policy Analysis and Management* 34, no 3 (2015a): 567–592.

Fox, Liana, Christopher Wimer, Irwin Garfinkel, Neeraj Kaushal, JaeHyun Nam, and Jane Waldfogel. "Trends in deep poverty from 1968 to 2011: The influence of family structure, employment patterns, and the safety net." *RSF: The Russell Sage Foundation Journal of the Social Sciences,* 1, no. 1 (2015b): 14–34.

Fox, Mary Kay, William L. Hamilton, and Biing-Hwan Lin. *Effects of food assistance and nutrition programs on nutrition and health: Volume 4, executive summary of the literature review.* No. 1481-2016-121334. 2004.

Frey, C. B., and M. A. Osborne. "The future of employment: How susceptible are jobs to computerization?" *Technological Forecasting & Social Change* 114 (2017): 254–280.

Frey, William H. "The nation is diversifying even faster than predicted according to new census data." *Brookings Institution*, July 2020.

Frey, William H. *Diversity explosion: How new racial demographics are remaking America.* Washington, DC: Brookings Institution Press, 2018.

Gabe, Thomas, and Julie M. Whittaker. "Antipoverty effects of unemployment insurance." (2012).

Ganong, Peter, and Jeffery Liebman. "The decline, rebound, and further rise in SNAP enrollment: Disentangling business cycle fluctuations and policy changes." *American Economic Journal: Economic Policy* 10, no. 4 (2018): 153–176.

Garcia, Jorge Luis, James J. Heckman, and Victor Ronda, "The lasting effects of early childhood education on promoting skills and social mobility of disadvantaged African Americans." National Bureau of Economic Research, 2021. No. w29057.

Garcia, Jorge Luis, James J. Heckman, Duncan Ermini Leaf, and Maria Jose Prados. "The life-cycle benefits of an influential and early childhood program." No. w22993. National Bureau of Economic Research, 2017.

Gibson-Davis, and Christina M. "Money, marriage, and children: Testing the financial expectations and family formation theory." *Journal of Marriage and Family* 71, no. 1 (2009): 146–160.

Gibson-Davis, Christina M., Kathryn Edin, and Sara McLanahan. "High hopes but even higher expectations: The Retreat from marriage among low-income couples." *Journal of Marriage and Family* 67, no. 5 (2005): 1301–1312.

Glynn, Sara Jane. *Gender wage inequality: What we know and how we can fix it.* Washington, DC: Washington Center for Equitable Growth, 2018.

Golden, Lonnie. *Part-time workers pay a big-time penalty.* Washington, DC: Economic Policy Institute, February 27, 2020.

Goldin, Claudia, and Cecilia Rouse. "Orchestrating impartiality: The impact of 'bind' auditions on female musicians." *American Economic Review* 90, no. 4 (2000): 715–741.

Goldin, Claudia, and Lawrence F. Katz. "Transitions: Career and family life cycles of the educational elite." *American Economic Review* 104, no. 4 (2008): 1091–1119.

Goldin, Claudia, and Lawrence F. Katz. *The race between education and technology.* Harvard University Press, 2009.

Goldin, Claudia, and Robert A. Margo. "The great compression: The wage structure in the United States at mid-century." *Quarterly Journal of Economics* 107, no. 1 (1992):1–34.

Goldin, Claudia, Sari Pekkala Kerr, Claudia Olivetti, and Erling Barth. "The expanding gender earnings gap: Evidence from the LEHD-2000 census." *American Economic Review* 107, no. 5 (2017): 1109–1114.

Goldin, Claudia. "A grand gender convergence: Its last chapter." *American Economic Review* 104, no. 40 (2014): 1091–1119.

Gonzalez-Barrera, Ana, and Mark Hugo Lopez. "Is being Hispanic a matter of race, ethnicity or both?" *Pew Research Center* 15 (2015). Available at: https://www.pewresearch.org/fact-tank/2015/06/15/is-being-hispanic-a-matter-of-race-ethnicity-or-both/.

Goodman-Bacon, Andrew. "The long-run effects of childhood insurance coverage: Medicaid implementation, adult health, and labor market outcomes." *American Economic Review* 111, no. 8 (2021): 2550–2593.

Gould, Elise, Jessica Schieder, and Kathleen Geier. "What is the gender pay gap and is it real?" Washington, DC: Economic Policy Institute, 2016.

Gould, Elise. *Wage inequality marches on—and is even threatening data reliability.* State of working America wages 2018, Washington, DC: Economic Policy Institute, 2019.

Gould, Eric D. "Torn apart? The impact of manufacturing employment decline on black and white Americans." *Review of Economics and Statistics* 103, no. 4 (2021): 770–785.

Gould, Eric D., and M. Daniele Paserman. "Waiting for Mr. Right: Rising inequality and declining marriage rates." *Journal of Urban Economics* 53, no. 2 (2003): 257–281.

Greenwood, Jeremy, Ananth Seshadri, and Mehmet Yorukoglu. "Engines of liberation." *Review of Economic Studies* 72, no. 1 (2005): 109–133.

Grogger, Jeffrey, and Lynn A. Karoly. *Welfare reform: Effects of a decade of change.* Harvard University Press, 2009.

Gundersen, Craig, and James P. Ziliak. "Poverty and macroeconomic performance across space, race, and family structure." *Demography* 41, no. 1 (2004): 61–86.

Gundersen, Craig, Brent Kreider, and John V. Pepper. "Reconstructing the supplemental nutrition assistance program to more effectively alleviate food insecurity in the United States." *The Russell Sage Foundation Journal of the Social Sciences* 4, no. 2(2018): 113–130.

Guzzo, Karen Benjamin, and Sarah R. Hayford. "Fertility and the stability of cohabiting unions: Variation by intendedness." *Journal of Family Issues* 35, no. 4 (2014): 547–576.

Hardy, Bradley, Timothy Smeeding, and James P. Ziliak. "The changing safety net for low income parents and their children: Structural or cyclical changes in income support policy?" *Demography* 55, no. 1 (2018): 189–221.

Hastings, Justine, and Jesse M. Shapiro. "How are SNAP benefits spent? Evidence from a retail panel." *American Economic Review* 108, no. 12 (2018): 3493–3540.

Haveman Robert, Rebecca Blank, Robert Moffitt, Timothy Smeeding, and Geoffrey Wallace. "The war on poverty: 50 years later." *Journal of Policy Analysis and Management* 34, no. 5 (2015): 593–638.

Hendren, Nathaniel, and Ben Sprung-Keyser. "A unified welfare analysis of government policies." *Quarterly Journal of Economics* 135, no. 3 (August 2020): 1209–1318.

Herbst, Chris M. "The rising cost of child care in the United States: A reassessment of the evidence." *Economics of Education Review* 64 (2018): 13–30.

Herd, Pamela, Melissa Favreault, Madonna Harrington Meyer, and Timothy Smeeding. "A targeted minimum benefit plan." *RSF: The Russell Sage Foundation Journal of the Social Sciences* 4, no. 2 (2018): 74–90.

Hipsman, Faye, and Doris Meissner. "Immigration in the United States: New economic, social, political landscapes with legislative reform on the horizon." *Migration Policy Institute* 16 (2013).

Hoffman, Saul D. "Abortion, contraception, and non-marital births: Re-interpreting the Akerlof-Yellen-Katz model of premarital sex and shotgun marriage." *Eastern Economic Journal* 43, no. 2 (2017): 352–361.

Hogan, Vincent. "Wage aspirations and unemployment persistence. *Journal of Monetary Economics* 51, no. 8 (2004): 1623–1643.

Holtz, Joseph, Charles H. Mullen, and John Karl Scholz. "Examining the effect of the earned income tax credit on the labor market participation of families on welfare." *National Bureau of Economic Research*, Working paper 11968. (2006).

Holzer, Harry. "Job market polarization and U.S. worker skills: A tale of two middles." *Economic Studies.* The Brookings Institute, 2015.

Hoynes Hilary W., Douglas Miller, and Jessamyn Schaller. "Who suffers during recessions?" *Journal of Economic Perspectives* 26, no. 3 (2012): 27–48.

Hoynes, Hilary W., and Ankur J. Patel. "Effective policy for reducing poverty and inequality? The earned income tax credit and the distribution of income." *Journal of Human Resources* 53, no. 4 (2018): 859–890.

Hoynes, Hilary W., and Diane Whitmore Schanzenbach. "Safety net investments in children." *Brookings Papers on Economic Activity* (Spring, 2018): 89–150.

Hoynes, Hilary W., and Jesse Rothstein. "Tax policy toward low-income families." No. 22080. National Bureau of Economic Research. 2016.

Hoynes, Hilary, and Diane Whitmore Schanzenbach. "Work incentives and the food stamp program." *Journal of Public Economics* 96, no. 1 (2012): 151–162.

Hoynes, Hilary, and Diane Whitmore Schanzenbach. *Strengthening SNAP as an automatic stabilizer*. Washington, DC: The Hamilton Project, Brookings Institution, 2019.

Kane, Joseph W. *Biden needs to create an infrastructure Talen pipeline, not just more jobs*. Washington, DC: Brookings Institution, 2021.

Kennedy, Sheela, and Catherine A. Fitch. "Measuring cohabitation and family structure in the United States: Assessing the impact of new data from the current population survey." *Demography* 49 no. 4 (2012): 1479–1498.

Kennedy, Sheela, and Larry Bumpass. "Cohabitation and children's living arrangements: New estimates from the United States." *Demographic Research* 19, p. 1663 (2008).

Khatiwada, Ishwar, and Andrew M. Sum. "The Widening socioeconomic divergence in the U.S. labor market." In *The dynamics of opportunity in America*, 197–252. Cham: Springer, 2016.

Kleven, Henrik. *The EITC and the extensive margin: A reappraisal*. No. w26405. National Bureau of Economic Research, 2021.

Koenig, Felix, Alan Manning, and Barbara Petrongolo. "Reservation wages and the wage flexibility puzzle." CEPR Discussion Paper No. DP11109, 2016. SSRN: https://papers.ssrn.com/sol3/papers.cfm?abstract_id=2733082

Kosar, Gizem, and Robert A. Moffitt. "Trends in cumulative marginal tax rates facing low-income families 1997–2007." *Tax Policy and the Economy* 31, no. 1 (2017): 43–70.

Krause, Eleanor, and Isabel Sawhill. *What we know and don't know about declining labor force participation: A review*. Washington, DC: Center on Children and Families, Brookings Institution, 2017.

Krogstad, Jens Manuel, and Mark Hugo Lopez. "Hispanic immigrants more likely to lack health insurance than U.S. born." *Pew Research Center*, September 26, 2014.

Krueger, Alan B. "The history of economic thought on the minimum wage." *Industrial Relations* 54, no. 4 (2015): 533–537.

Kruger, Alan B. "Where have all the workers gone?" Working paper. Princeton University and NBER, 2016.

Kuperberg, Arielle. "Premarital cohabitation and direct marriage in the United States: 1956–2015." *Marriage and Family Review* 55, no. 5 (2019): 447–475.

Lang, Kevin, and Jee-Yeon K. Lehmann. "Racial discrimination in the labor market: Theory and empirics." *Journal of Economic Literature* 50, no. 4 (2012): 959–1006.

Laughlin, Lyda. "Who's minding the kids? Child care arrangements: Spring 2011. Current Population Reports. P70-135. US Census Bureau, Washington, DC." (2013).

Leftin, Joshua, Esa Eslami, and Mark Strayer. *Trends in supplemental nutrition assistance program participation rates: Fiscal year 2002 to fiscal year 2009*. No. 58390a9977d04407ab6427. Mathematica Policy Research, 2011.

Lundberg, Shelly, Robert A. Pollak, and Jenna Stearns. "Family inequality: Diverging patterns in marriage, cohabitation, and childbearing." *Journal of Economic Perspectives* 30, no. 2 (2016): 79–102.

Malik, Rasheed. "Working families are spending big money on child care." *Center for American Progress* (2019).

Manning, Wendy D. "Cohabitation and child well-being." *The Future of Children* 25 no. 2 (2015): 51–66.

Manning, Wendy D., Susan L. Brown, and Krista K. Payne. "Two decades of stability and change in age at first union formation." *Journal of Marriage and Family* 76, no. 2 (2014): 247–260.

Marr, Chuck, Kris Cox, and Arlos Sherman. *Build back better's child tax credit changes would protect millions from poverty-permanently*. Washington, DC: Center on Budget and Policy Priorities, 2021.

Matsudaira, Jordan D., and Rebecca M. Blank. "The impact of earnings disregards on the behavior of low-income families." *Journal of Policy Analysis and Management* 33, no. 1 (2014): 7–35.

Matthews, Hannah, Karen Schulman, Julie Bogtman, Christine Johnson-Staub, and Helen Blank. "Implementing the child care and development block grant reauthorization: A guide for states." *Center for Law and Social Policy, Inc. (CLASP)* (2015).

McLanahan, Sara, and Christine Percheski. "Family structure and the reproduction of inequalities." *Annual Review of Sociology* 34 (2008): 257–276.

McLanahan, Sara, and Wade Jacobsen. "Diverging destinies revisited." In *Families in an era of increasing inequality*, edited by Paul R. Amato, Alan Booth, Susan M. McHale, and Jennifer Van Hook, 3–23. Springer International Publisher, 2015.

McLanahan, Sara. "Diverging destinies: How children are faring under the second demographic transition." *Demography* 41, no. 4 (2004): 607–627.

Meyer, Bruce D., and Dan T. Rosenbaum. "Welfare, the earned income tax credit, and the labor supply of single mothers." *The Quarterly Journal of Economics* 116, no. 3 (2001): 1063–1114.

Meyer, Bruce D., and Nikolas Mittag. "Using linked survey and administrative data to better measure income: Implications for poverty, program effectiveness, and holes in the safety net." *American Economic Journal: Applied Economics* 11, no. 2 (2019): 176–204.

Mishel, Lawrence. *Yes, manufacturing still provides a pay advantage, but staffing firm outsourcing is eroding it*. Washington, DC: Economic Policy Institute, 2018.

Moffitt, Robert A. "The deserving poor, the family, and the US welfare system." *Demography* 52, no. 3 (2015): 729–749.

Moffitt, Robert A., and John Karl Scholz. "Trends in the level and distribution of income support." *Tax Policy and the Economy* 24, no. 1 (2010): 111–152.

Monte, Lindsay M. "Multiple-partner fertility in the United States: A demographic portrait." *Demography* 56, no. 1 (2019): 103–127.

Morgan, S. Philip, Erin Cumberworth, and Christopher Wimer. "The great recession's influence on fertility, marriage, divorce, and cohabitation." In *The great recession*, edited by David B. Grusky, Bruce Western, and Christopher Wimer, 220–245. New York: Russell Sage Foundation, 2011.

Morrissey, Taryn W. "Child care and parent labor force participation: A review of the research literature." *Review of Economics of the Household* 15, no. 1 (2017): 1–24.

Moss-Racusin, Corine A., John F. Dovidio, Victoria L. Brescoll, Mark J. Graham, and Jo Handelsman. 2012. "Science faculty's subtle gender biases favor male science students." *Proceedings of the National Academy of Science* 90, no. 41 (2012): 16474–16479.

Moulton, Jeremy G., Alexandra Graddy-Reed, and Lauren Lanahan. "Beyond the EITC: The effect of reducing the earned income tax credit on labor force participation." *National Tax Journal* 69, no. 2 (2016): 261–284.

Muro, Mark, and Siddarth Kulkarni. "Voter anger explained—in one chart." *The Avenue*, March 15, 2016. https://www.brookings.edu/blog/the-avenue/2016/03/15/voter-anger-explained-in-one-chart/.

Murray, Charles. *Losing ground: American social policy, 1950–1980.* New York: Basic Books, 2008.

National Academies of Sciences, Engineering, and Medicine. *A roadmap to reducing child poverty.* National Academies Press, 2019.

National Academy of Sciences, Engineering, and Medicine. *The economic and fiscal consequences of immigration.* National Academies Press, 2017.

National Center for Health Statistics, National Vital Statistics Reports, Births: Final Data for 2016, Volume 67, no. 1 (January 31, 2018).

National Employment Law Project. "Unemployment insurance kept 4.7 million people out of poverty in 2020." Policy Brief, September 2021.

National Research Council. "Measuring poverty: A new approach (CF Citro and RT Michael, Eds.)" (1995).

Neuman, David, Roy J. Bank, and Kyle D. van Nort. "Sex descrimination in restraurant hiring: An audit study." *Quarterly Journal of Economics* 111, no. 3 (1996): 915–941.

OECD. Poverty rate (indicator), 2020. https://doi.org/10.1787/0fe1315d-en (Accessed on 07 December 2020).

Orrenius, Pia M., and Madeline Zavodny. "The effect of minimum wages on immigrants' employment and earnings." *ILR Review* 61, no. 4 (2008): 544–563.

Osborne, Cynthia, and Sarah McLanahan. "Partnership instability and child well-being." *Journal of Marriage and Family* 69, no. 4 (2007): 1065–1083.

Pal, Ipshita, and Jane Waldfogel. "The family gap in pay: New evidence for 1967 to 2013." *The Russell Sage Journal of the Social Sciences* 2, no. 4 (2016). https://doi.org/10.7758/RSF.2016.2.4.04.

Parker, Emily, Louisa Diffey, and Bruce Atchison. *How states fund pre-K. Education: A primer for policy makers.* Education Commission of the States, 2018.

Parker, Kim, and Renee Stepler. "Americans see men as the financial providers, even s women's contributions grow." *Pew Research Center* (2017).

Parker, Kim, Rich Morin, Juliana Menasce Horowitz, Mark Hugo Lopez, and Molly Rohal. *Multiracial in America: Proud, diverse and growing in numbers*, 98–109. Washington, DC: Pew Research Center, 2015.

Paul, Mark, William Darity, Jr., Darrick Hamilton, and Khaing Zaw. "A path to ending poverty by way of ending unemployment: A federal job guarantee." *The Russell Sage Foundation Journal of the Social Sciences* 4, no. 3 (2018): 44–63.

Pew Research Center. "Marriage and cohabitation in the U.S." November 2019.

Provencher, Ashley. "Unit of analysis for poverty measurement: A comparison of the supplemental poverty measure and the official poverty measure." *Census Bureau*, August 2, 2011.

Raley, R. Kelly, and Elizabeth Wildsmith. "Cohabitation and children's family instability." *Journal of Marriage and Family* 66, no. 1 (2004): 210–219.

Raley, R. Kelly, Megan M. Sweeney, and Danielle Wondra. "The growing racial and ethnic divide in US marriage partners." *The Future of Children/Center for the Future of Children, the David and Lucile Packard Foundation* 25, no. 2 (2015): 89.

Reeves, Richard V., and Eleanor Krause. "Cohabiting parents differ from married ones in three big ways." Social Mobility Papers, Brookings Institution, April 5, 2017. https://www.brookings.edu/research/cohabiting-parents-differ-from-married-ones-in-three-big-ways/.

Reeves, Richard V., and Joanna Venator. "Sex, contraception, or abortion? Explaining class gaps in unintended childbearing." *Research Paper for the Brookings Institution*, 2015. brookings.edu/research/papers/2015/02/26-class-gaps-inuninte nded-childbearings-reeves.

Renwick, Trudi, and Liana Fox. "The supplemental poverty measure: 2015." *Current Population Reports*, 1–23.

Reuben, Ernesto, Paola Sapienza, and Luigi Zingales. "How stereotypes impair women's careers in science." *Proceedings of the National Academy of Sciences* 111, no. 12 (2014): 4403–4408.

Romich, Jennifer, and Heather D. Hill. "Coupling a federal minimum wage hike with public investments to make work pay and reduce poverty." *The Russell Sage Foundation Journal of the Social Sciences* 4, no. 3 (2018): 22–43.

Saenz, Rogelio, and Kenneth Johnson. "White deaths exceed births in a majority of US states." (2018). https://apl.wisc.edu/data-briefs/natural-decrease-18.

Sawhill, Isabel V. *Generation unbound: Drifting into sex and parenthood without marriage.* Brookings Institution Press, 2014.

Sawhill, Isabel V., and Morgan Welch. "The American families plan: Too many tax credits for children?" Up Front, Brookings Institution, Washington, DC. May 27, 2021.

Sawhill, Isabel, and Joanna Venator. "Is there a shortage of marriageable men?" *Center on Children and Families*, 2015. https://pdfs.semanticscholar.org/a051/eb2 8b75a12253034006a1b7120dbb22e0cb0.pdf.

Schanzenbach, Diane Whitmore, Lauren Bauer, Ryan Nunn, and Megan Mumford. "Who is out of the labor force?" *Economic Analysis* (2017).

Schanzenbach, Diane Whitmore, Ryan Nunn, Lauren Bauer, David Boddy, and Greg Natz. *Nine facts about the great recession and tool for fighting the next downturn.* Washington, DC: The Hamilton Project, Brookings Institution, 2016.

Schmidt, Erik. "For the first time, 90 percent completed high school or more. *US Census Bureau* (2018). https://www.census.gov/library/stories/2018/07/educational-attainment.html.

Schmidt, Lucie. *The new safety net? Supplemental security income after welfare reform.* Williams College Economics Department, 2013.

Schmitt, John, Elise Gould, and Josh Bivens. *America's slow-motion wage crisis: Four decades of slow and unequal growth.* Washington, DC: Economic Policy Institute, 2018. https://www.epi.org/publication/americas-slow-motion-wage-crisis-four-decades-of-slow-and-unequal-growth-2/.

Schneider, Daniel, and Alison Gemmill. "The surprising decline in the nonmarital fertility rate in the United States." *Population and Development Review* 42 (2016): 627–649.

Semega, Jessica, Melissa Kollar, Emily A. Shrider, and John F. Creamer. "Income and poverty in the United States: 2019. Current population reports (P60-270)." (2020).

Shaefer, H. Luke, Sophie Collyer, Greg Duncan, Kathryn Edin, Irwin Garfinkel, David Harris, Timothy M. Smeeding, Jane Waldfogel, Christopher Wimer, and Hirokazu Yoshikawa. "A universal child allowance: A plan to reduce poverty and income inequality among children in the United States." *The Russell Sage Foundation Journal of the Social Sciences* 4, no. 2 (2018): 22–42.

Shambaugh, Jay, Lauren Bauer, and Audrey Breitwieser. *Returning to education.* The Hamilton Project on Human Capital and Wages, 2018.

Shambaugh, Jay, Lauren Bauer, and Audrey Breitwieser. *Who is poor in the United States? A Hamilton project annual report.* Washington, DC: Economic Facts, the Hamilton Project, 2017.

Shapiro, Isaac, Robert Greenstein, Danilo Trisi, and Bryann Da Silva. *It pays to work: Work incentives and the safety net.* Center on Budget and Policy Priorities, 2016.

Short, Kathleen. "The supplemental poverty measure: 2013." *Current Population Reports* (2014): 60–251.

Smeeding, Timothy. "Gates, gaps and intergenerational mobility: The importance of an even start." In *The dynamics of opportunity in America*, edited by Irwin Kirsch and Henry Brown, 255–295. Cham: Springer, 2016.

Solomon-Fears, Carmen. *Nonmarital births: An overview.* Washington, DC: Congressional Research Service, 2014.

Song, Jae, and Til Von Wachter. "Long-term nonemployment and job displacement." In *Evaluating labor market dynamics, proceedings from the Jackson Hole economic policy symposium sponsored by the federal reserve board of Kansas City, Jackson Hole Wyo* (August 2014). www.kansascityfed.org/publicat/sympos/2014/2014vonWachter.pdf.

Srivastava, Anjali, and Milliam M. Rodgers III. "The motherhood wage gap for U.S. first-generation immigrant and native women." *National Poverty Center* working paper series no. 13-08. 2013. Ann Arbor: University of Michigan. Accessed

July 26, 2019. https://studylib.net/doc/13982630/the-motherhood-wage-gap-for-u
.s.-first-generation-immigra.

Stevenson, Betsey, and Justin Wolfers. "Marriage and divorce: Changes and their driving forces." *Journal of Economic Perspectives* 21, no. 2 (2007): 27–52.

Sullivan, Dennis H., and Andrea L. Ziegert. "Hispanic immigrant poverty: Does ethnic origin matter?" *Population Research and Policy Review* 27, no. 6 (2008): 667–687.

Sullivan, Dennis H., and Andrea L. Ziegert. "Prevalence and demography of insufficient earnings." *The Journal of Applied Business and Economics* 23, no. 5 (2021): 213–228.

Tax Policy Center. "How does the federal tax system affect low-income households?" *The Tax Policy Center Briefing Book*, May 2020.

Tuzeman, Didem. "Why are prime-age men vanishing from the labor force? *Economic Review—Federal Reserve Bank of Kansas City* 103, no. 1 (2018): 5–30.

Ullrich, Rebecca, Stephanie Schmit, and Ruth Cosse. "Inequitable access to child care subsidies." *Center for Law and Social Policy (CLASP)* (2019). Available at: www
.clasp.org/sites/default/files/publications/2019/04/2019_inequitableaccess.pdf.

United States Census Bureau. "Foreign-Born Population by Region of Birth: 1960-2010." *Newsroom*, December 2011. https://www.census.gov/newsroom/pdf/cspan
_fb_slides.pdf.

United States Census Bureau. CPS historical time series visualizations, educational attainment (2019). Accessed 12, 2019. https://www.census.gov/library/visualizations/time-series/demo/cps-historical-time-series.html.

United States Census Bureau. Historical living arrangements of children (November 2017). https://www.census.gov/data/tables/time-series/demo/families/children
.html.

United States Census Bureau. Table A-2 CPS educational attainment historical times series (2018). Accessed 12, 2019. https://www.census.gov/data/tables/time-series/demo/educational-attainment/cps-historical-time-series.html.

United States Department of the Treasury. "The economics of child care supply in the United States," September, 2021. https://home.treasury.gov/system/files/136/The
-Economics-of-Childcare-Supply-09-14-final.pdf.

United States, Bureau of Labor Statistics, Employment Projections, Table 3.4 Civilian labor force by age, sex, race and ethnicity, 1996, 2006, 2016 and projected 2026. https://www.bls.gov/emp/tables/civilian-labor-force-detail.htm.

United States, Bureau of Labor Statistics. 2021. "A profile of the working poor, 2019." Report 1093. https://www.bls.gov/opub/reports/working-poor/2019/home.htm.

United States, Census Bureau, Current Population Reports, P60, *Income and Poverty in the United States*, select years, US Government Publishing Office, Washington DC.

United States, Department of Agriculture. "Trends in supplemental nutrition assistance program participation rates: Fiscal year 2010 to fiscal year 2016." July 2018.

United States, Department of Agriculture. *Thrifty food plan, 2021*. August 2021. FNS-916. https://FNS.usda.gov/TFP.

United States, Government Accountability Office. *Child care: Access to subsidies and strategies to manage demand across states*. Report to congressional committees, GAO-17-60. Washington, DC: Government Accountability Office (December 2016). https://www.gao.gov/assets/690/681652.pdf.

United States, Health and Human Services, Low Income Home Energy Assistance Program. "Fact Sheet." November 2018. www.acf.hhs.gov/ocs/programs/liheap.

United States, Internal Revenue Service. "Child tax credit and credit for other dependents," Publication 972, US Department of the Treasury, Revised February 2020.

United States, Internal Revenue Service. "Earned income credit." Publication 596, US Department of the Treasury, January 2021.

United States, Social Security Administration. "Annual statistical supplement to the social security bulletin, 2018." November 2018.

Urahn, Susan K. Erin Currier, Dana Elliott, Lauren Wechsler, Denise Wilson, and Daniel Colbert. *Pursuing the American dream: Economic mobility across generations*, 2012. Available at: wwwpewtrustsorg/reports/economic_mobility/pursuingamericandreampdf.pdf.

Urban Institute. "Part of us: A data-driven look at children of immigrants." *Features*, March 14, 2019. https://www.urban.org/features/part-us-data-driven-look-children-immigrants.

Valetta, Robert, Leila Bengali, and Catherine van der List. "Cyclical and market determinants of involuntary part-time employment." Federal Reserve Bank of San Francisco Working Paper 2015-19, 2018.

Ventura, Stephanie J. *Changing patterns of nonmarital childbearing in the United States*. Hyattsville, MD: National Center for Health Statistics. (NCHS) Data Brief No 18 (2009).

Vespa, Jonathan, David M. Armstrong, and Lauren Medina. "Demographic turning points for the United States: Population projections for 2020 to 2060." Current Population Reports, P25-1144. U.S. Census Bureau. Washington, DC (2018).

Waller, Maureen R., and Sara S. McLanahan, "His" and "her" marriage expectations: Determinants and consequences." *Journal of Marriage and Family* 67, no. 1 (2005): 53–67.

Western, B. *Punishment and inequality in America*. New York: Russell Sage Foundation, 2006.

Western, B., and Becky Pettit. "Incarceration and social inequality." *Daedalus* 13, no. 3 (2010): 8–19.

Wheaton, Laura, and Victoria Tran. "The antipoverty effects of the supplemental nutritional assistance program." Urban Institute Research Report, 2018.

Williams, Wendy M., and Stephen J. Ceci. "National hiring experiments reveal 2:1 Faculty preference for women on STEM tenure track." *Proceedings of the National Academy of Sciences* 112, no. 17 (2015): 5360–5365.

Wilson William Julius, and Kathryn M. Neckerman. "Poverty and family structure: The widening gap between evidence and public policy issues." In *Fighting poverty: What works and what doesn't*, edited by S. H. Danziger, and D. H. Weinberg, 232–259. Cambridge, MA: Harvard University Press, 1987.

Wimer, Christopher, Liana Fox, Irwin Garfinkel, Neeraj Kaushal, and Jane Waldfo-gel. "Progress on poverty? New estimates of historical trends using an anchored supplemental poverty measure." *Demography* 53, no. 4 (2016): 1207–1218.

Wimer, Christopher, Sophie Collyer, and Sara Kimberlin. "Assessing the potential impacts of innovative new policy proposals on poverty in the United States." *The Russell Sage Foundation Journal of the Social Sciences* 4, no. 3 (2018): 167–183.

Wu, Lawrence L. "Effects of family instability, income, and income instability on the risk of a premarital birth. *American Sociological Review* 61 (1996): 386–406.

Wu, Lawrence L., and Brian C. Martinson. "Family structure and the risk of a pre-marital birth." *American Sociological Review* 58 (1993): 210–232.

Wu, Lawrence L., and Nicholas D. E. Mark. "Could we level the playing field? Long-acting reversible contraceptives, nonmarital fertility, and poverty in the United States." *RSF: The Russell Sage Foundation Journal of the Social Sciences* 4, no. 3 (2018): 44–166.

Young, Justin R., and Marybeth J. Mattingly. "Underemployment among hispan-ics: The case of involuntary part-time work." *Monthly Labor Review* (December, 2016). Available at: https://www.bls.gov/opub/mlr/2016/article/underemployment-among-hispanics.htm.

Ziliak, James P. "Temporary assistance for needy families." In *Economics of means-tested transfer programs in the United States*, 303–393. National Bureau of Economic Research Conference Report. Chicago, IL and London: University of Chicago Press, 2016.

Ziliak, James P. *Temporary assistance for needy families*. Chicago: University of Chicago Press, 2016.

Zong, Jie, Jeanne Batalova, and Hallock, J. "Frequently requested statistics on immigrants and immigration in the United States." Migration Policy Institute. (2018). https://www.migrationpolicy.org/article/frequently-requested-statistics-immigrants-and-immigration-united-states.

.

Index

Note: Page numbers in *italics* refer to figures and tables.

187

poverty by providing services, 158, 159; tax credits, 159–61. *See also* policy proposals

birth control, 18

births: inequality of opportunity at, 1; non-marital, 24–25

Bitler, Marianne, 77, 84, 149–51

Black, Sandra E., 2, 39

blacks, 6

Blank, Rebecca M., 96

Blau, David, 46, 132

Borowczyk-Martins, Daniel, 54

Bosworth, Barry P., 37

Bound, John, 95

Bureau of Labor Statistics. *See* US Bureau of Labor Statistics

Burkhauser, Richard V., 95

Cajner, Tomaz, 55–56

Carnevale, Anthony P., 158–59

Case, Ann, 41

cash transfers: social insurance programs, 89–95. *See also* means-tested cash transfers

CBO. *See* US Congressional Budget Office

Charles, Kerwin Kofi, 48

Cherlin, Andrew J., 20, 50

Chester, Alisa, 2

Chetty, Raj, 1

child allowances (CA), 11, 160–62, 166, 167; combining work and wages with, 132–34; cost-effectiveness, 155; policy package, 157–58; policy proposals for, 149–51; policy simulations, 119, 120, 132–35

Child and Dependent Care Tax Credit (CDCTC), 77, 148–49, 157, 159, 161

childcare, subsidies for, 40

Child Care and Development Block Grant (CCDBG), 40

childcare costs, 39–40; eliminating, 131–32

childcare credit: refundable, policy proposal for, 148–49, 155, 166–67. *See also* tax credits

Child Health Insurance Program (CHIP), 78, 79

child poverty, 1, 7; effects of policies and policy packages, *154*; National Academies report, 156–58; National Academy of Sciences on, 2–3, 153; policy packages for, 156–58. *See also* policy proposals; policy simulations

children: cohabiting families, 24; investment in, 1–2; living arrangements of, 17–26; as nation's future, 1; poverty rates, 1; safety net investments, 2; underinvestment in, 2. *See also* families; SPM families

Child Tax Credit (CTC), 71, 75, *76*, 77, *77*, 79, 82, 85–89, 119, 120, 133, 149, 150, 155, 159, 160

China, immigration from, 15

CHIP. *See* Child Health Insurance Program

Churchill, Brandon F., 146

civilian labor force, 35. *See* labor force participation

cohabitation/cohabiting couples, 23–24; benefits, 23; children born into, 24; married couples *vs.*, 23–24; relationship satisfaction and trust, 23; transition to marriage, 24; unintended childbirth, 23

college education: completion rates, 17; fatherhood bonus, 47; gender wage gap, 19, 45, *46*; racial differences, 17. *See also* education/educational attainment

college wage premium, 44

Congressional Budget Office. *See* US Congressional Budget Office (CBO)

Consumer Expenditure Survey, 4

Consumer Price Index for Urban Wage Earners and Clerical Workers (US Bureau of Labor Statistics), 89

contraception, use of, 21

Cooper, David, 57

Corinth, Kevin, 160

Fox, Liana, 4, 100
Frey, C. B., 15, 38
full-time employment, 165

Gabe, Thomas, 90
Garcia, Jorge Luis, 2
Geier, Kathleen, 44
Gemmill, Alison, 25
gender gap in labor-force participation, 164–65
gender wage gaps: education and, 45, *46*; fatherhood bonus, 47; human capital variables and, 46; labor-market characteristics, 45–47; marital and parenthood status, 47–48; motherhood wage penalties, 47, 48
Gibson-Davis, Christina M., 20
Glaeser, Edward, 75
Glaeser, Edward Ludwig, 75
globalization, 36, 37, 39, 51
Glynn, Sara Jane, 46
Golden, Lonnie, 47
Goldin, Claudia, 45, 47
Goodman-Bacon, Andrew, 2
Gould, Elise, 19, 37, 44
government cash transfers, social insurance programs, 89–95. *See also* Social Security
government programs, means-tested cash transfers: Aid to Families with Dependent Children (AFDC), 72, *76*, 78, 96; Supplemental Security Income (SSI), 71, *76*, 77, 78, 95–97, *98*, 121; Temporary Assistance for Needy Families (TANF), 40, 71–72, 75, *76*, 78, 95–97, *98*, 100, 121, 141
government programs, means-tested in-kind benefits, 97–102; Low-Income Home Energy Assistance Program (LIHEAP), 102–4, *103*; National School Lunch Program (NSLP), 100; School Breakfast Program (SBP), 100; SNAP. *See* Supplemental Nutrition Program; Women's Infants and Children (WIC), 72, *76*, 78, 79, 100, 102, 104

Graddy-Reed, Alexandra, 84
graduation rates, 17
"Great Compression," 42
Great Depression, 50
"Great Divergence," 42
Great Recession, 5, 49–51, 59; fertility and, 25, 50; as longest recession, 50; marriage and divorce rates, 50; unemployment rates, 50; wage growth and, 48
Grogger, Jeffrey, 96–97
Gundersen, Craig, 7, 151

Hanson, Gordon H., 37
Hardy, Bradley, 85–86
Head Start, 131
Hendren, Nathaniel, 2
Herbst, Chris M., 131
HHS. *See* US Department of Health and Human Services
Hill, Heather D., 144–46, 154
Hispanics, 6
Hobijn, Bart, 48
Hogan, Vincent, 38
Holtz-Eakin, Douglas, 143
Holzer, Harry, 38
Household Food Consumption Survey of 1955, 3
Housing Act of 1937, 101
housing assistance, 101–2
Housing Choice Voucher program, 101–2. *See also* housing vouchers
housing vouchers, 72, 101–2, 121, 152, 153, 155–57, 162, 167
Hoynes, Hilary, 2, 77, 80, 84–85, 99
HUD. *See* US Department of Housing and Urban Development

immigration, 14–15; employment-based visas, 14; permanent, 14; principles shaping, 14
incentives, work, 73, 74, 82, 84, 119, 121, 134, 141, 146, 147, 150–51, 156, 160–62, 167
India, immigration from, 15
inflation-adjusted wages, 42

US Government Accountability Office (GAO), 40
US Internal Revenue Service, 82
US Social Security Administration. *See* Social Security Administration
US Treasury, 95

Valletta, Robert, 56
Venator, Joanna, 20–21

wages, 42–49; college wage premium, 44; education and, 42, 44, *45*; fatherhood bonus, 47; gender and, *43*, 43–44. *See also* gender wage gaps; Great Recession, 49–51; inflation-adjusted, 42; low wages/earnings, 56–59; middle-wage workers, 42–43; motherhood wage penalty, 47, 48; racial and ethnic groups, 44, *45*, 48–49, *49*
Waldfogel, Jane, 48
Welch, Morgan, 160–61
welfare spending, 71–75; assistance-family structure conundrum, 74; cash assistance or tax credits, 71–72; changes in, 72; health-care spending, 71, 72; housing expenditures, 72; means-tested, 71, 72; nutrition programs, 72; poverty policy and, 72–75; security-work conundrum, 73–74; target-isolation conundrum, 74–75; work disincentives of, 73–74.

See also in-kind transfer programs; means-tested cash transfers
Welty, Elisabeth D., 143, 155
Western, B., 38, 39
Wheaton, Laura, 99
whites, 6
Whittaker, Julie M., 90
Wimer, Christopher, 5, 6, 50, 145, 150
Women's Infants and Children (WIC), 72, *76*, 78, 79, 100, 102, 104
Wondra, Danielle, 21, 22
work and childcare expenses, 104, 106–12
Work and Well-Being of Poor Families with Children: When Work Is Not Enough, 3
work-based policy, 165
work disincentives, 73–74, 84, 121, 131, 141, 146, 147, 150, 155, 157
Workers' Compensation, 91–95
work gap, 121–22
work incentives, 73, 74, 82, 84, 119, 121, 134, 141, 146, 147, 150–51, 156, 160–62, 167
working poor, 52–53
work requirements, 140–41

Young, Justin R., 55–56

Ziegert, Andrea L., 66
Ziliak, James P., 7, 85–86, 151

About the Authors

Dennis H. Sullivan is emeritus professor of economics at Miami University in Oxford, Ohio. After receiving his PhD from Princeton University, he joined the faculty at Miami University and has also held sabbatical appointments at Vanderbilt University and at Syracuse University. The majority of his published research addresses policy issues in the economics of income distribution, primarily involving taxation or poverty alleviation.

Andrea L. Ziegert is Julian H. Robertson, Jr. Professor of Economics at Denison University, where she teaches courses in microeconomics, public finance, poverty, and income inequality. Her primary research is focused on poverty and income distribution, particularly centered on families with children. Her second area of research is economic education, particularly service learning and experiential education. She developed the "Service Learning" website for the National Science Foundation–supported pedagogy portal, *Starting Point: Teaching and Learning Economics, A Source for Pedagogical Resources*. Finally, with Robin Bartlett, she developed the National Science Foundation–supported mentoring workshop, CCOFFE: Creating Career Opportunities for Female Economists, a precursor to today's American Economic Association–supported mentoring workshops, CeMent.

Ziegert earned her BS and MA in economics at Miami University (Oxford, Ohio) and PhD at the University of North Carolina-Chapel Hill.